STANDING ON THE WALLS OF TIME

STANDING ON THE WALLS OF TIME

Ancient Art of Utah's Cliffs and Canyons

KEVIN T. JONES

Photographs by LAYNE MILLER

THE UNIVERSITY OF UTAH PRESS

Salt Lake City

The Defiance House Man colophon is a registered trademark of The University of Utah Press. It is based on a four-foot-tall Ancient Puebloan pictograph (late PIII) near Glen Canyon, Utah.

LIBRARY OF CONGRESS CATALOGING-IN-PUBLICATION DATA
Names: Jones, Kevin T., 1951- author. | Miller, Layne, photographer (expression)
Title: Standing on the walls of time : ancient art of Utah's cliffs and canyons / Kevin T. Jones ; photographs by Layne Miller.
Description: Salt Lake City : University of Utah Press, [2019] | Includes bibliographical references and index. |
Identifiers: LCCN 2018047498 (print) | LCCN 2018049736 (ebook) | ISBN 9781607816751 | ISBN 9781607816744 (pbk. : alk. paper)
Subjects: LCSH: Art, Prehistoric--Utah. | Rock paintings--Utah.
Classification: LCC E78.U55 (ebook) | LCC E78.U55 J65 2019 (print) | DDC 709.01/12--dc23
LC record available at https://lccn.loc.gov/2018047498

Errata and further information on this and other titles available online at UofUpress.com.
Printed and bound in the United States of America.

DEDICATION

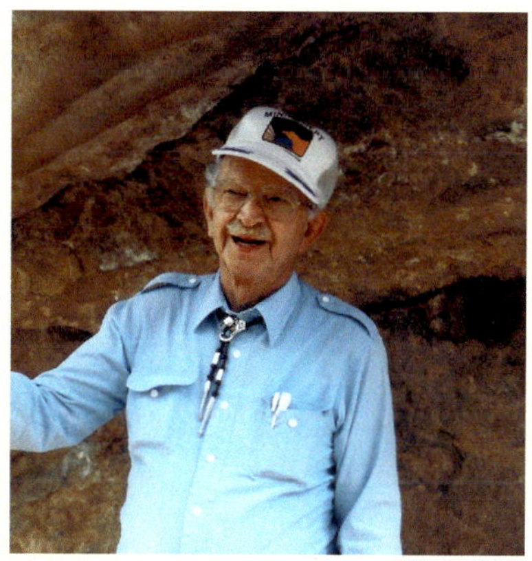

This book is dedicated to the memory of J. Eldon "Doc" Dorman, friend, mentor, and passionate advocate for the appreciation and protection of Utah's archaeological resources, especially rock art. Doc was an inspiration to us and to legions of friends and neighbors who accompanied him on his famous "Jeep Safaris" to the San Rafael Swell and beyond. Doc had a lasting influence on the region as a founder of the Prehistoric Museum in Price, and we remember him fondly.

TABLE OF CONTENTS

ACKNOWLEDGMENTS

We thank our wives, Barbara Evert and Karen Miller, for their support and encouragement. We especially thank Reba Rauch, our editor at the University of Utah Press, for shepherding this book through its long gestation process. Thanks to the Bill Barrett Corporation for a generous grant to assist with the cost of printing the color photographs. Many others helped us out along the way, including Nick Jones, Melissa Bond, Sally Cole, Brenda Cowley, Dorothee Kocks, Kurt Proctor, Tim Riley, Steve Trimble, and Amie Tullius. Special thanks to artist Skyler Chubak for creating the beautiful map of the area. And we extend a gracious and heartfelt thank-you to the members of the Utah Statewide Archaeological Society and the Utah Rock Art Research Association for their efforts over the years to document and protect Utah's precious archaeological and cultural heritage.

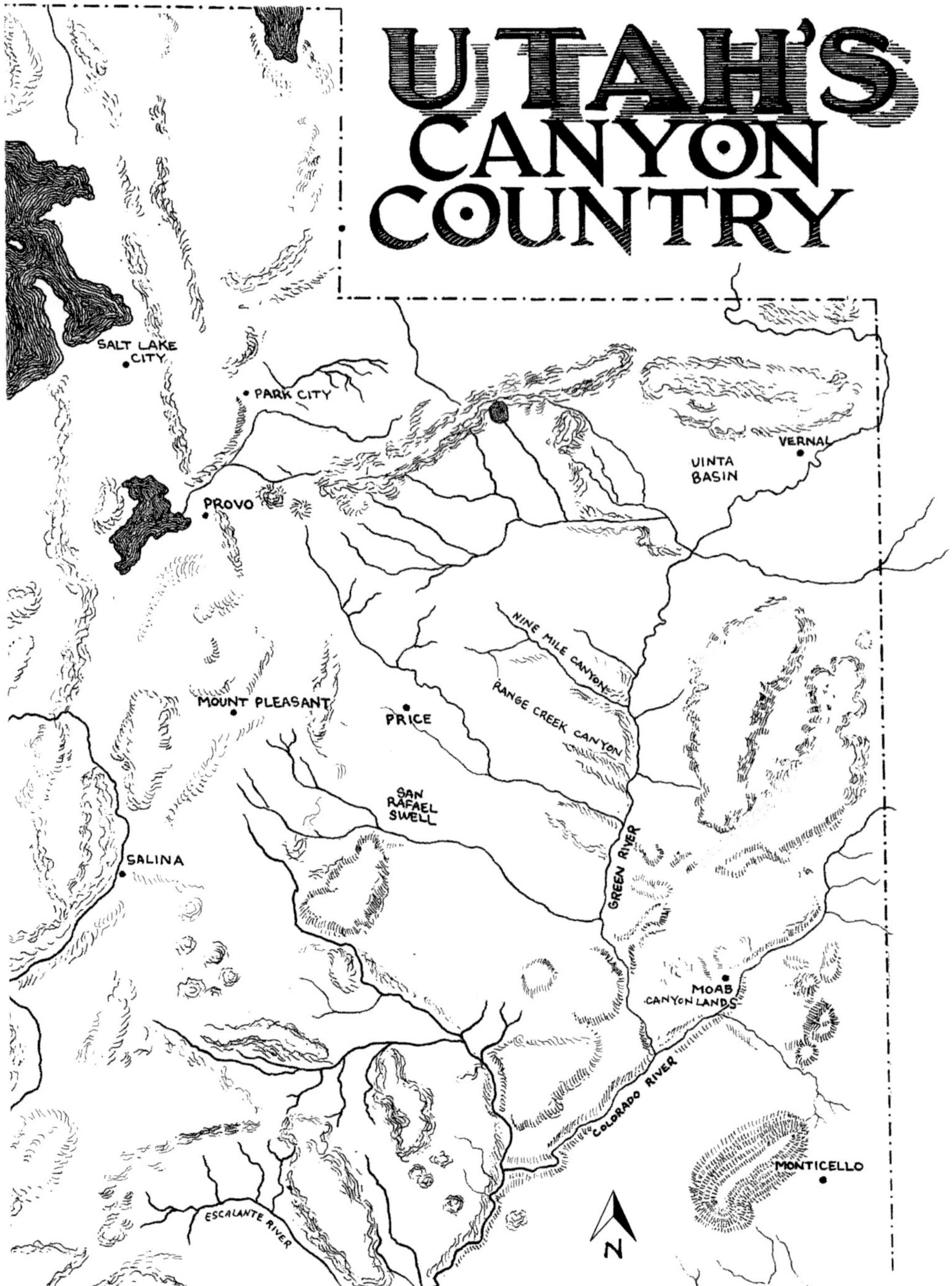
UTAH'S CANYON COUNTRY
SALT LAKE CITY
PARK CITY
PROVO
UINTA BASIN
VERNAL
NINE MILE CANYON
RANGE CREEK CANYON
MOUNT PLEASANT
PRICE
SAN RAFAEL SWELL
SALINA
GREEN RIVER
MOAB
CANYON LANDS
COLORADO RIVER
MONTICELLO
ESCALANTE RIVER
N

1

ABOUT THIS BOOK

The canyons of the American Southwest are magnificent geological structures—stark sandstone cliffs in rich hues of gold and flaxen, pinks and burgundy—and they stand as grand testaments to the forces of nature and deep time, leaving many visitors in awe. These panoramic vistas have long drawn artists—filmmakers, photographers, printmakers, and painters—who strive to capture images that harken to vast, wide open landscapes. Devoid of all but the slightest hints of human presence, their works seek to convey the great beauty of the natural world. Yet, as we look closer, we can see, subtly gracing the stone, the unmistakable signatures of millennia of artists whose carvings and paintings of figures familiar and fantastic express their humanity on these walls, their marks speaking across the ages. The cliffs and canyons exhibit in sublime silence the work of masters who expressed their most precious and personal feelings on these walls of time. This book is a small reminder of the thousands of artists, artisans, and visionaries who speak across the centuries, whose genius enriches lives and inspires those who experience their work. We have been moved by our encounters with the creations of ancient artists and are grateful we are able to share our love and enthusiasm with our readers.

For many thousands of years before Europeans drove the inhabitants of the rugged sandstone cliffs and canyons of western North America from their homes, cultures of great knowledge and richness thrived. Until the invaders spread disease and brought their monolithic gods to this rugged and beautiful part of the world, the citizens of this land hunted, gathered, farmed, raised families, fought, played, sang, danced, prayed, and expressed some of their most personal and sacred thoughts through images on stone for all to see. Today only a scant record of those rich lives exists, but what a remarkable legacy the artists of the ancient canyons have left behind.

Countless books and articles attest to the profound impression these ancient works have had on modern viewers. Many have tried to assign meaning to the symbols, often with absurd and facile results. Some Native Americans see familiar sym-

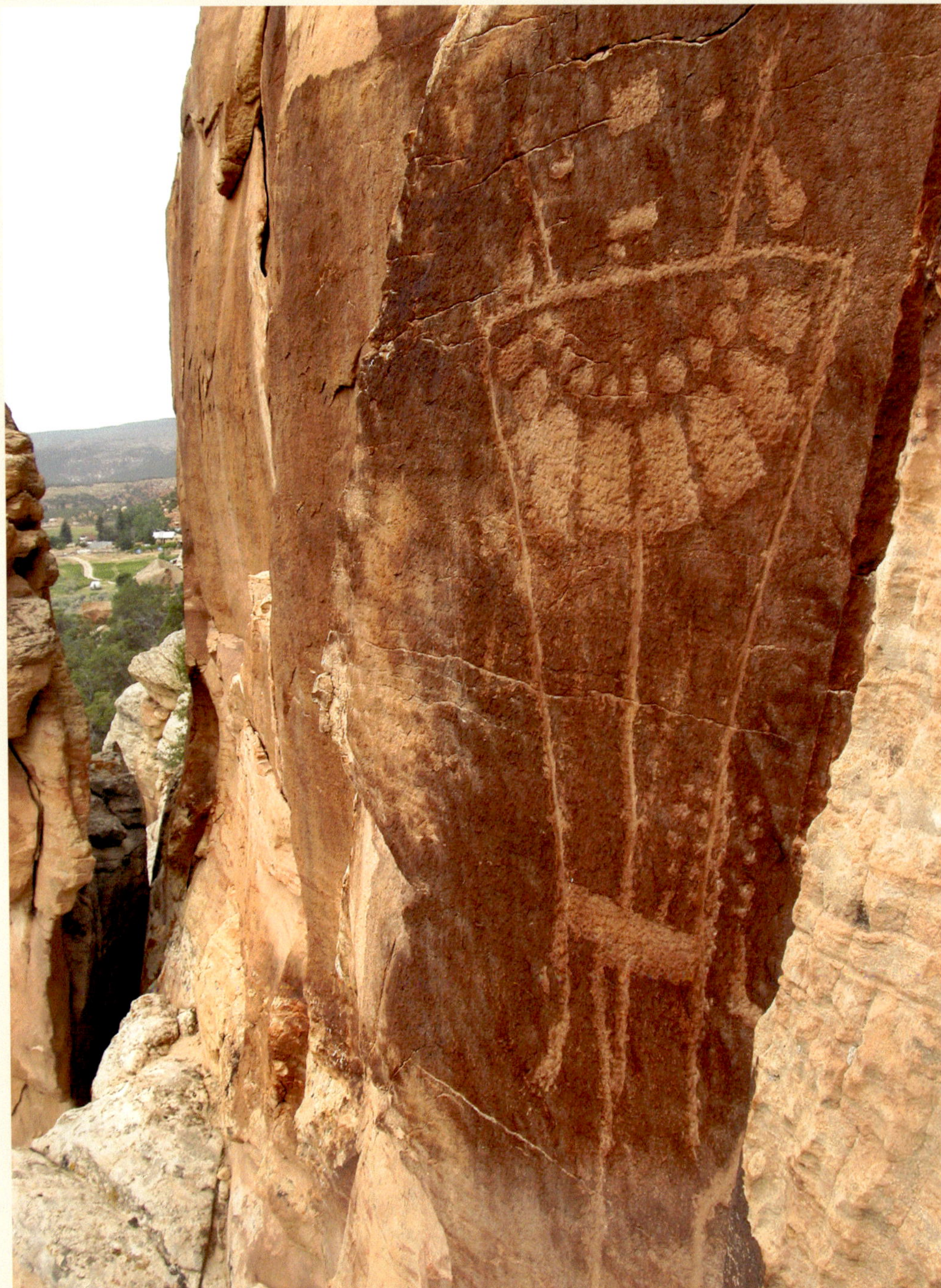

FIGURE 1.2. A beautiful Fremont-style anthropomorph above Dry Fork Canyon near the McConkie Ranch in the Uinta Basin.

bols that may reveal cultural meaning, but can be reluctant to share their observations and thoughts. Even when symbols are recognized, the passage of time may have diminished their relevance to the present. Academic researchers usually (but not always) shy away from trying to decipher meanings, and instead work to identify patterns in the iconography to learn about past cultures and their geographic and temporal positions as expressed on stone. Some view the art of early cultures as code for something knowable through induction, such as representing maps, stories, calendars, astronomical markers, and even validation of Western religious teachings.

This book represents a departure from nearly all of these approaches. I am not going to try to interpret the artists' meanings or symbols. In fact, I am strongly opposed to that approach. I do not try to match or categorize symbols in an attempt to advance culture history studies. I advocate for a much simpler, more human approach—to view the work of ancient artists purely as art. Let it reach you on more of an emotional, as opposed to intellectual, level. Appreciate the creativity, the technique, the place—the entirety of the work—and let the artist speak directly to you. Immerse yourself in the beauty, the mystery, the genius of these works and allow yourself to glimpse, however briefly and equivocally, another culture through the wall of time.

Layne Miller has spent much of his life on a quest to visit and document the masterpieces that haunt the canyons and cliffs of eastern Utah. His passion is to record and capture the remarkable artistry with camera and lens so he can share his love of these majestic testaments to rich, spiritually infused lives. His photographs are incredible, indeed are works of art themselves, but without intruding into the creativity of the original artist. More than simple documentation, they reveal a true insight into the ancient art form itself.

Layne's photographs transport us to a time when the lines we draw today between work, play, belief, creativity, family, spirituality, and landscape did not exist. A person's life was integrated and complete. Work did not start at eight; church was not on Sunday. Each act of each day of each life was part of a contiguous, continuous whole, and the expressions drafted on the cliff faces and canyon walls yield insights and allow entry into lives that are, for the most part, lost and inaccessible to us today.

These remarkable images—invitations by artists now long gone to partake of their humanity—are a rare gift, wrapped and delivered to us by an incredibly talented archaeologist and photographer. And they are more than images. They are glimpses into human souls, and the depth and complexity of humanity they reveal are astounding.

While there is incredible rock art all over the world, and particularly in the American Southwest, the photographs presented here are nearly all from central and eastern Utah, especially the San Rafael Swell and Nine Mile Canyon, areas with great concentrations of magnificent rock art. Some of Layne's photos are from outside this region, but we have selected photos primarily from his home territory. There are many, many other places in the state and region that have noteworthy rock art, and while we would like to have included more, we were forced by practical matters to make this book less than the thousands of pages it might have been. We hope you'll understand.

I too brought a lifetime of interest in and study of ancient cultures to this project. My ideas and observations are intended to provoke and bring thought and contemplation to the appreciation of rock art. My goal is to elevate appreciation of the work of the ancient creators from being considered ancient graffiti, the scratchings of primitive people, or mere folk art to its deserved status as fine art of great value and historic significance. Let these photos and essays move you to visit and experience the grand works of art that enhance the canyon walls of the American Southwest, and join us in recognizing their value to us and the generations to come.

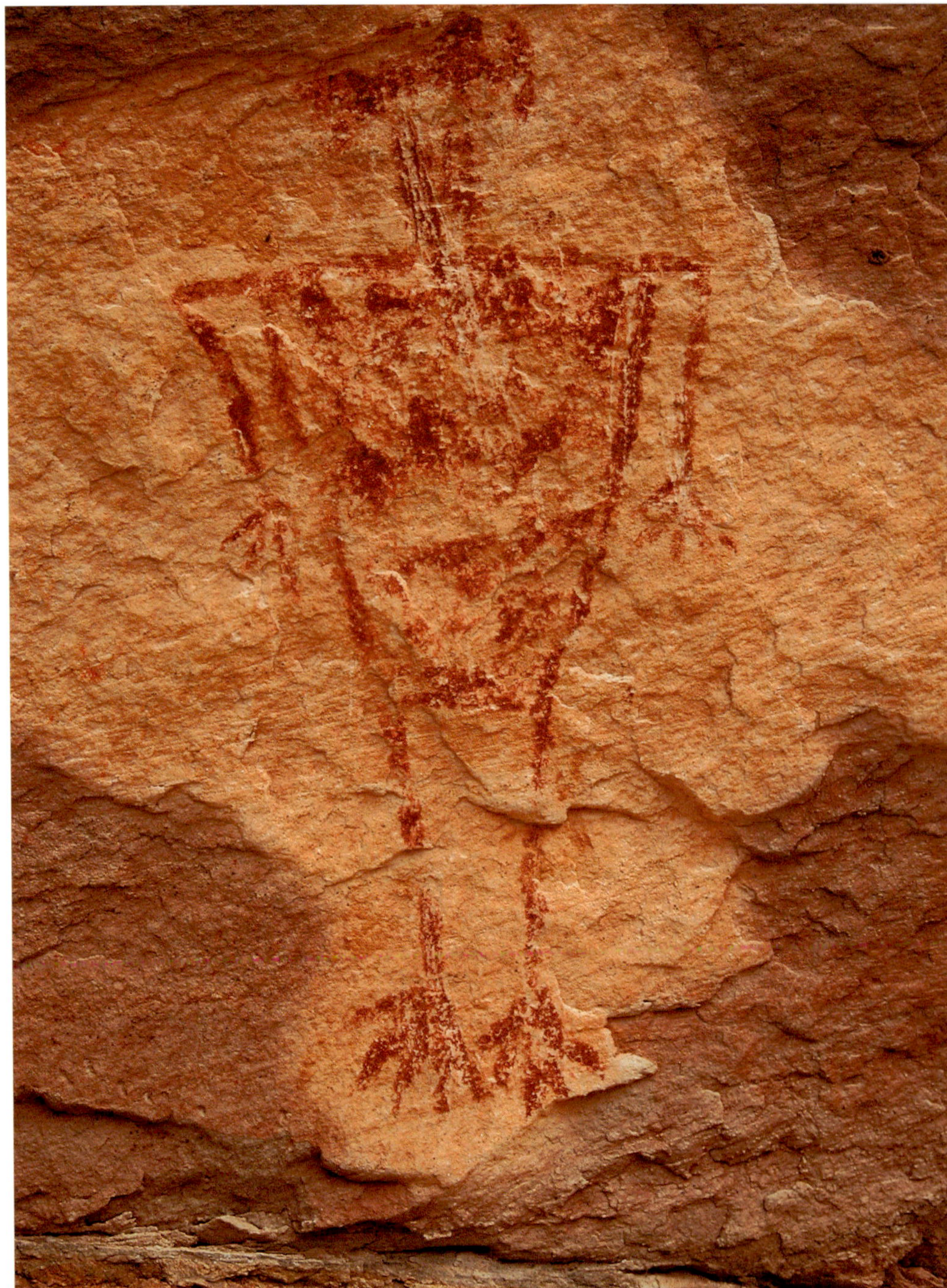

FIGURE 1.3. A San Juan Basketmaker-style anthropomorph on Comb Ridge, southern Utah.

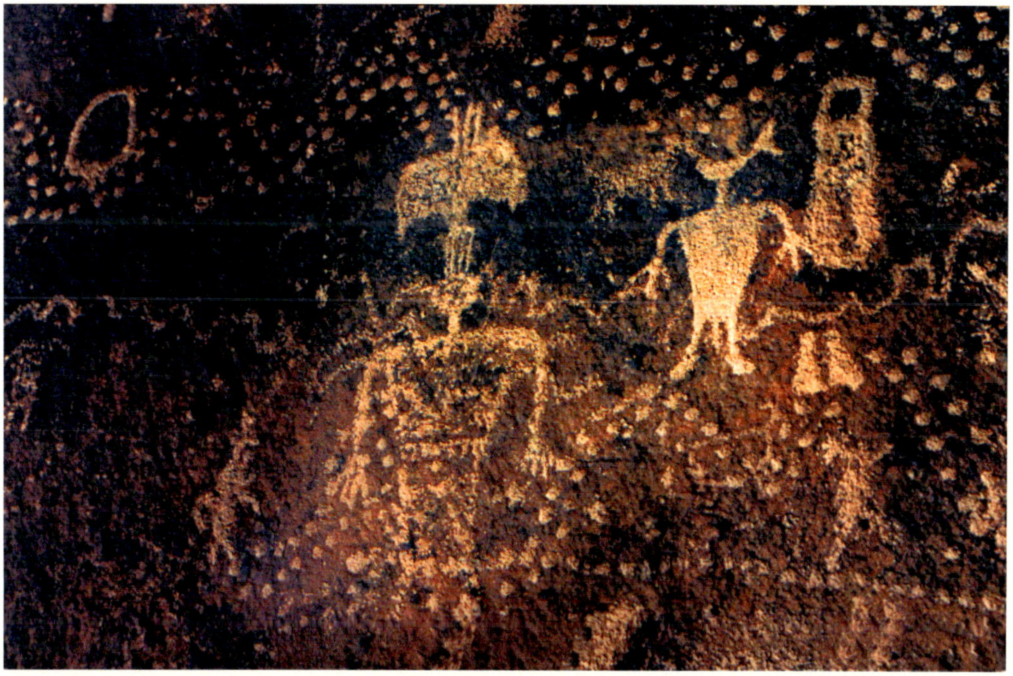

FIGURE 1.4. A San Juan Basketmaker-style panel on a large boulder near the base of Cedar Point, southern Utah.

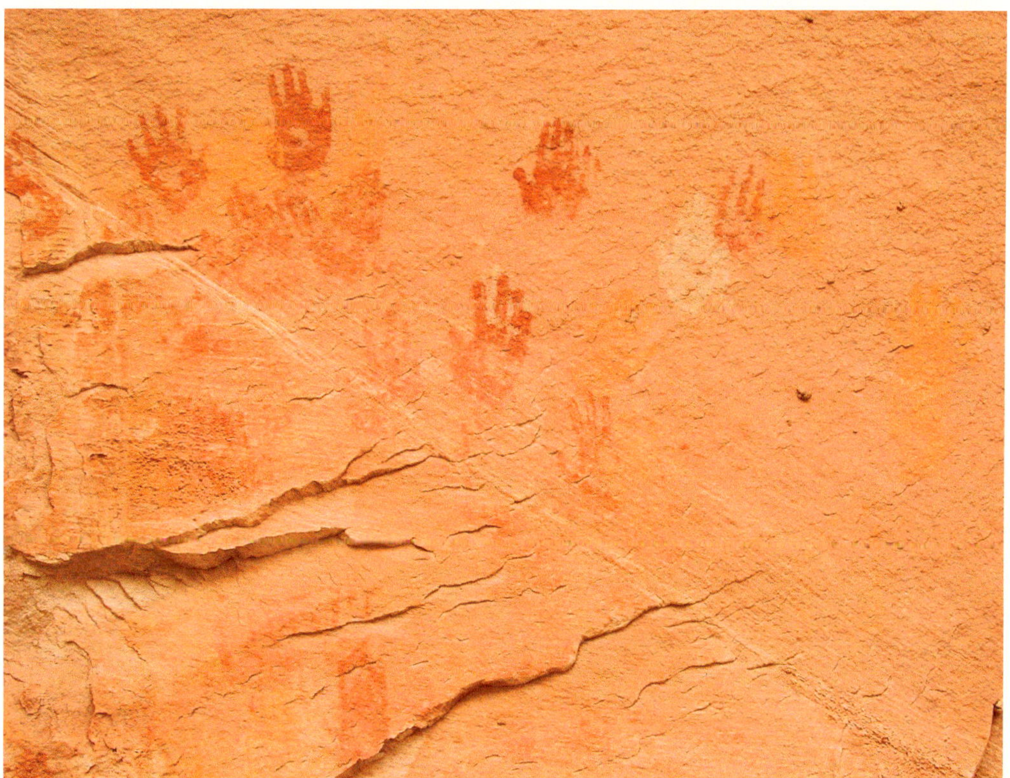

FIGURE 1.5. Positive handprints in a large alcove in southern Utah. Their cultural affiliation is unknown.

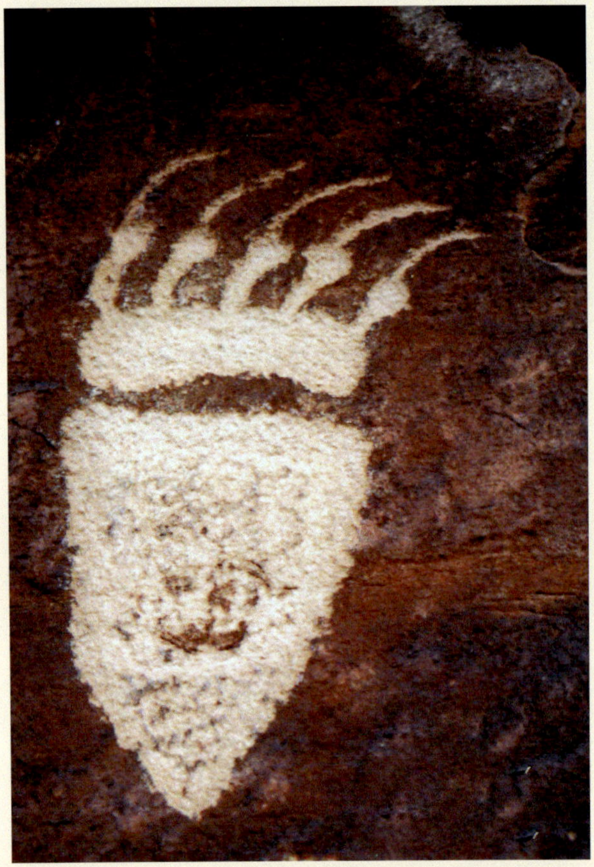

FIGURE 1.6. A large Ute-style bear paw from Nine Mile Canyon. It may relate to the Ute Bear Dance performed by tribal members each spring.

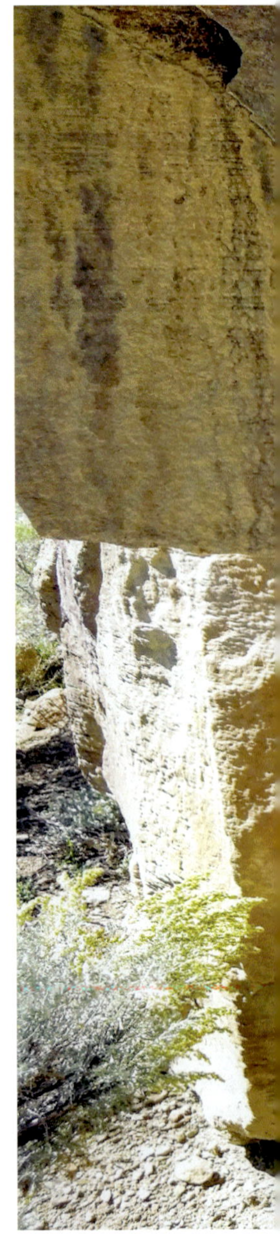

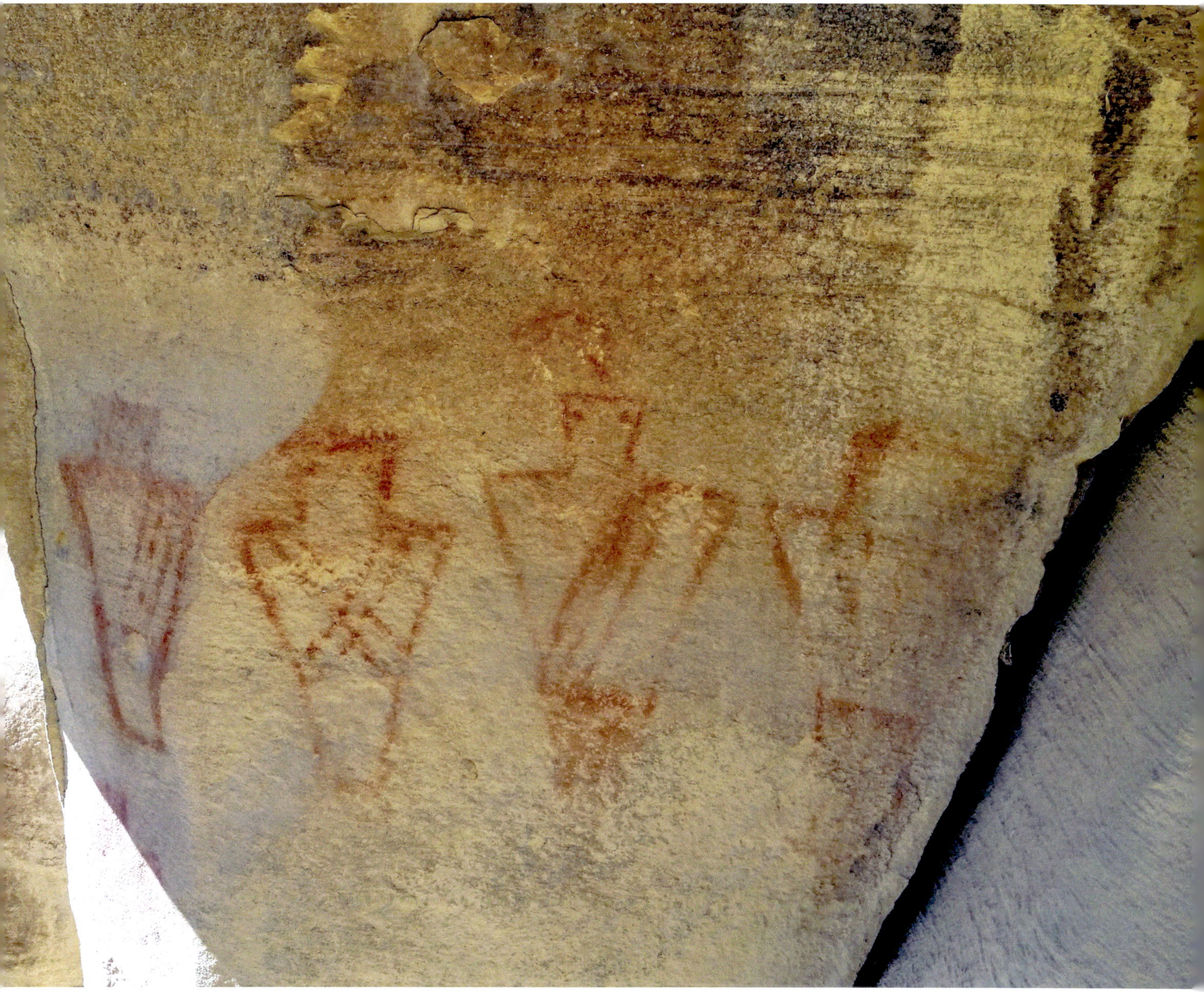

FIGURE 1.7. Anthropomorphic Fremont-style pictographs in Nine Mile Canyon.

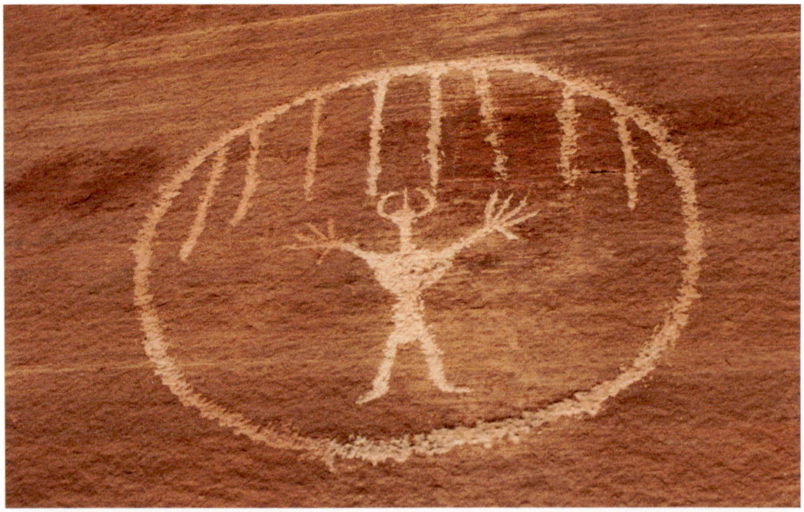

FIGURE 1.8. An Ancestral Puebloan–style shield figure with an enclosed anthropomorph in Montezuma Creek, southern Utah.

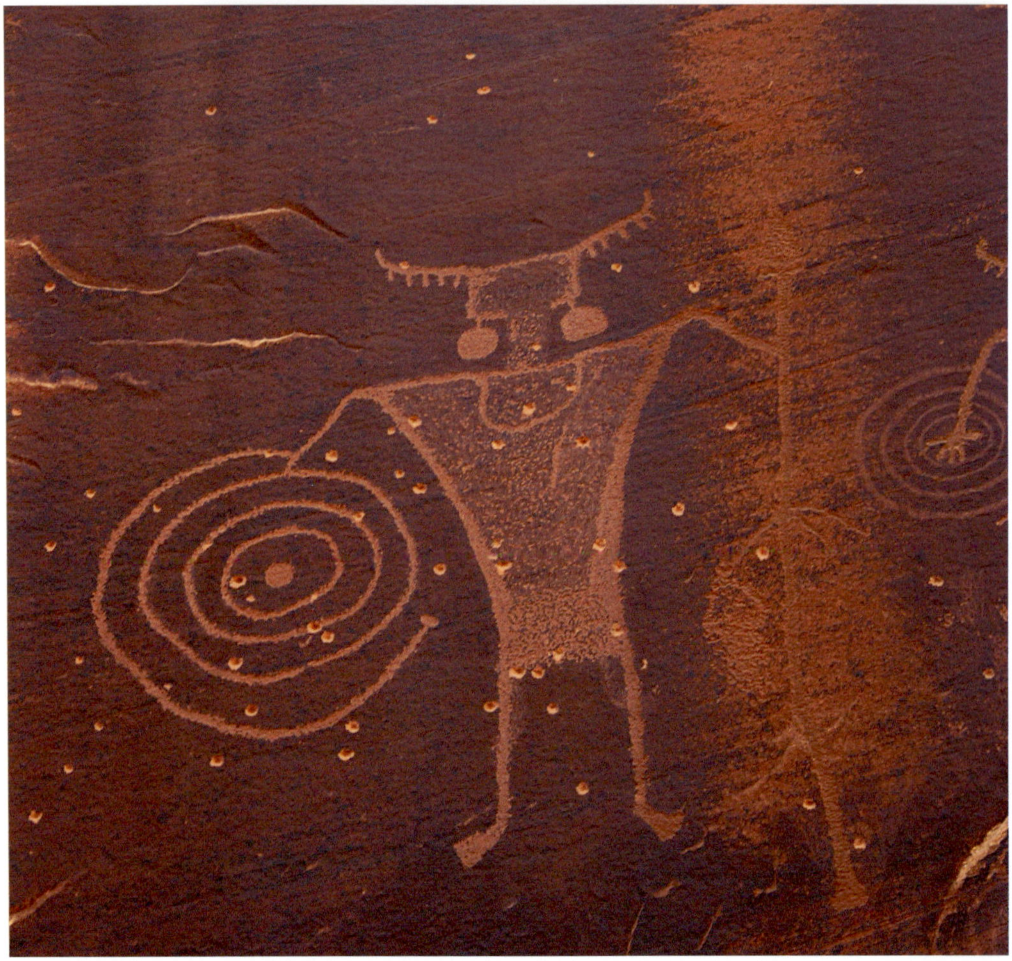

FIGURE 1.9. A Fremont-style anthropomorph in Mill Creek Canyon, near Moab, holding a shield and spear. The panel is riddled with bullet holes.

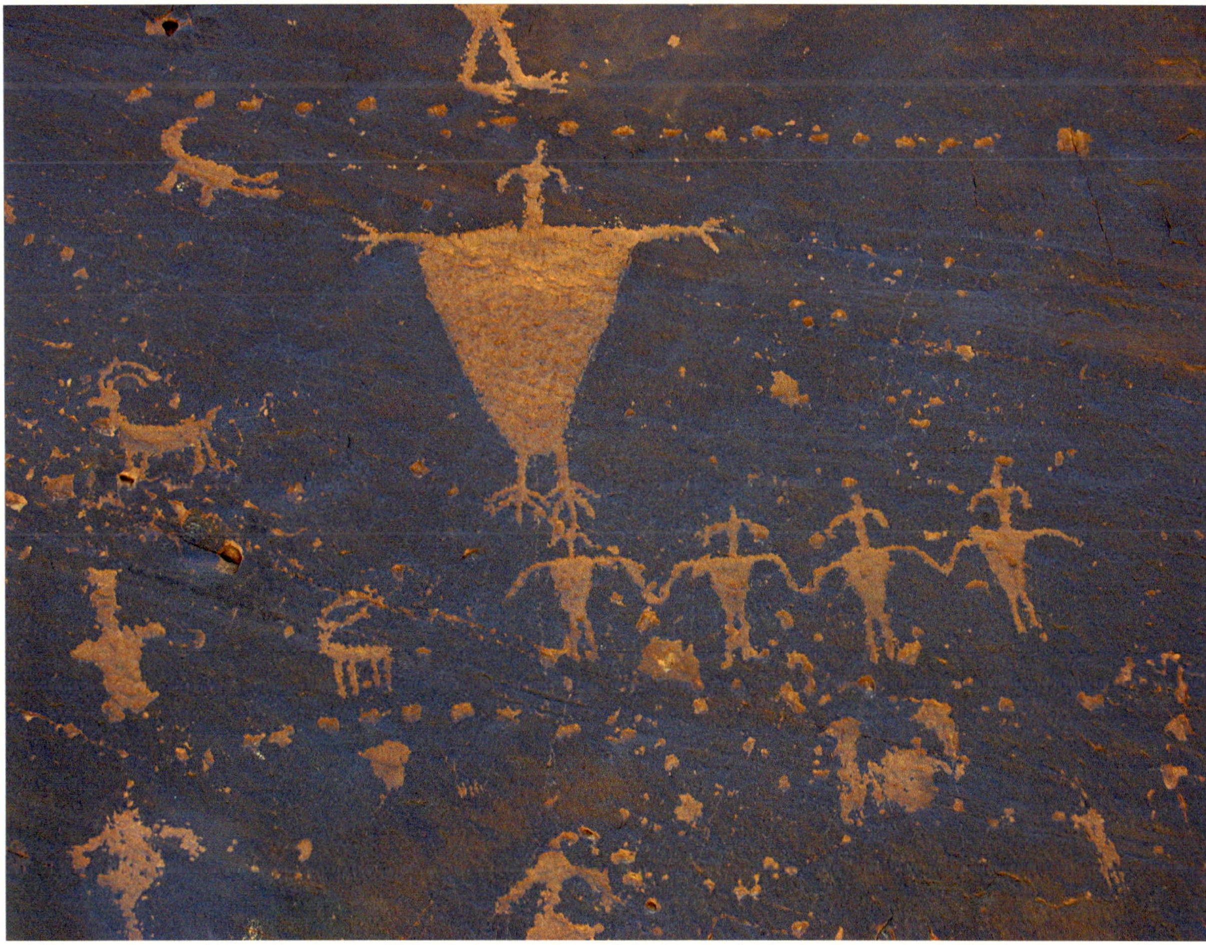

FIGURE 1.10. An Ancestral Puebloan–style petroglyph in Mill Creek Canyon near Moab.

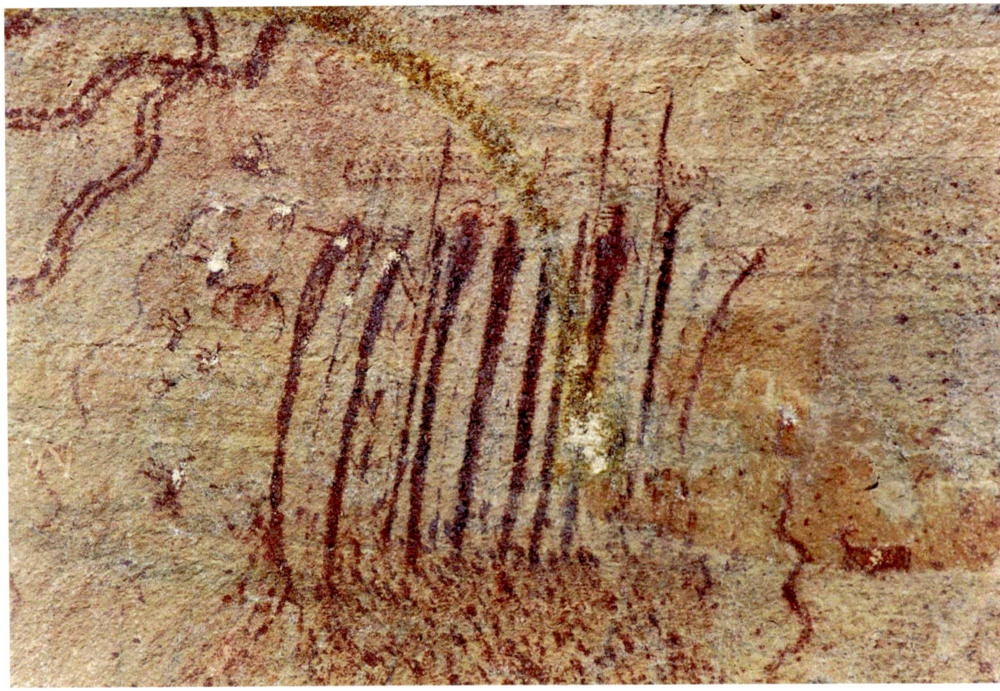

FIGURE 1.11. A close-up view of the upper portion of a pictograph panel in Buckhorn Draw in the San Rafael Swell with what appear to be Barrier Canyon–style bighorn sheep, snakes, birds, and stylized anthropomorphs.

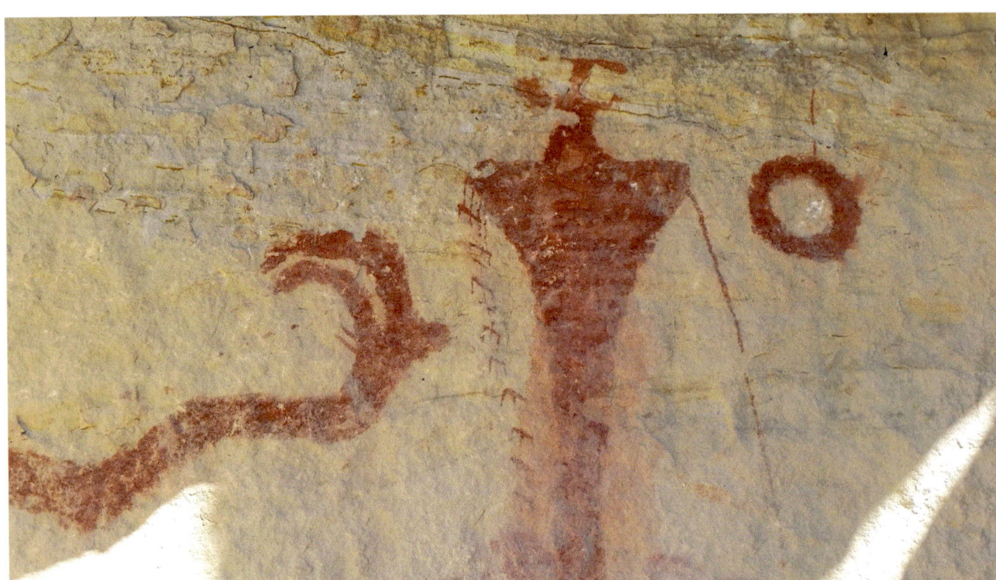

FIGURE 1.12. A horned snake and other details on a pictograph panel in a small canyon in eastern Utah.

2

WHEN AND WHERE (AND WHY)

For archaeological research to have any chance of making sense of the scant remnants of the past, we have to be able to understand how old something is, and to know where it came from or where it was made. For artifacts, this process involves an almost obsessive quest to know the provenience of each piece: where was it found, in what stratigraphic context, what material(s) it was made from and where they were obtained, and what was found with it. The trends and details discernable through the study of artifacts and their proveniences have allowed us to develop—through association, seriation, and absolute and relative dating techniques—fairly comprehensive cultural-historical reconstruction of past technologies, use of different materials, and patterns through time and over geographic space.

Assigning dates to rock art is difficult and generally imprecise. For an archaeologist, rock art is an artifact, not unlike pottery sherds, projectile points, and basketry, albeit with some significant, unique attributes. It is not found in buried contexts and is thus not easily determined to be in direct association with other kinds of artifacts, making dating and attributing cultural affiliation difficult. A confounding matter involves its very nature: it is art, the embodiment of human creative expression, and it is thus, due to its incredibly diverse content and variety of styles, remarkably difficult to classify, to assign to a style or time period or archaeological culture.

Despite these limitations, the scientific study of rock art remains an important undertaking, along with the more humanities-based appreciation of its artistic, cultural, spiritual, and symbolic content and expression. We recognize the challenges of studying prehistoric art and know that while location and temporal assignment are critical to understanding it, revealing precise locations for rock art sites can lead to undesirable consequences, and assignment of cultural affiliation can be fraught with difficulties. Accordingly, the images presented in this book are principally intended to show the incredible humanity of the artists and to reveal the vast depth of the artistry displayed on the canyon walls and cliff faces. As an organizational theme, we present the images in rough temporal/cultural-histori-

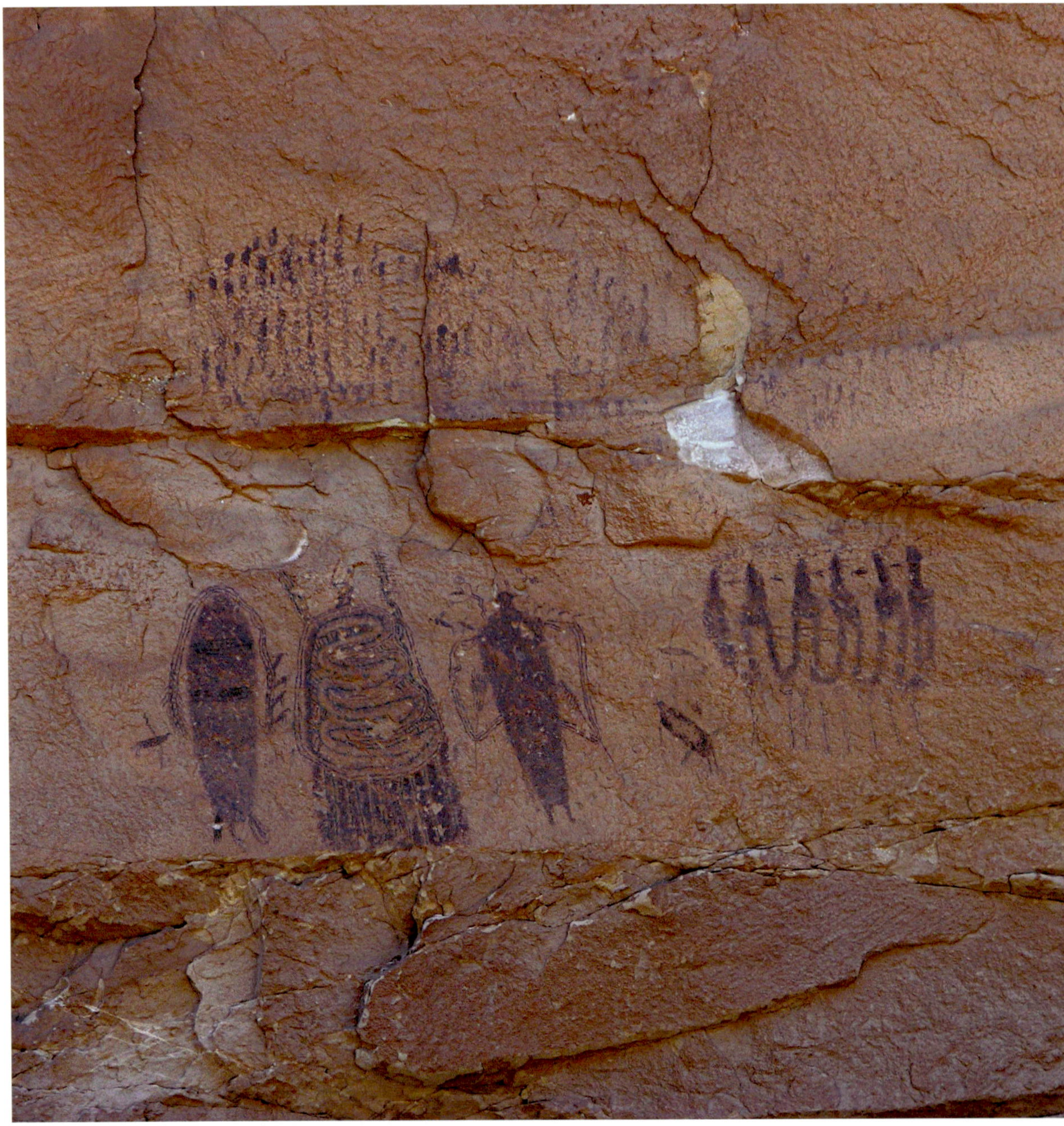

FIGURE 2.1. A Barrier Canyon–style pictograph near Moab often referred to as the Intestine Man.

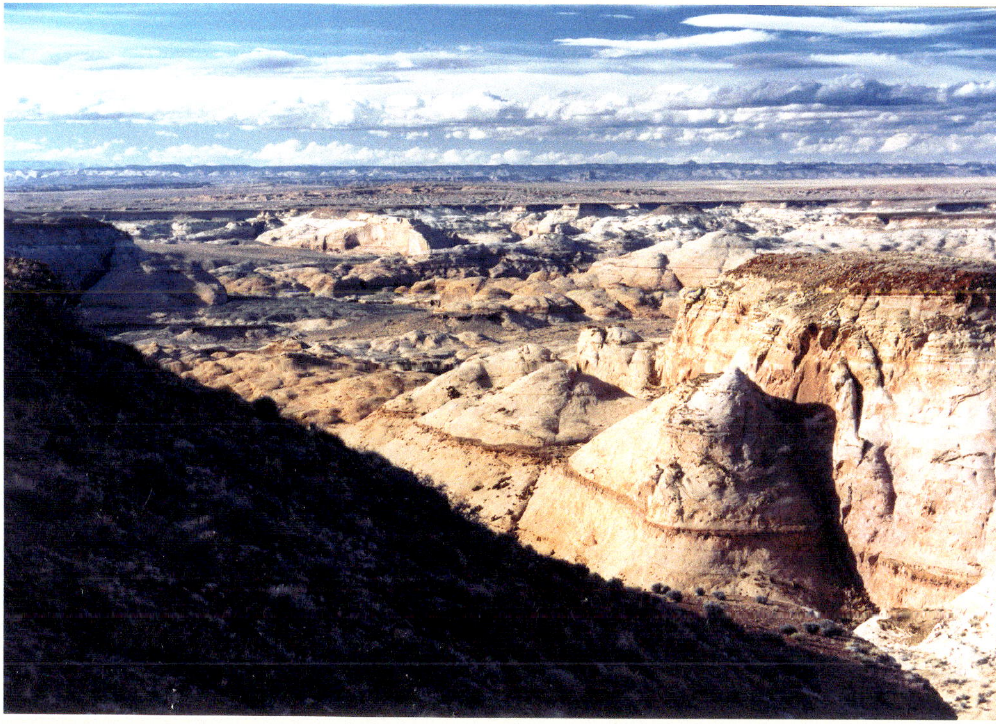

FIGURE 2.2. A view of the Robbers Roost area in southern Utah, home of many rock art panels.

cal order, beginning with the earliest images and concluding with the more recent. In addition, for each image we provide locational information that will enable readers to understand the general geographic placement of the various pieces of art, but not with the level of precision that will allow ready directions to the spot. The art presented in this volume is centered in eastern Utah, focusing on the Nine Mile Canyon/San Rafael Swell area, but includes examples of the most interesting works surrounding that area as well, including the Uinta Basin, Canyonlands, Range Creek, and beyond. In order to provide the reader with the general geographic area of sites, we most often refer to the drainage basin in which they are found, such as Nine Mile Canyon, Range Creek Canyon, Clear Creek Canyon, and so on.

Please recognize that rock art is fragile, and if you choose to visit a site, do so with care. Remember that you are in an archaeological site. Be careful where you walk, sit, and climb so you do not inadvertently damage something of importance. And never, ever touch the art or do anything to enhance it, such as adding chalk or moisture. Some of the rock art in this area might be over 10,000 years old. Please treat it with respect!

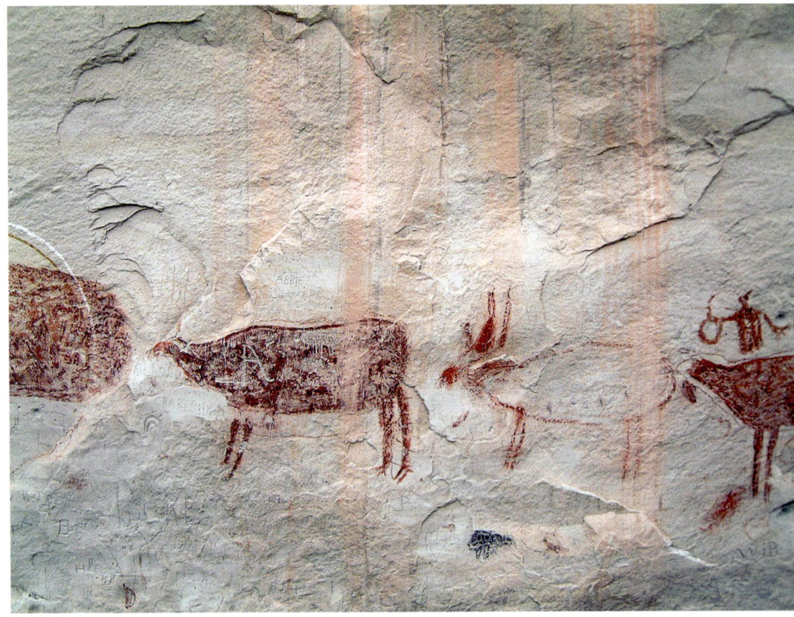

FIGURE 2.3. Large elk-like figures in Fish Creek Cove near Capitol Reef. They appear to be headless, but a close examination reveals that the heads were originally painted in white and have since faded and been mostly washed away.

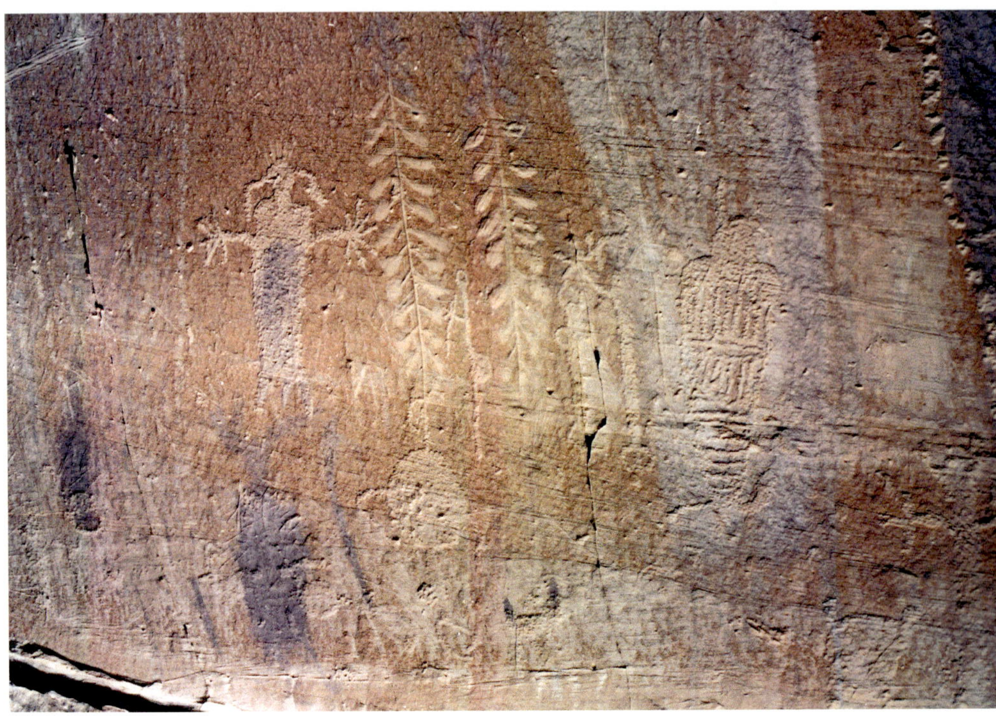

FIGURE 2.5. A Barrier Canyon–style and/or Basketmaker-style panel with a mix of petroglyphs and pictographs featuring what appear to be yucca plants with blossoms or fruit.

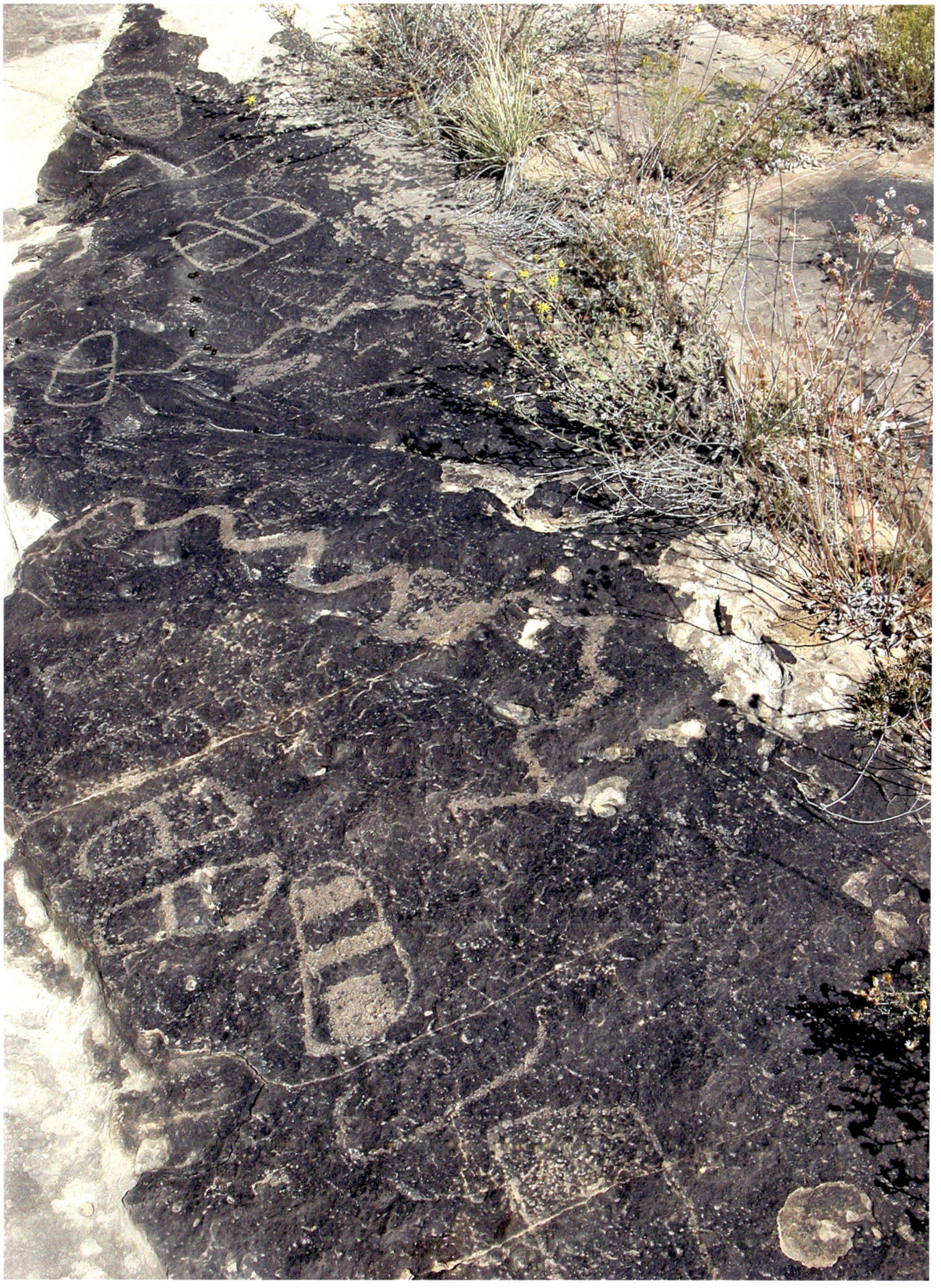

FIGURE 2.4. Sandal track petroglyphs on bedrock in eastern Utah. The cultural affiliation is unknown but may be Ancestral Puebloan.

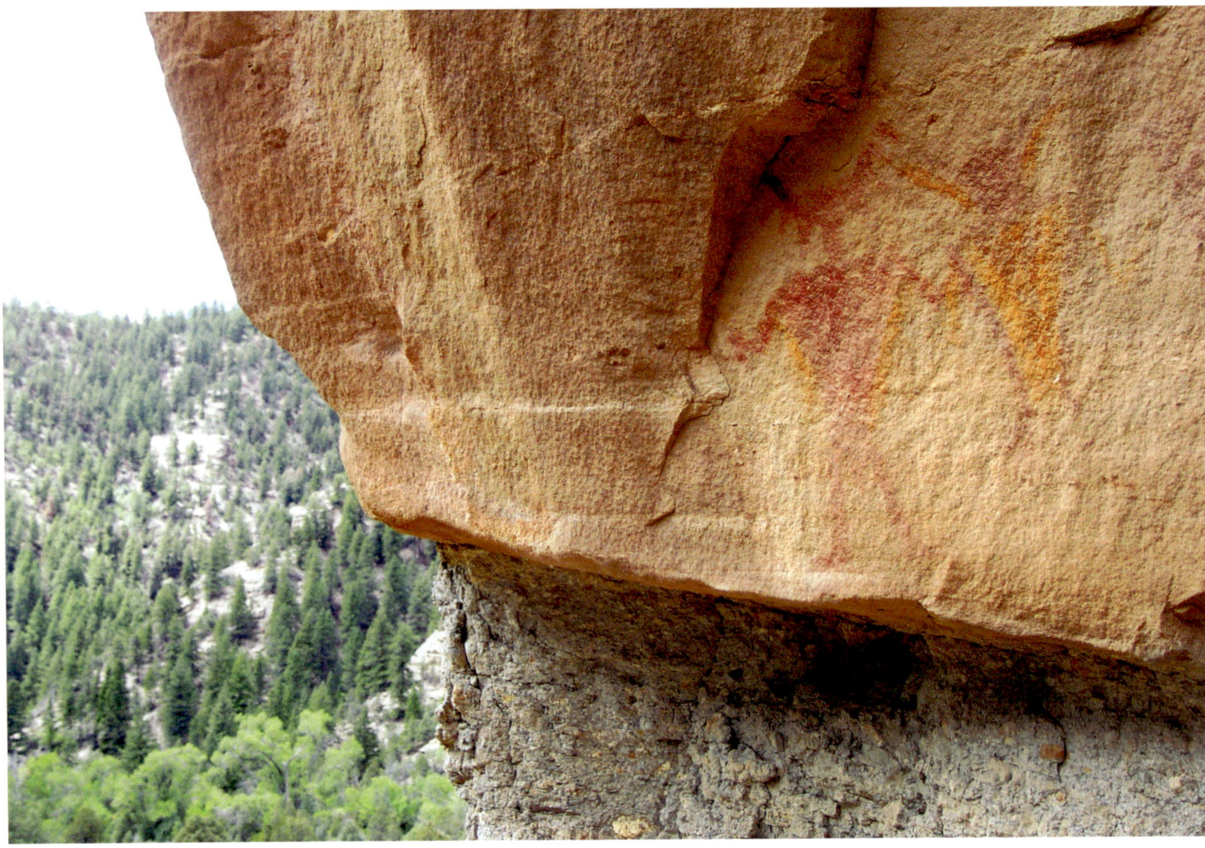

FIGURE 2.6. Two Fremont-style pictographs in Range Creek Canyon. These red and orange anthropomorphs are reminiscent of Fremont figurines.

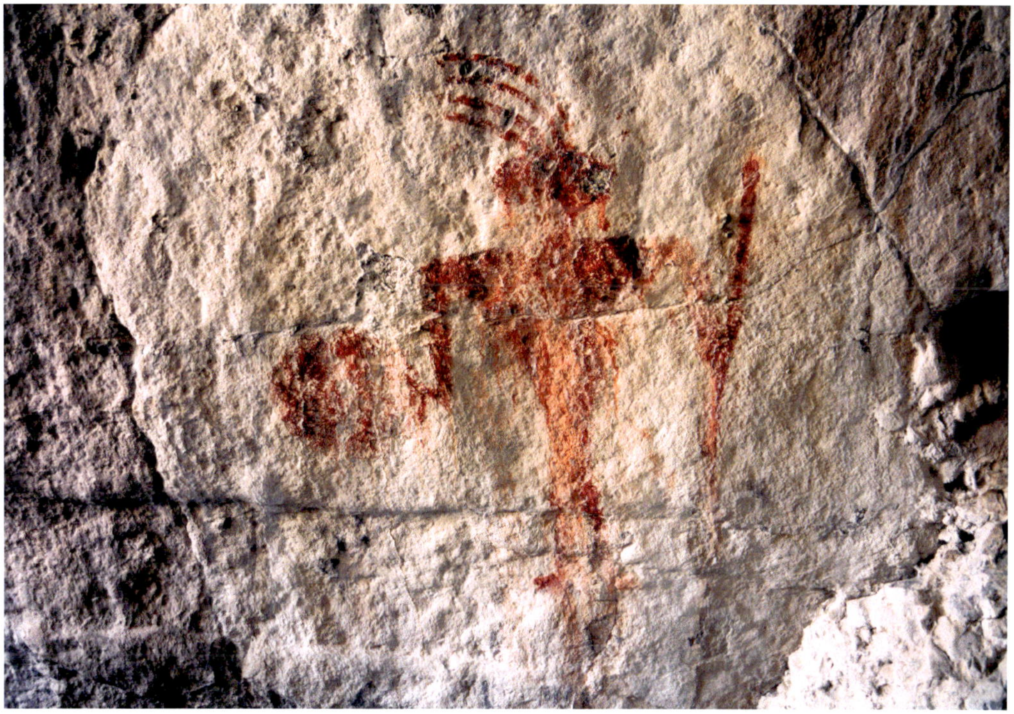

FIGURE 2.7. A Fremont-style pictograph in Ferron Canyon, in eastern Utah.

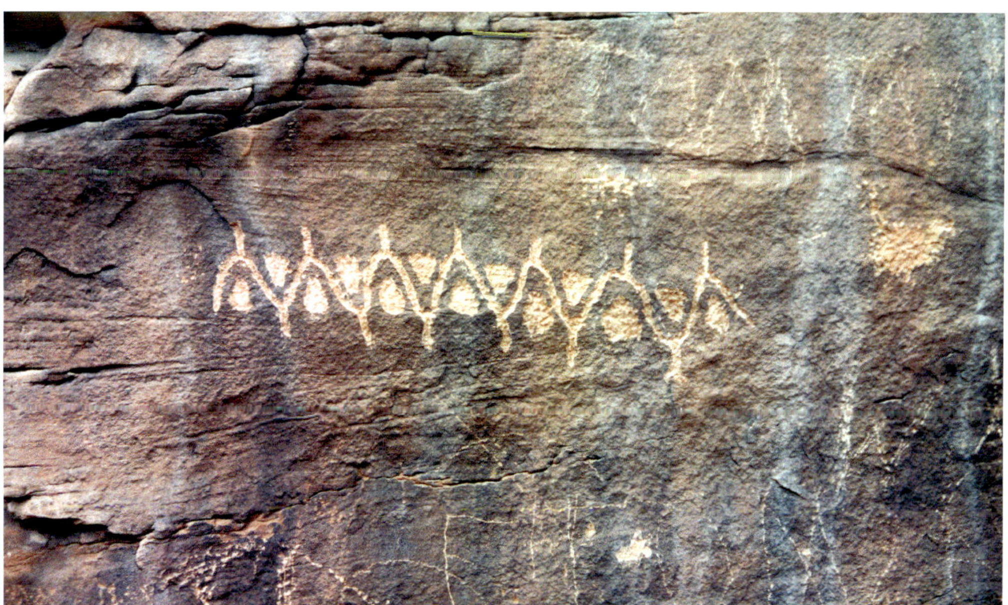

FIGURE 2.8. An unusual petroglyph in Nine Mile Canyon. Note the scratchings of vandals who defaced the panel.

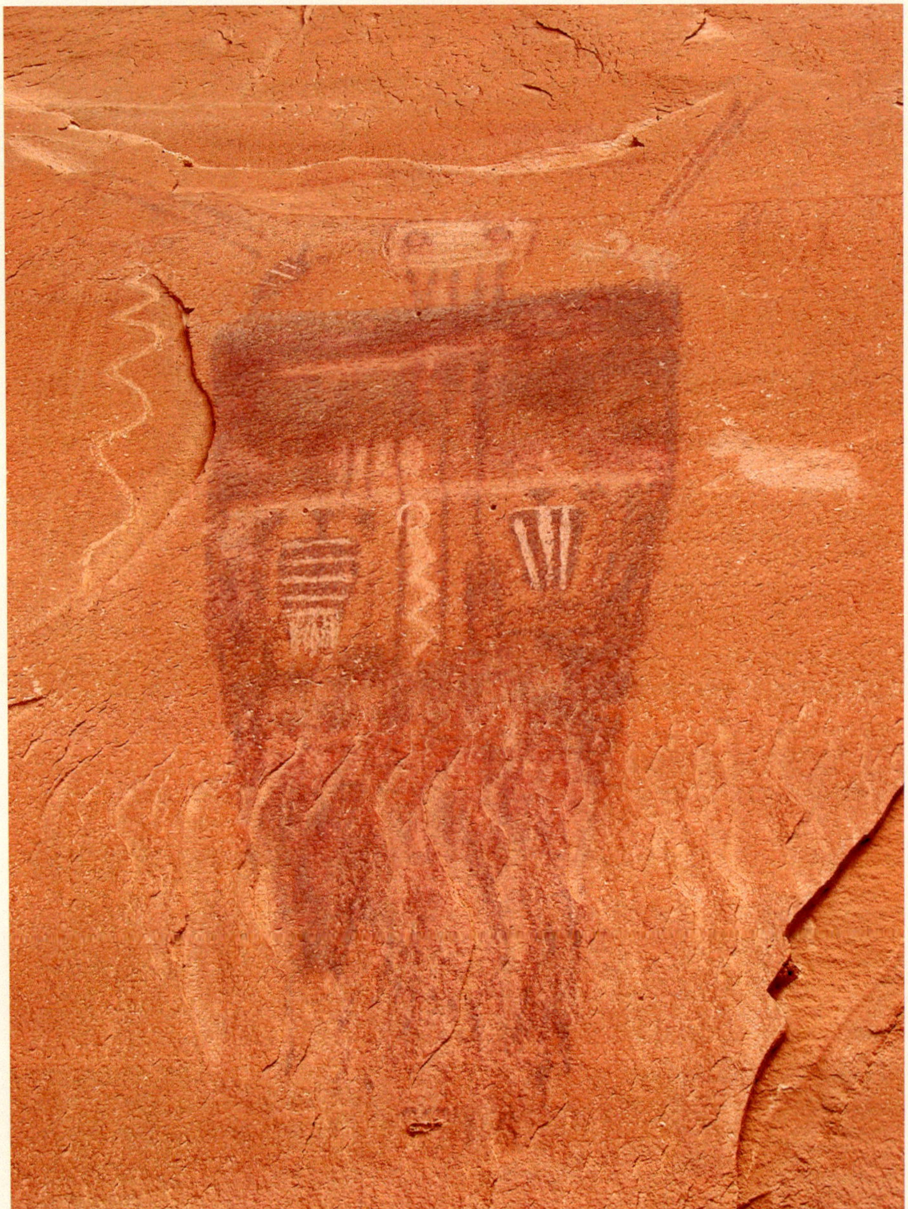

FIGURE 2.9. An intricately decorated Barrier Canyon–style anthropomorph in Horseshoe Canyon with interior decorations and figures resting on its shoulders.

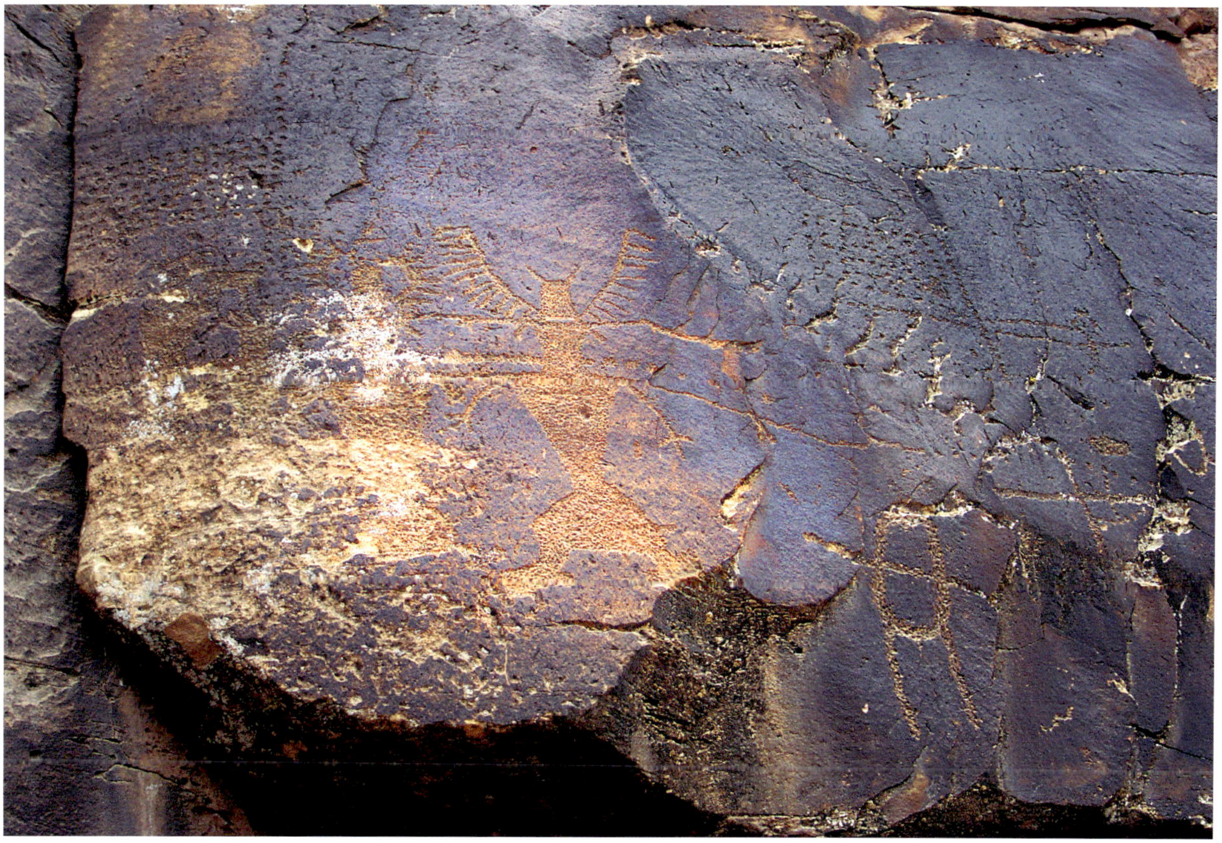

FIGURE 2.10. A beautiful Fremont-style anthropomorph in Nine Mile Canyon with a rake-like headdress.

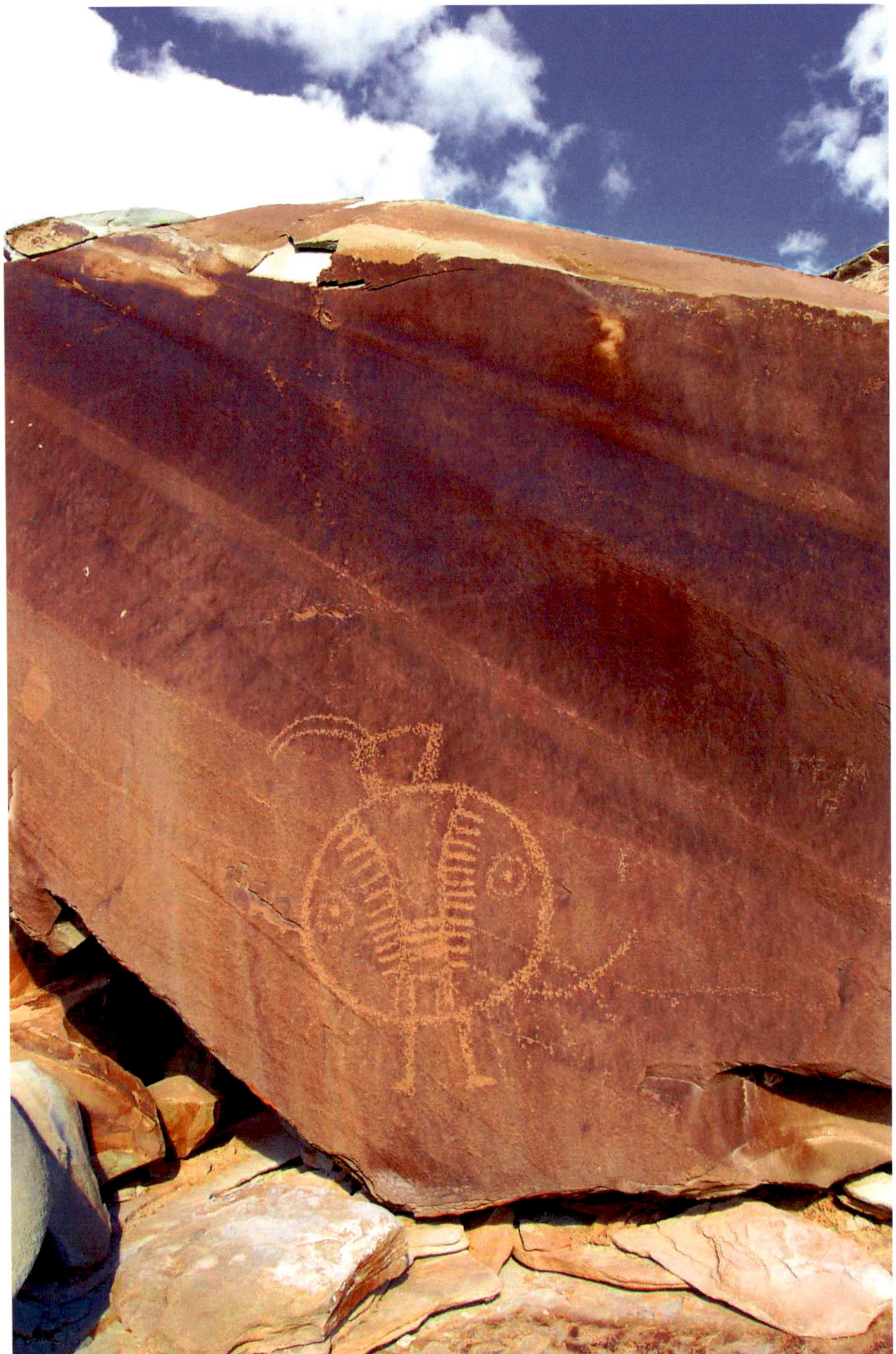

FIGURE 2.11. The Silent Sentinel, who seems to be standing guard over the canyons of the San Rafael Swell.

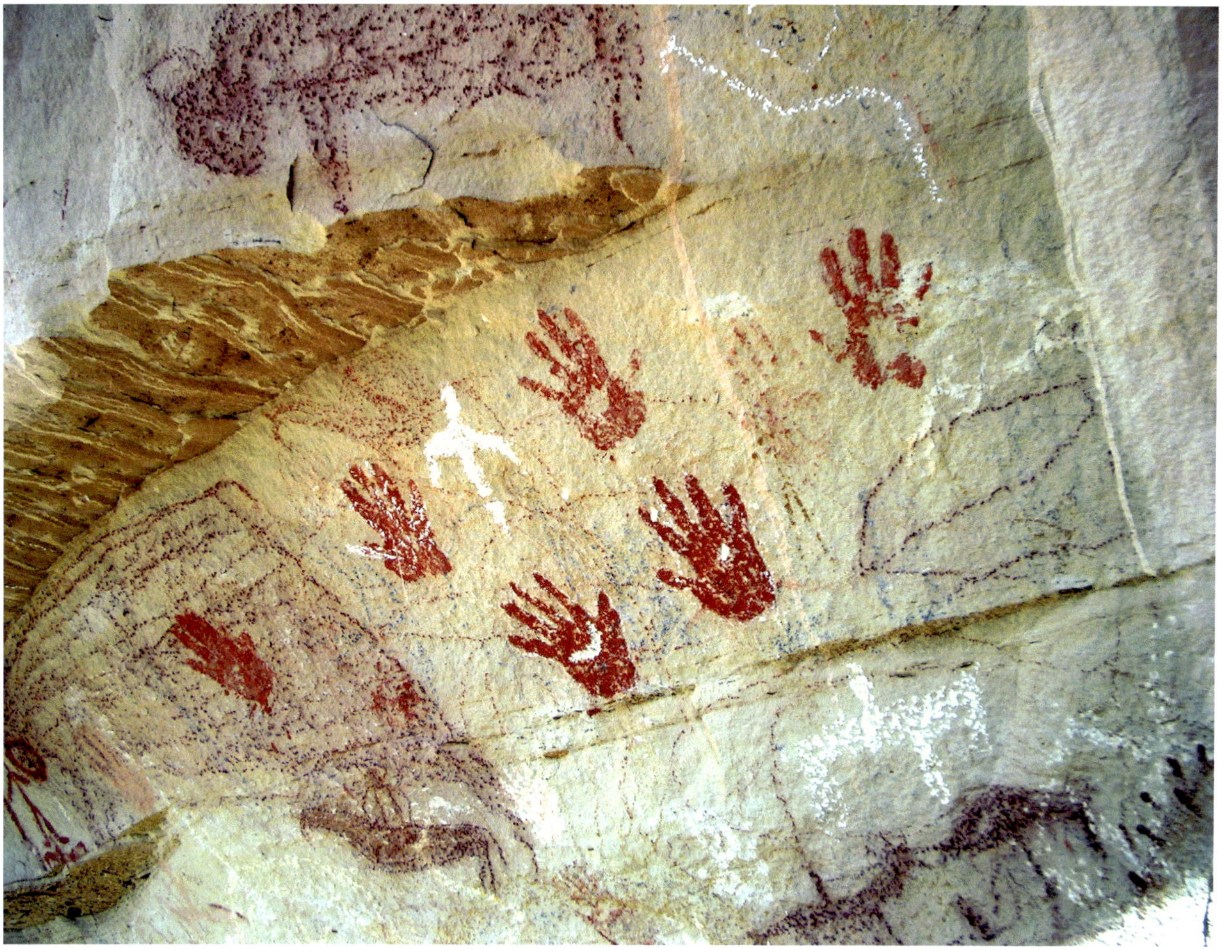

FIGURE 2.12. Ute-affiliated painted handprints and other elements in Westwater Canyon of the Colorado River, eastern Utah. Some of them appear to have been drawn with sticks of pigment.

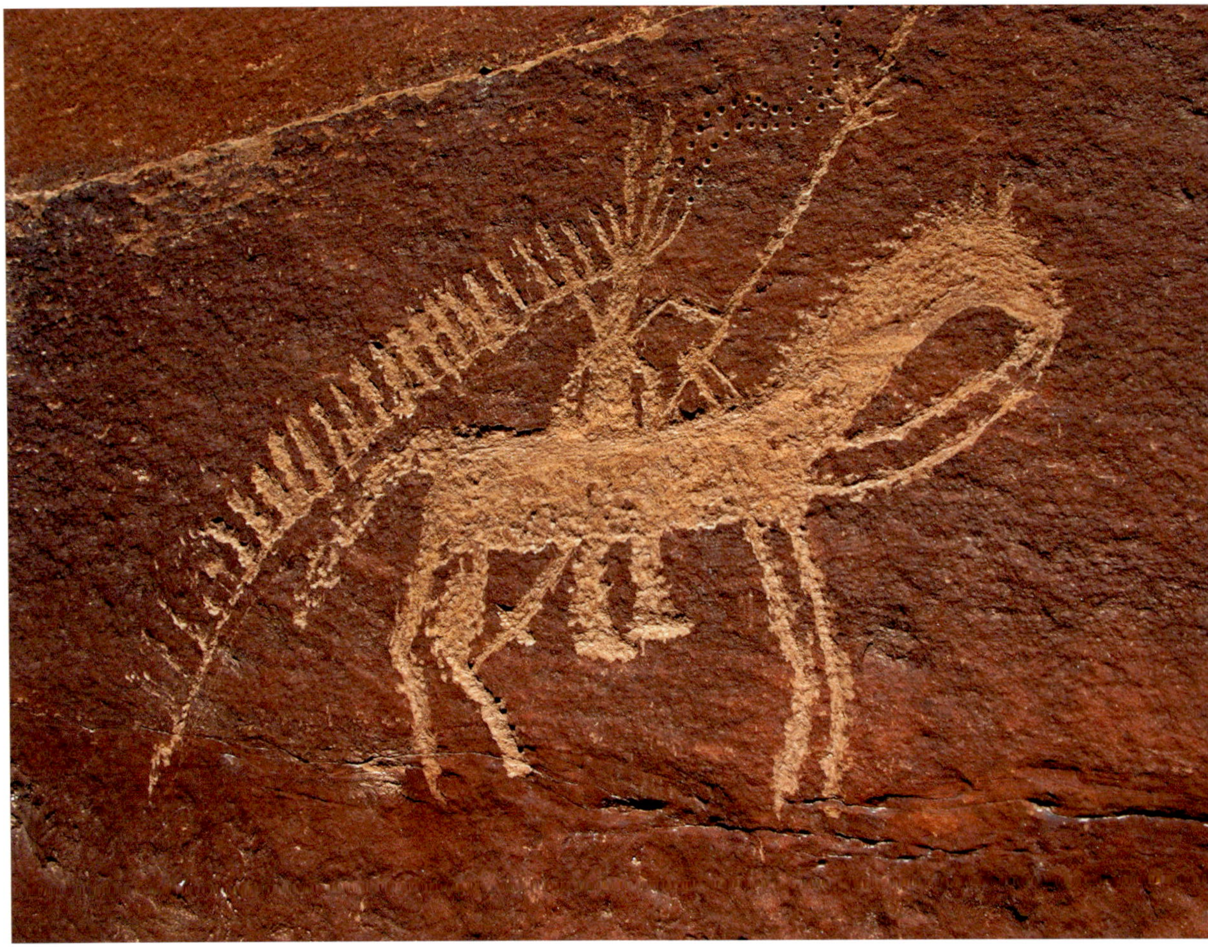

FIGURE 2.13. One of several Ute-style petroglyphs in Nine Mile Canyon that may depict mounted warriors. This one appears to have a feather headdress, lance, and other items obtained after the Utes obtained horses.

3

ANCIENT ART

People have inhabited the Intermountain West for over 10,000 years. From the craggy peaks of the Wasatch Range to the mile-deep riverine gorges, the starkly barren salt flats to the rugged piñon-juniper woodlands, people have been part of this place for hundreds of generations. Not some dull-witted cave people, as depicted in romanticized mass-market fiction, these were people like you and me. Yes, people with the same range of human characteristics as you, your family, your neighbors, friends, leaders, teachers, and enemies. Some were as brilliant as Einstein, as gifted storytellers as Hemingway, as compelling spiritual leaders as Jesus, and as talented artists as Picasso and Michelangelo. Einstein, Hemingway, Jesus, Picasso, and Michelangelo all lived in just the last 2,000 years. Think of how many incredible humans have walked the trails of the West before us. How can we connect with them? How can we know them?

The time before Europeans arrived in the New World is generally regarded as prehistoric, meaning that there exists almost no history recorded by the people who were here. Other than some written records from Mesoamerica (many more of which were destroyed by the Spanish conquerors), oral traditions and stories, and paintings and renderings on ceramics, in sculptures, and on stone, no real record exists. What we know of people who lived thousands of years ago, well beyond the reach of oral tradition, comes from the archaeological record.

Archaeologists attempt to understand and explain the past behavior of people and cultures using only what was left behind as keys to the lives long since ended. We study the ruins of their houses and camps, the bones of animals they consumed, the tools they lost or broke and discarded, sometimes their bodies and bones, and other material traces they left on the landscape—cairns, ditches, pits, fire pits, and markings on stone, wood, baskets, and pottery.

Archaeologists study the material remains of past lives. We have gotten pretty good at reconstructing prehistoric diets, technologies, and settlement patterns. We can posit a fairly detailed culture history of a place, complete with dates and places showing when a particular type of animal was hunted, when a style of stone tool was made, when a kind of pottery was introduced, when farming started. What we are not good at is reconstructing or understanding prehistoric cultures.

Think about your own culture. How would you define yourself? What aspects of your life set you and those like you apart from others in the world? One thing most of us would use to identify ourselves is the language we speak. That is a clear identifier. We learn our language from those closest to us, usually our family. The language we speak clearly identifies us as distinct from those who speak differently. What else? Religion is often an important component of identity. How about the music we listen to? The stories that are passed down from generation to generation? These tend to be the primary ways we distinguish ourselves from other peoples.

In addition, we might mention clothing. Our clothing is different than that of people of other places and cultures, as is our art. Do our tools and economies distinguish us from other cultures? Not so much. What does this mean for archaeologists? It means that the most important ways people identify themselves, those items of their behavior that distinguish them from others, are not generally expressed in the concrete objects that may be accessible to archaeologists.

Archaeologists cannot dig up a language. We cannot tell what language a person spoke from looking at that person's house, tools, or bones. We cannot dig up beliefs. We cannot dig up stories. What are we left with? We sometimes find clothing. We do find tools and can learn about prehistoric economies, but what a shallow understanding that leaves us. And we do sometimes find artistic embellishment of everyday items and places in the environment. Would you feel that someone knew you and your culture if all they knew about you was the basics of your economy, what tools you used, and what kind of house you lived in? I do not think you would.

Of the aspects of our lives that make us most human, those things that we all share and which we use to distinguish ourselves from others—our language, beliefs, stories, and art—sometimes only our art remains to be studied and appreciated by those who come after. The designs on a fragment of pottery, the embellishments on a piece of basketry or cloth, the figures painted or scored on stone—these may be the only glimpse we will ever have of the true humanity, the soul, of those who preceded us.

And of those things, it is the purposeful creation of images on stone, the most lasting part of any environment, that is the legacy of our forebears. And while we can appreciate and marvel at the art of the earlier ones because it was created by people, the most complicated organisms to ever exist, we can never know what those images and symbols meant to their creators or what they intended to convey. Never. If we pretend to, we are only fooling ourselves, for the keys to understanding ancient art died with the artists and cultures that created them, sometimes many thousands of years ago.

You might say that some things can be understood, such as a depiction of a deer or a snake. We can surely tell that the artist painted a snake. However, we do not have any idea what meaning that depiction carried. Think of a modern painting depicting Adam and Eve in the Garden of Eden, Eve holding an apple and facing a snake. For someone from a culture not privy to the biblical story, it would be a painting of a man and woman eating fruit and looking at a snake. They would not understand that the painting is intended to portray the first man and woman being seduced into committing the first sin by Satan, who has taken the form of a serpent. None of the intended meaning of the piece of art would be understandable to a person from outside the culture. And for someone who came along thousands of years later, when no other interpretations or keys to the symbolism exist, it would be impossible to even guess at the meaning.

The same goes for the ancient rock art of western North America. Or anywhere, for that matter. The art was created by people, just like you, who created art to convey thoughts, emotions, ideas, and beliefs using symbols germane to their own culture. The keys to the symbolism are cultural, not universal. For people who lived thousands of years ago, the keys to those symbols have been lost.

What appears to be a bighorn sheep depicted on a rock art panel might have represented an element of a story that we have never heard, a symbol for something we cannot decipher. And once we get beyond the apparently simple renderings of familiar entities such as animals and people, the meanings become even more obscured: wavy lines, geometric designs, spirals, circles, human-like figures with horns or features that appear so different as to make it clear that regular humans are not what is being pictured.

I do, however, think it is important to acknowledge the relationships between modern Native American beliefs and teachings, and some of the symbols and meanings expressed in rock art. I have visited rock art with elders from several regional tribes, and they pointed out symbols they recognized as being similar to ones they use to represent cultural elements such as clans, human and animal figures that may depict elements of traditional teachings and stories, and physical features such as mountains and streams. Please keep a couple of things in mind. Native people may be reluctant to divulge the significance of the symbols to non-Native people for a variety of reasons. And many of the elements in rock art date to the deep past, before the ancestors of the modern regional tribes arrived in the area, thus the symbolism is also likely not accessible to them. In general, for non-Native people, it is best to refrain from trying to assign meaning to the rock art and its symbols.

Our human desire to figure something out tends to dominate our thinking when viewing ancient art. We want to make some sense of it. Decipher it. Understand it. We cannot bear to be dumbfounded by art so beautiful, frightening, and mysterious. We want to know what it means.

So we tend to try to use our own cultural background to figure out what the ancients were saying. We think we can pick out symbols for the sun and moon, water and animals, plants and people. We borrow items from modern Native American symbolism to interpret ancient art.

But we shouldn't. We will always be wrong. Always. Even in trying to show that a figure has an astronomically significant placement, we are imposing our own way of thinking on ancient works, and we are likely to be wrong.

I am not saying that we should view ancient art as so foreign that we cannot hope to get any meaning from it, as if listening to a completely unknown tongue being spoken. No, not at all. I am saying that rather than trying to decipher the ancient artist's meaning, we can try to find the meaning the art has for us.

Try this experiment. Go to an art show or gallery. Look at the paintings, photographs, or whatever is being displayed. Do not read the artists' statements. Some pieces may for some reason disgust you. Some will do nothing at all for you. Some will draw you in, capture your interest somehow. Some may move you to smile, or frown, or puzzle over the piece. Some may anger you. Art is a uniquely human way of communicating with others at a deep, emotional level. To appreciate art is to invite it into your emotional world, to let the artists' creations affect you. This is one of the most profound forms of communication we as humans have, and we invented it. We probably invented it before we even had language to communicate at an entirely different level.

So I am advocating that we invite the ancient artists into our most human world: our emotional world. The photographs Layne Miller has taken are most astounding to me in that they capture the image's emotional content. Look at them, absorb them, let the artist in. Let's take a stroll through this ancient landscape and see where it takes us. Let's allow the ancient artists, these messengers from antiquity to speak to us, and maybe we will hear a tiny bit of what they have to say. And that will surely be a good thing.

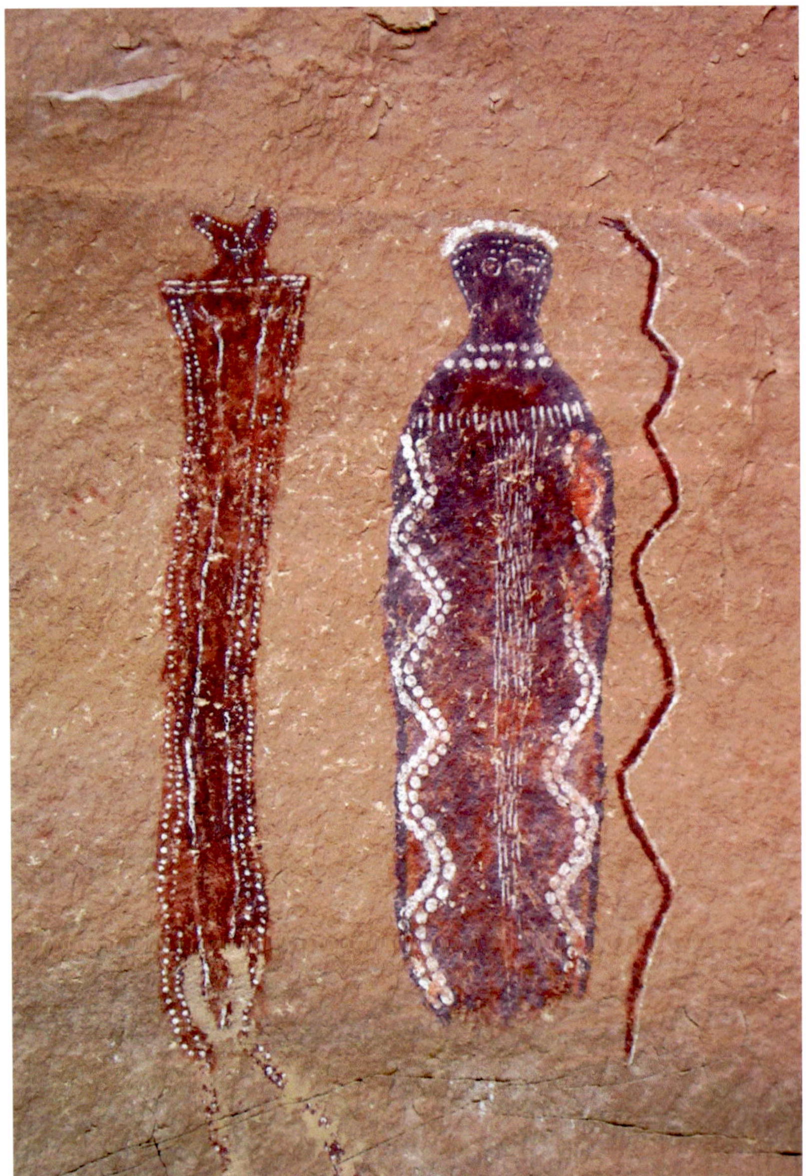

FIGURE 3.1. Exquisite Barrier Canyon–style pictographs on what is commonly known as the Perfect Panel.

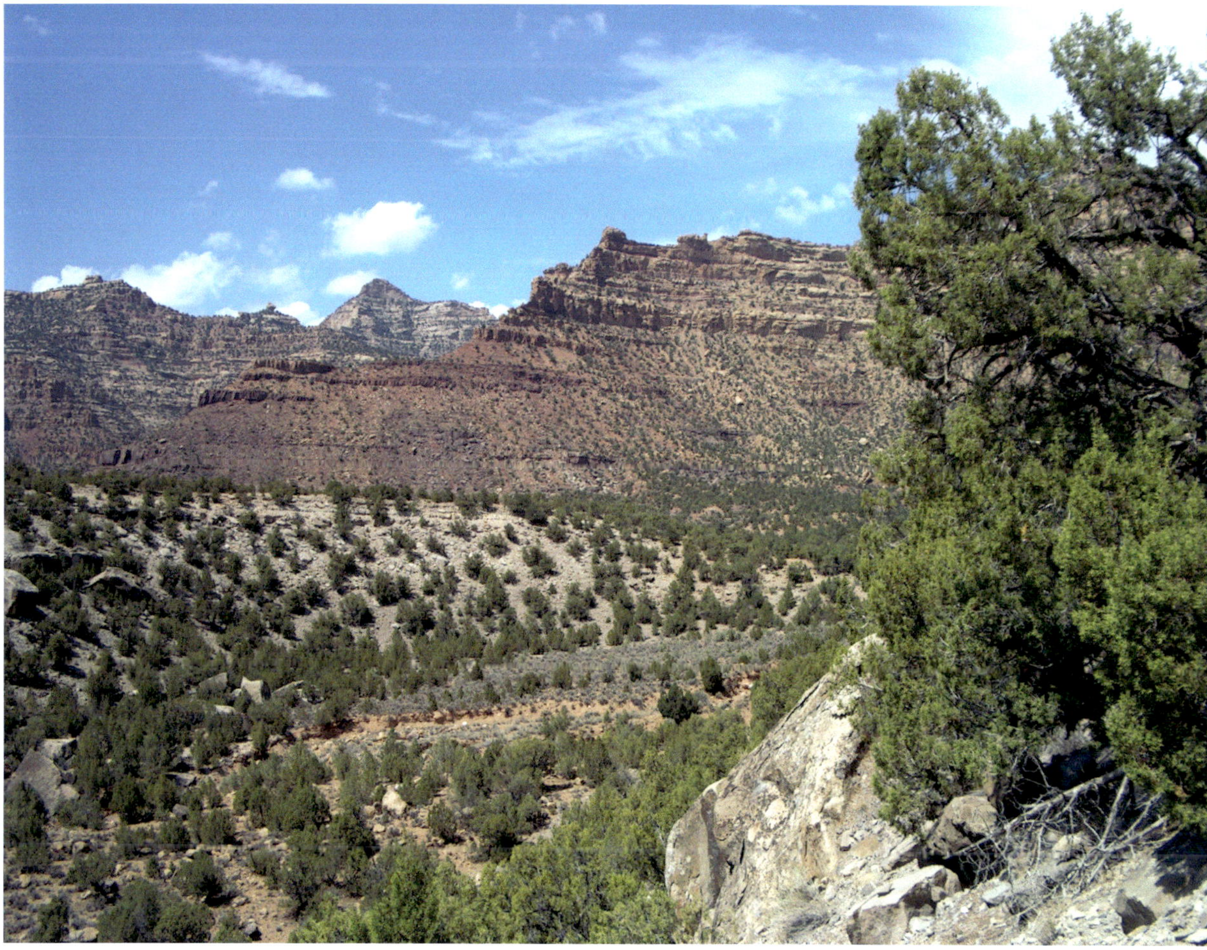

FIGURE 3.2. A view of Range Creek Canyon in the Book Cliffs region.

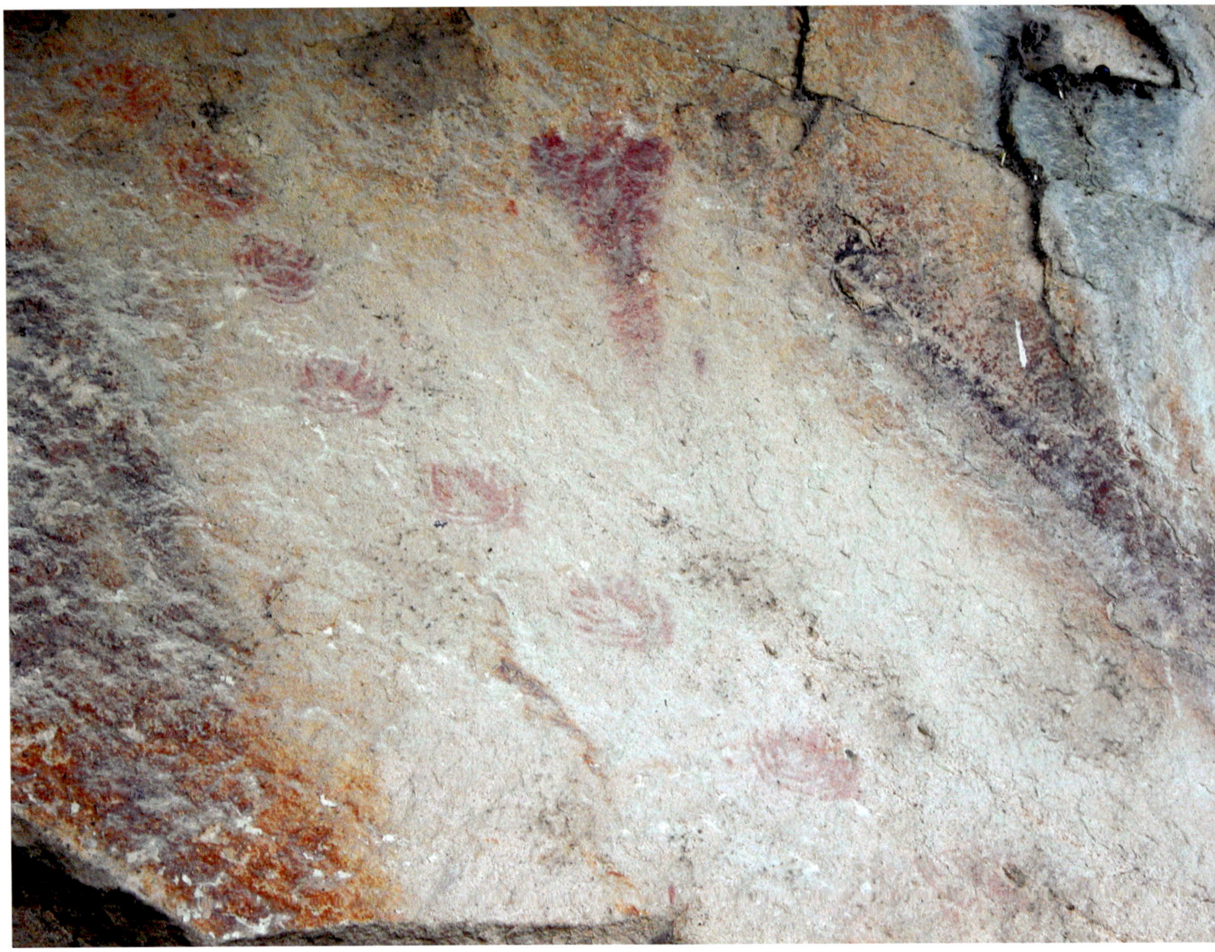

FIGURE 3.3. A faint painted panel in an alcove near Joe's Valley, central Utah.

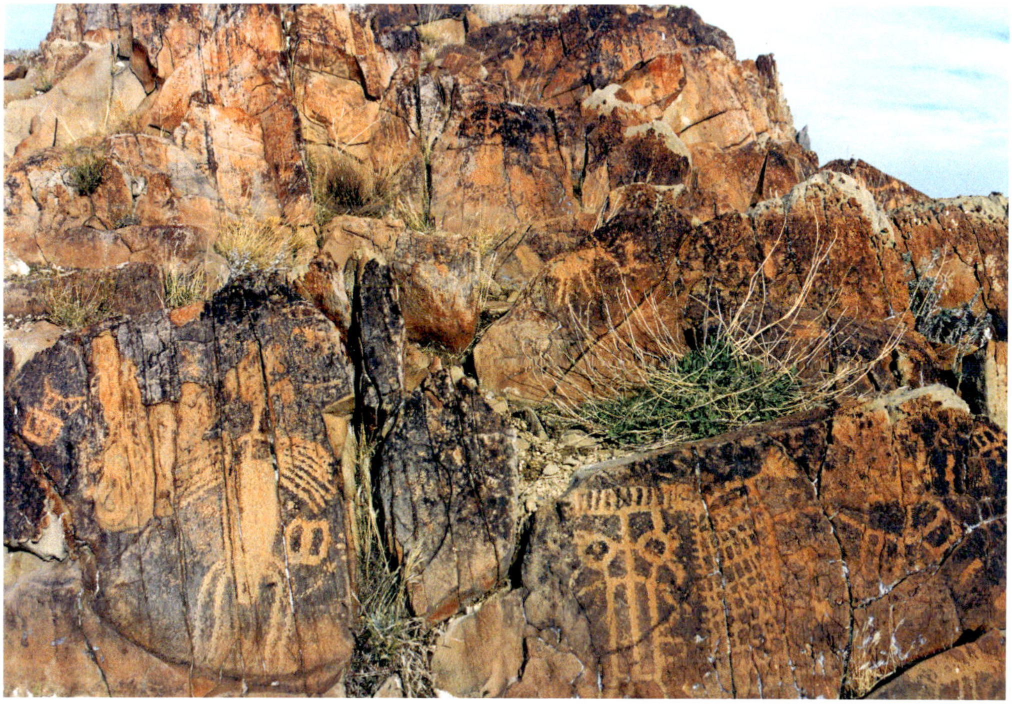

FIGURE 3.4. A petroglyph panel near the shores of the Great Salt Lake, possibly Archaic or Fremont.

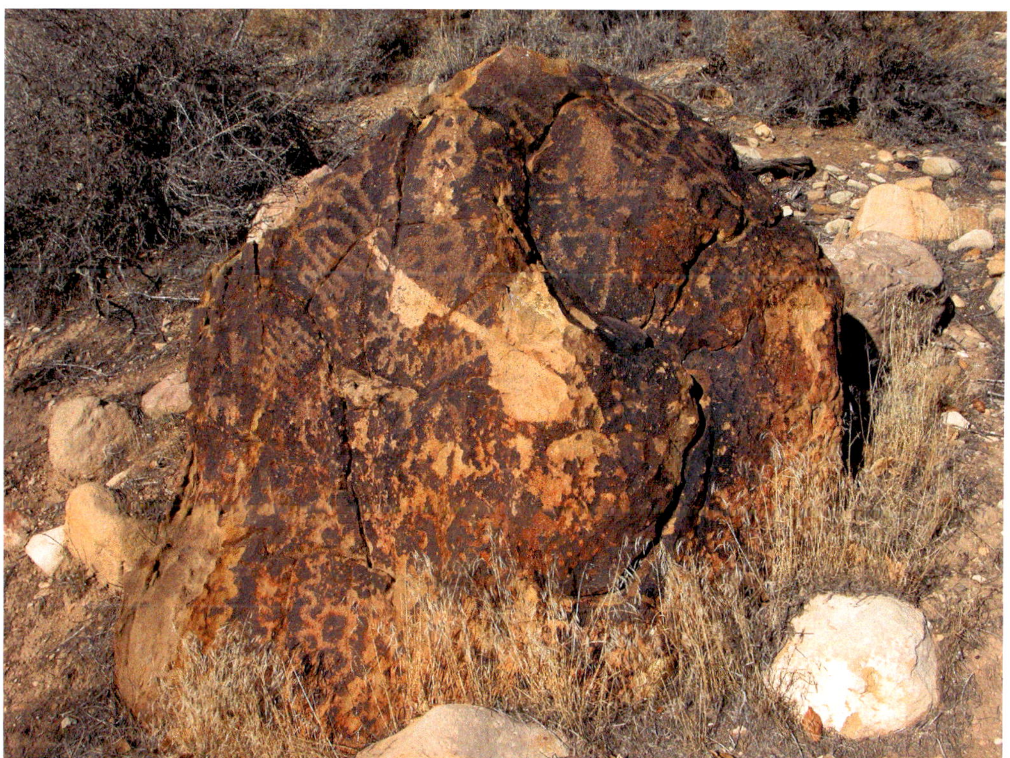

FIGURE 3.5. A decorated boulder next to a ranch house near Sunnyside, Utah. The curvilinear style is thought by some to be one of the oldest styles found in Utah.

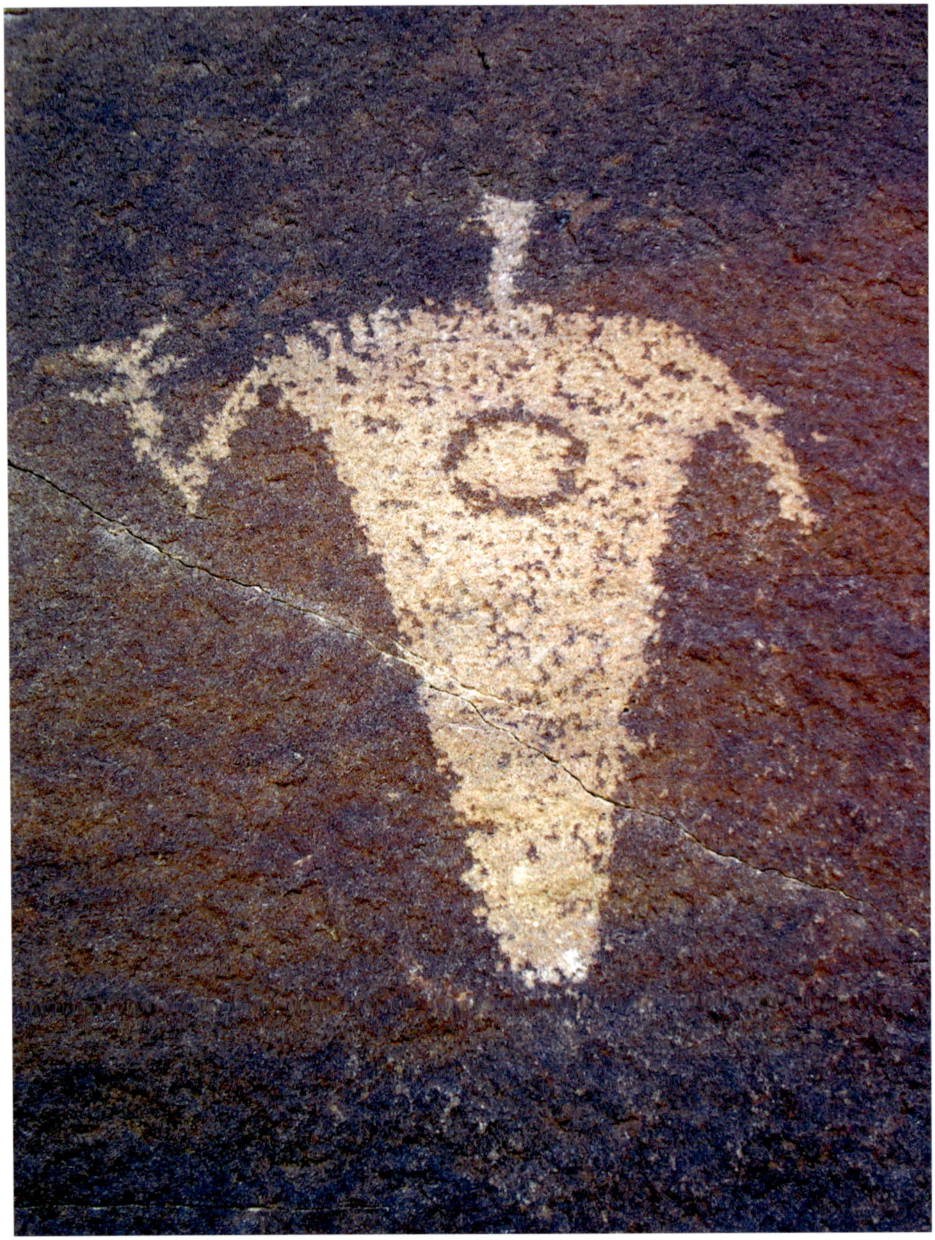

FIGURE 3.6. A Basketmaker-style anthropomorph in Range Creek Canyon with an arm transforming into what some interpret as an open-mouthed horned snake.

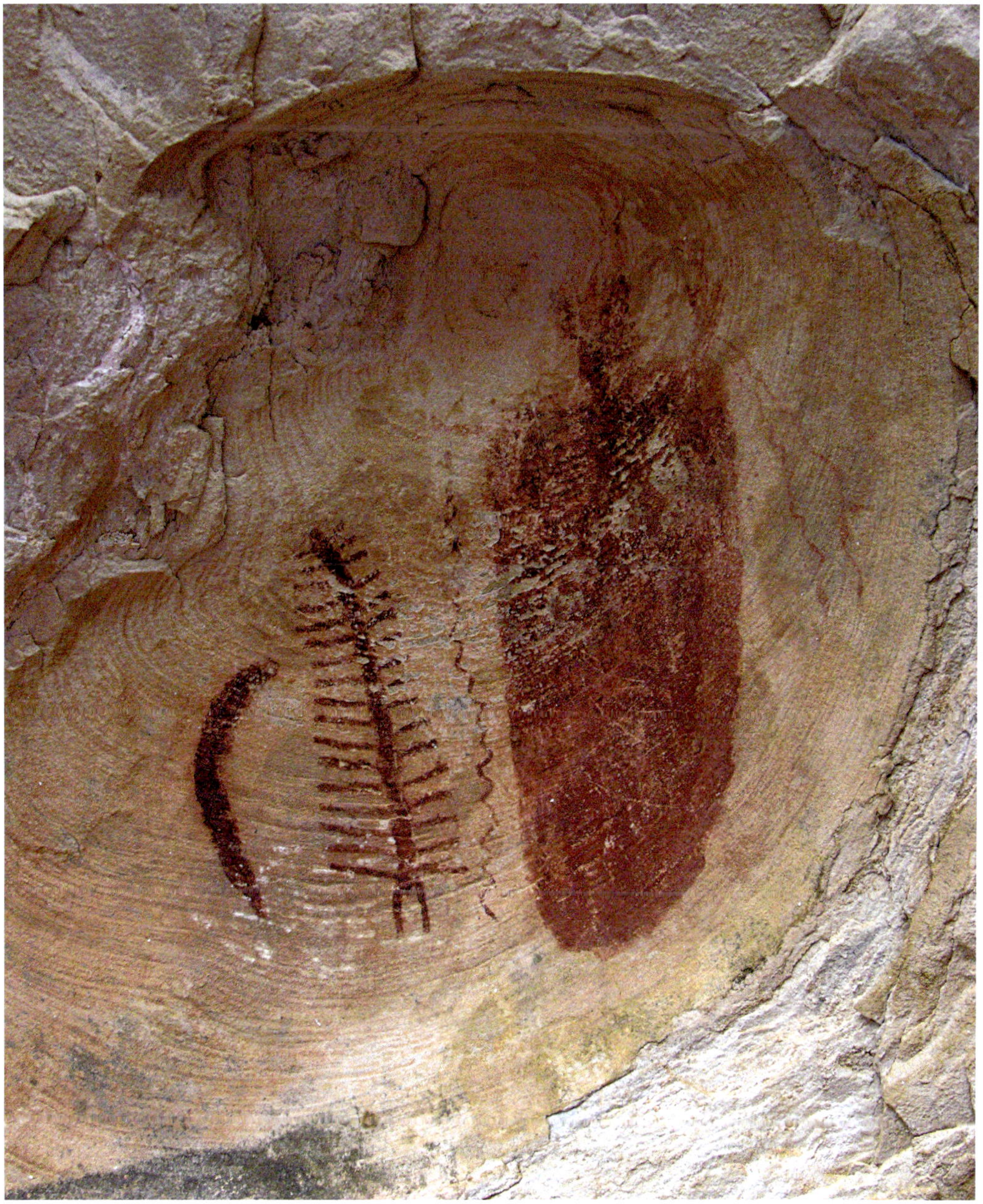

FIGURE 3.7. A pictograph from Seven Mile Canyon near Moab. Among its unusual figures is one that looks like a centipede.

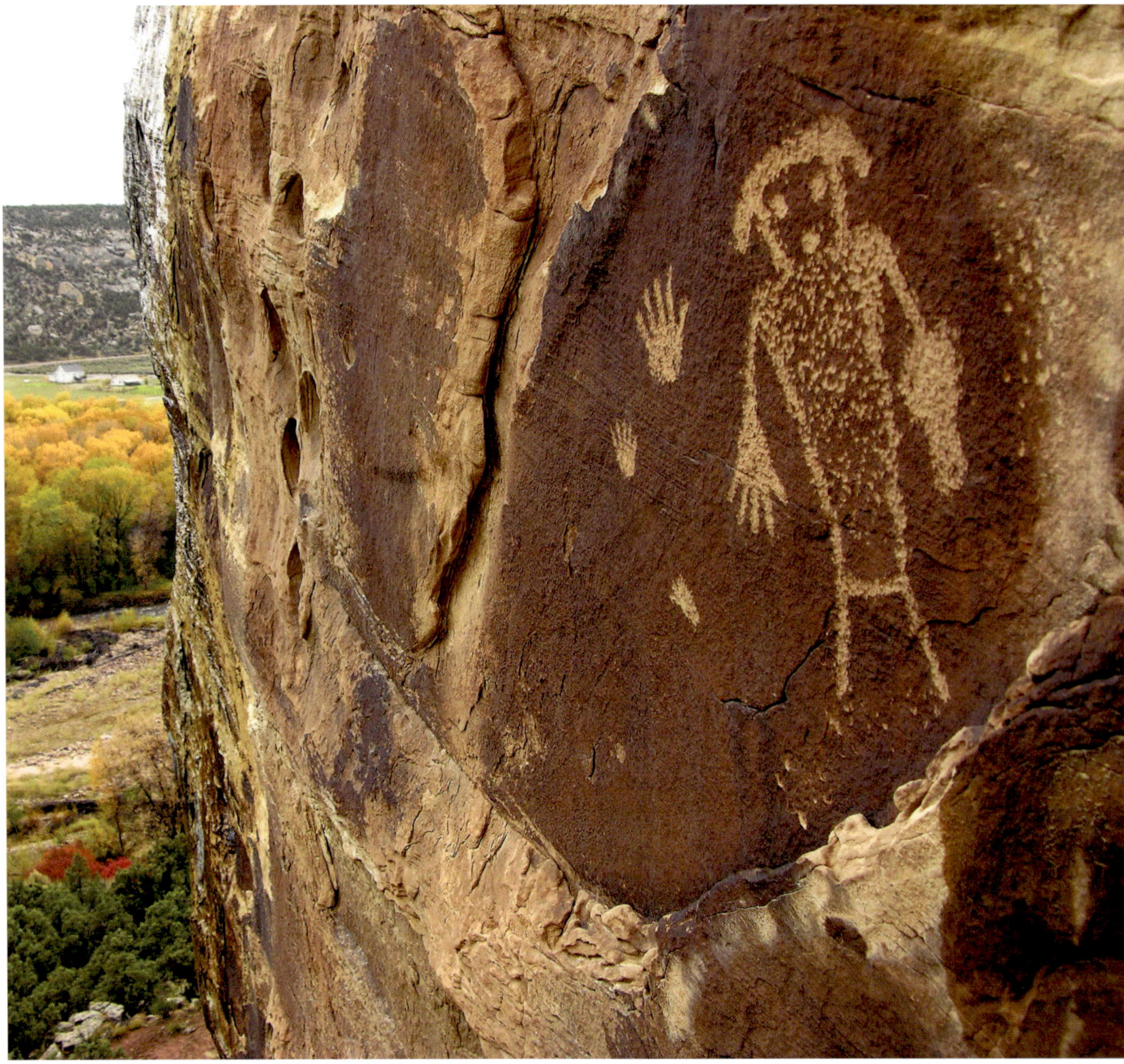

FIGURE 3.8. Fremont-style figures gracing a cliff in the Ashley Creek area of the Uinta Basin.

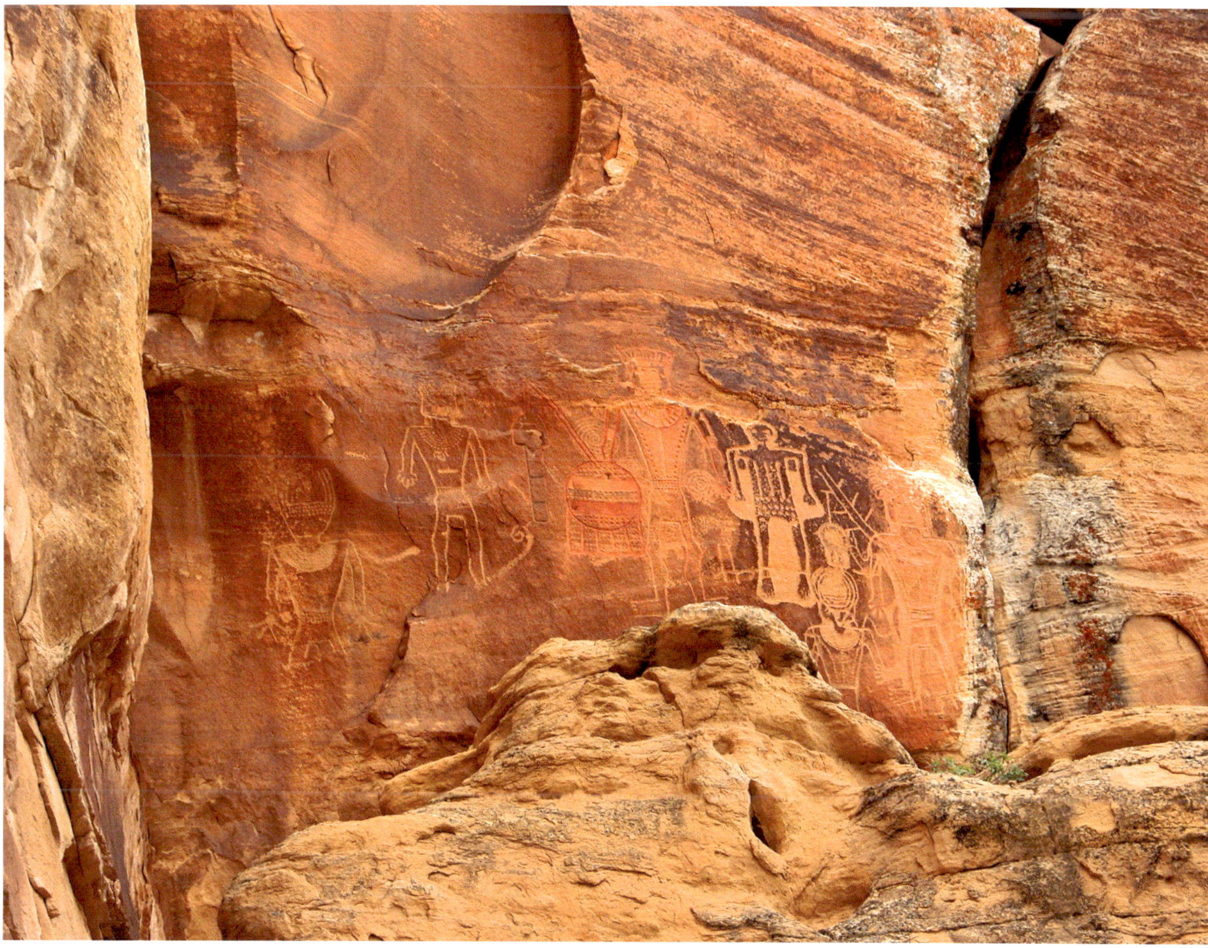

FIGURE 3.9. The Three Kings panel near Vernal, Utah. This incredible example of Utah rock art is often called classic Fremont, but it's actually not typical of that style.

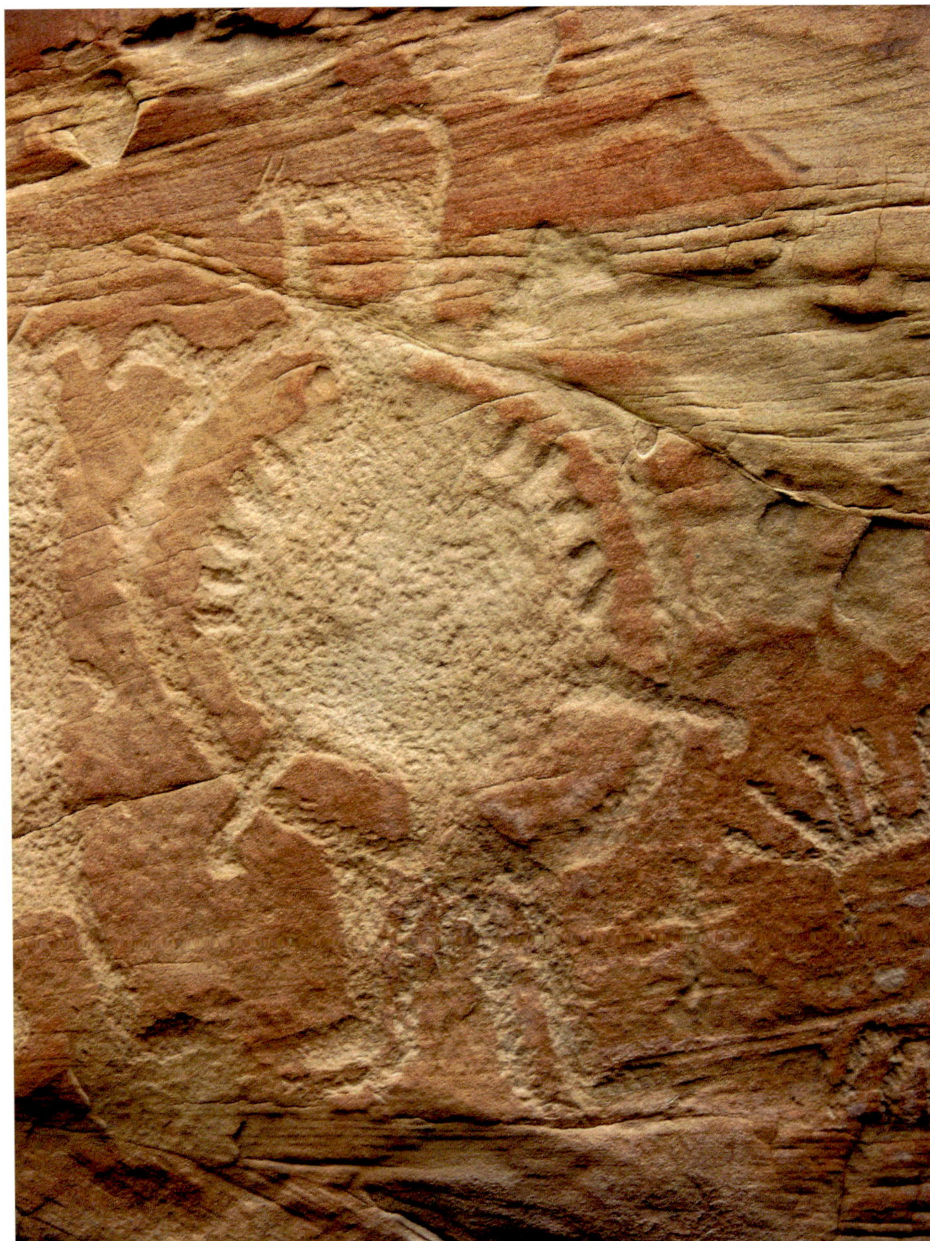

FIGURE 3.10. A Fremont-style shield figure in the Ashley Creek area of the Uinta Basin.

4

TIME, SPACE, CULTURE, AND SYMBOLISM ON THE WALLS OF TIME

When someone took tools and paints and created an image on the cliff face of a remote canyon alongside a great, flowing river, little thought was likely given to how the work might be interpreted a thousand years hence. Unlike the practice of many modern creators, no date or signature (that we know of or can recognize) was carved to give credit and reference to the image. Many who visit rock art sites are content to view the ancient engravings and paintings and let the symbolism and flow of the creation wash over them, as any good art will. Some, however, especially archaeologists and art historians, are compelled to assign a date to the creation, determine how it relates to other art and objects in the region, and speculate about the style and traditions embodied in the symbols. As to the meaning of the piece—such as whether the apparent bighorn sheep depicted on the stone represents actual bighorn sheep, or references a story, or even depicts mythical creatures or persons—we will never know and should not speculate. As to dates, times, relationships, and styles, however, we can make some determinations, inferences, and guesses.

One initial caveat: rock art, while considered a class of artifact by archaeologists, is—by its very nature of being immovably attached to a stone, monolith, or cliff face—not readily assigned dates or associations, as are other artifacts such as ceramic sherds or chipped stone tools. A potsherd found in stratigraphic context with other artifacts and naturally deposited materials can be assigned a date because it is associated with other objects that can be accurately dated, such as bits of organic material. So when potsherds of the same type are found in other contexts, even on the surface, they can be confidently assigned to a specific time period. Other objects, such as projectile points of certain styles, can be affiliated with that pottery type, and those too can be used to assign dates to deposits or sites. Not so with rock art.

Rock art is not portable; therefore it is not found in buried deposits in association with other objects and features. For rock art to be dated, it must be dated

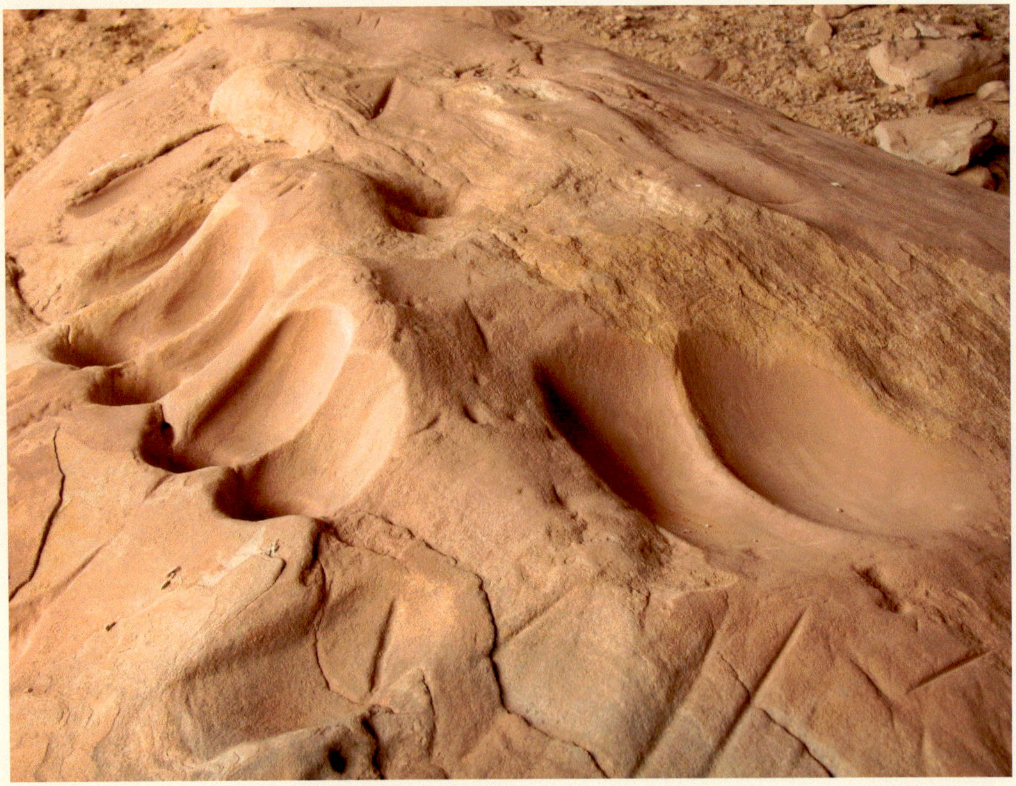

FIGURE 4.1. Grinding slicks below pictograph handprints in southern Utah.

directly by some physical method or assumed to be associated with other features and deposits nearby. The age of some rock art can be estimated by radiocarbon dating of pigments or components of its paint, or by the amount of patina acquired since its creation. On rare occasions, rock art can be found in buried contexts, and the art can be assigned a date on that basis (that is, the art is older than dateable material in the sediments that buried it). Beyond these limited tools, rock art is most often assigned dates by affiliating it with a dated archaeological "culture." Also, sometimes items depicted in the art can offer clues. For example, a depiction of a mammoth in rock art was likely created when mammoths were present; an image of a bow and arrow (e.g., figures 10.2 and 11.11) cannot pre-date the introduction of the bow and arrow; and pictures of horses and guns (e.g., figures 2.13 and 12.3) surely date to after the arrival of Europeans.

Given the limitations on dating, we can generally assign only very approximate time estimates to most rock art. Rock art of the Fremont culture, for instance, could have been created at any time between 600 and 1,500 years ago. And those beginning and end dates are not set in stone. Rock art considered to be from the Archaic period might be anywhere from 2,000 to 8,000 years old. And again, those dates should not be cited without allowing for some wiggle room.

So while we would certainly like to know exactly when each figure was created and something about the cultural milieu of that time and place, we must keep in mind that those aspects of rock art studies are far from precise. Just as some rock art is faded, eroded, and losing definition as the forces of time and nature bear upon it, we must know that we are only viewing it through a clouded lens, that our desire for factual precision will not be fulfilled, and that there are some things about these wonderful gifts left by those who lived long ago that we will never fully comprehend or appreciate. Surely our methods of study and the tools provided by technology will only get better, but even if some of the limitations on dating are eliminated in the future, it may be best if we allow for some obscurity of fact when viewing rock art. Perhaps the mystery is something to appreciate—and sometimes let be.

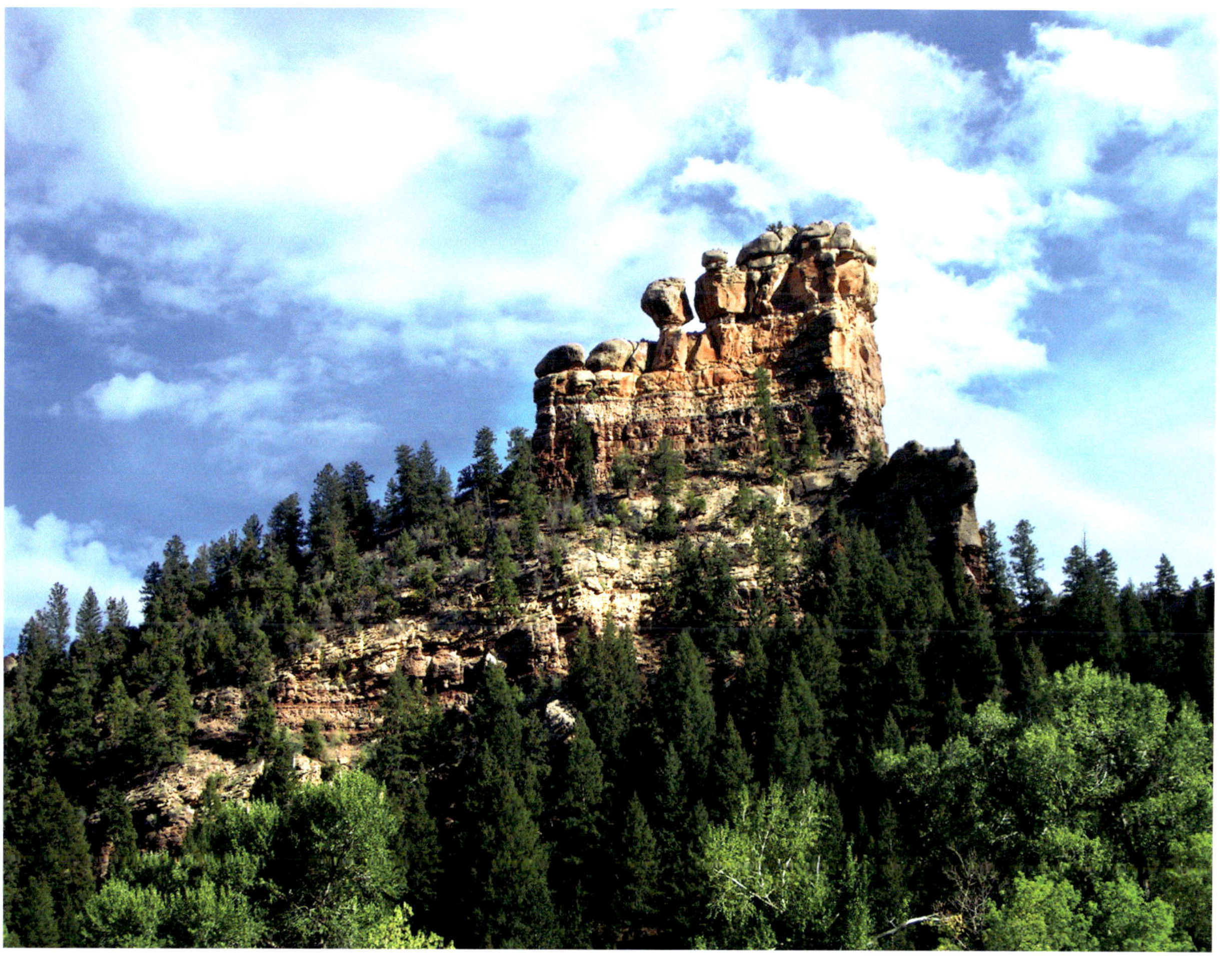

FIGURE 4.2. The formation called Locomotive Rock near the entrance to Range Creek Canyon. Waldo Wilcox, the former owner of the ranch there, said his family called it Waldo's Choo-Choo.

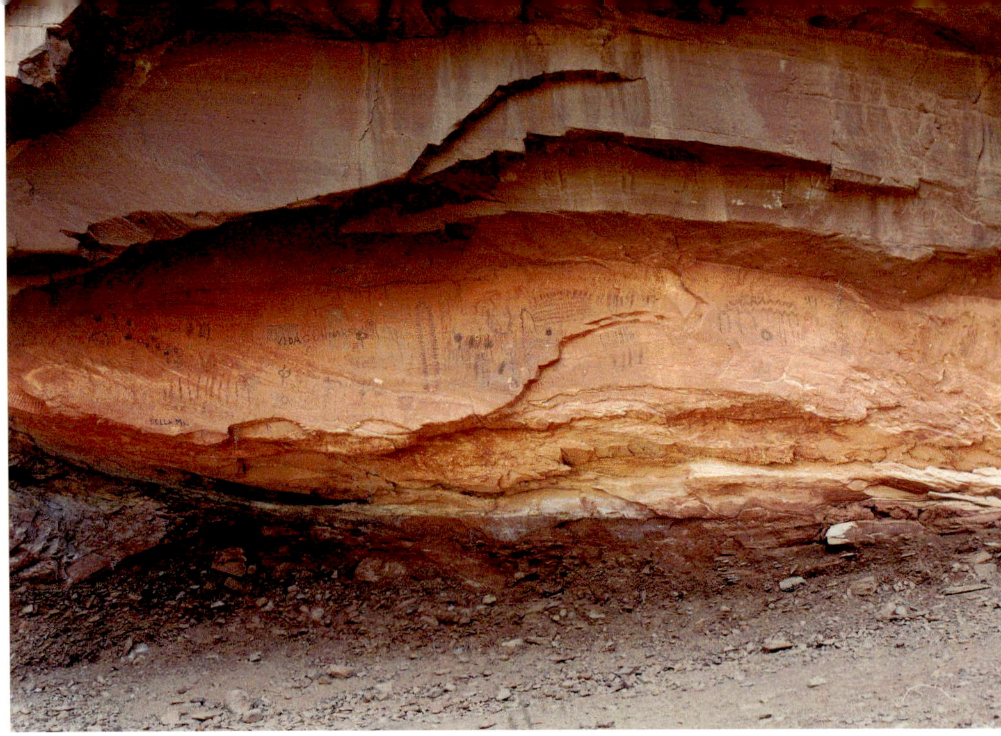

FIGURE 4.3. A pictograph panel in Black Dragon Canyon in eastern Utah. The figures are different from the Barrier Canyon–style figures found elsewhere at the site.

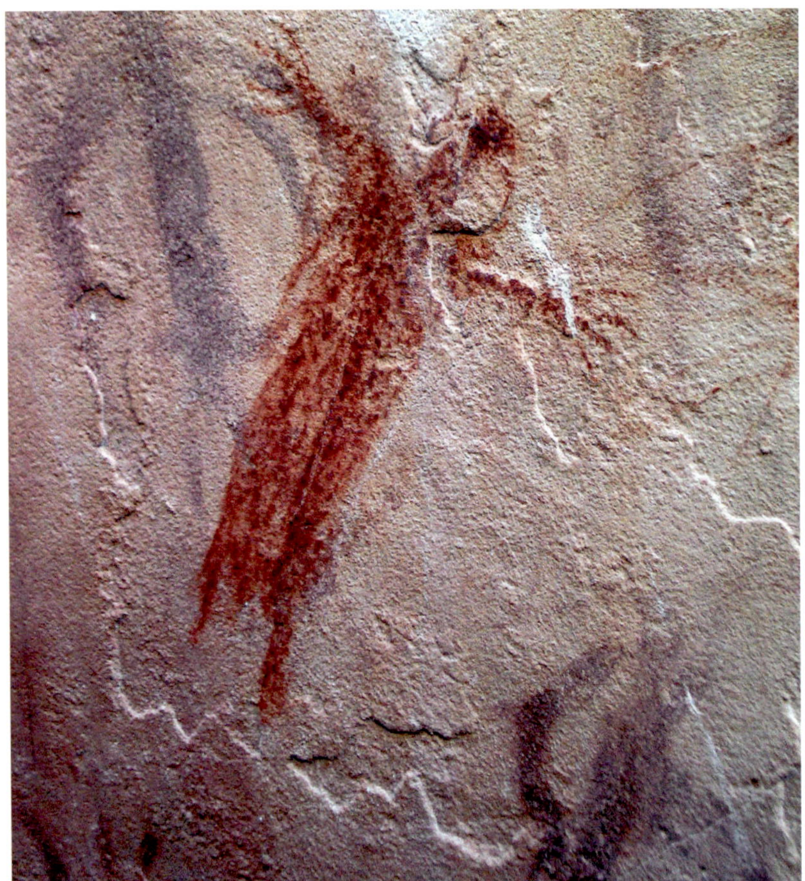

FIGURE 4.4. A figure on a panel in a shallow wash near Moab. The panel contains very unusual pictographs that might be Ute. Some, like this one, appear to have been drawn with a stick of pigment that worked like a crayon.

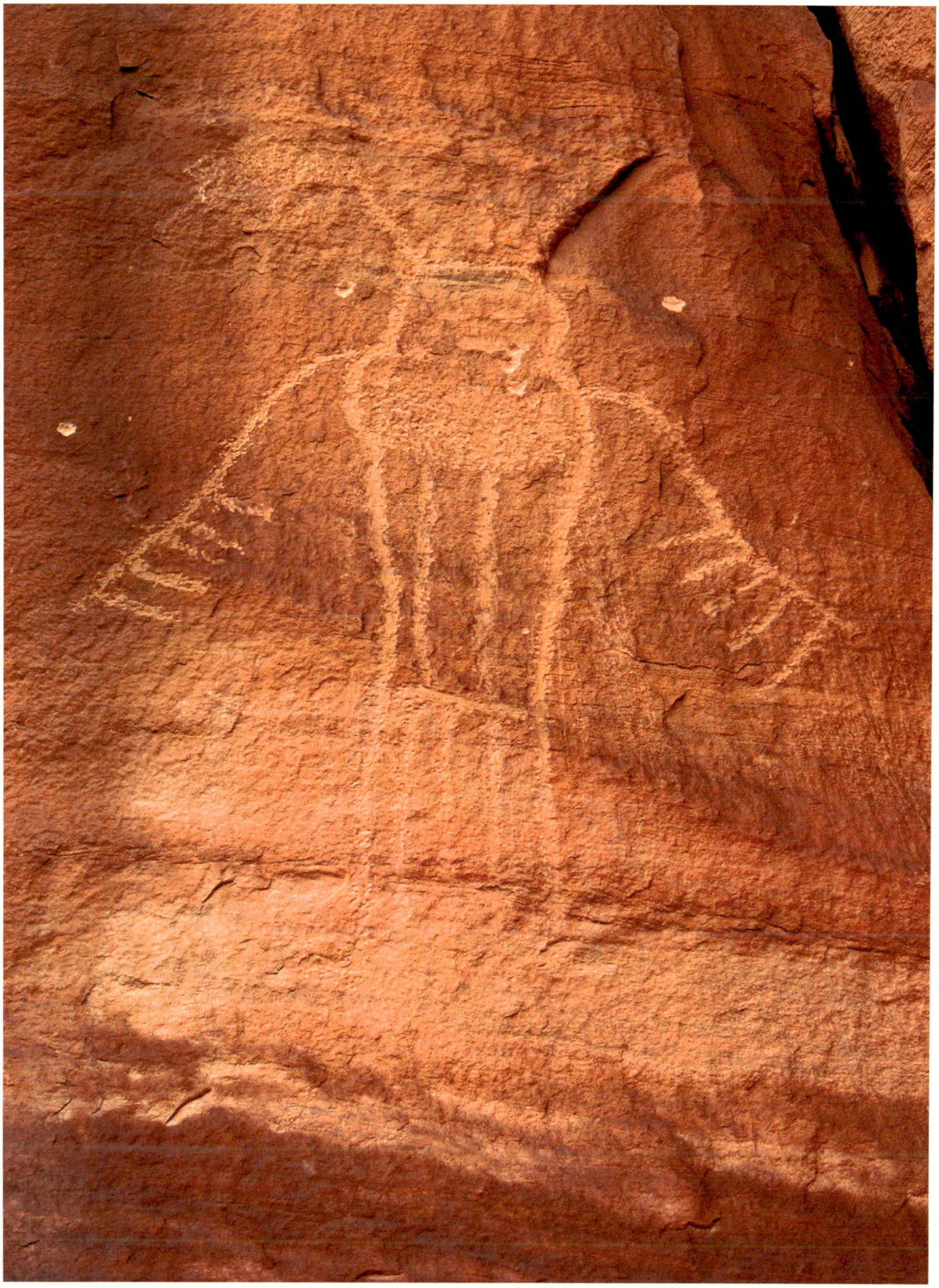

FIGURE 4.5. A winged Fremont-style anthropomorph near the McConkie Ranch outside Vernal, Utah. Bullet scars mar this unusual figure.

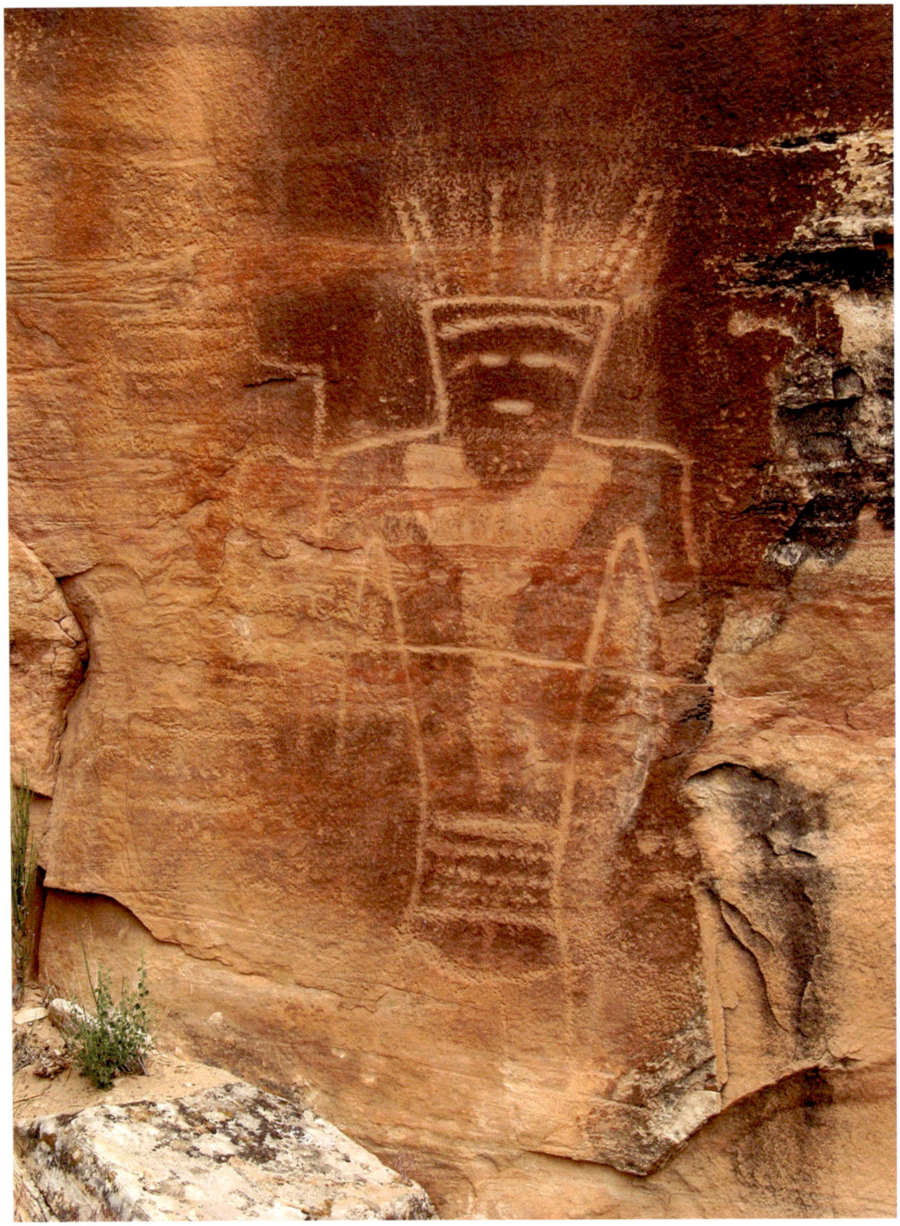

FIGURE 4.6. A Fremont-style anthropomorph on the McConkie Ranch near Vernal, Utah.

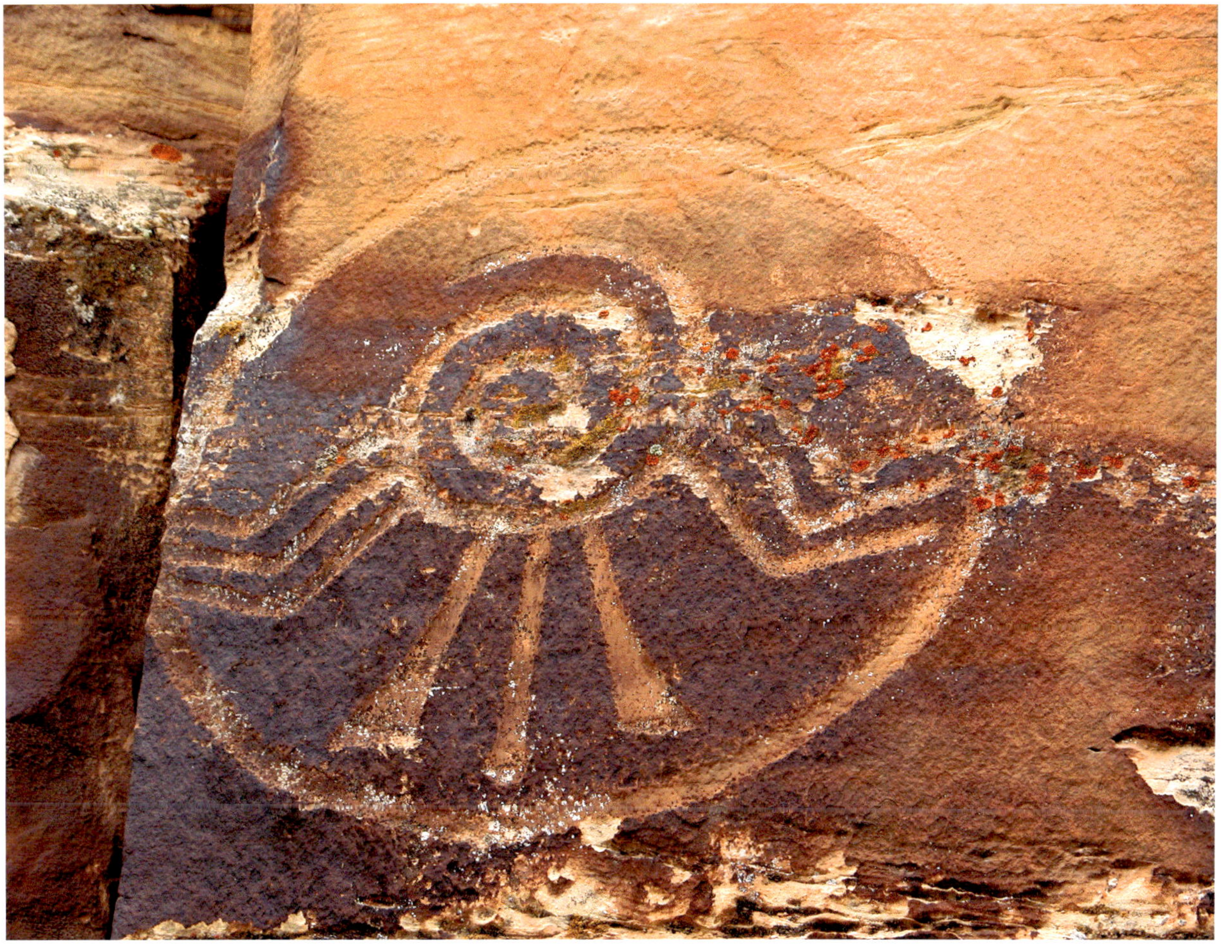

FIGURE 4.7. A Fremont-style shield-like petroglyph near Vernal, Utah.

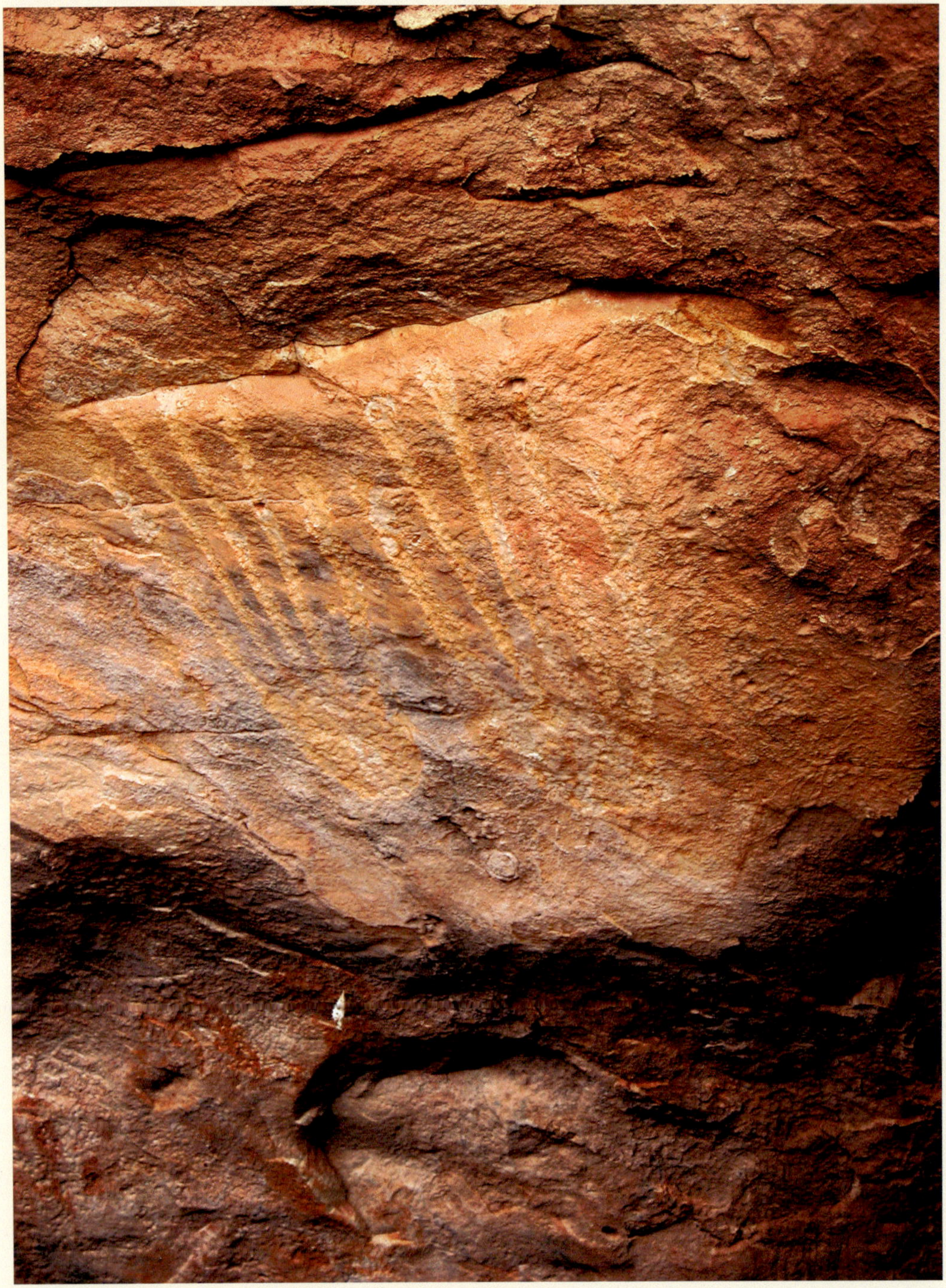

FIGURE 4.8. Graceful pictographs on the roof of an alcove in southern Utah. The associated Ancestral Puebloan site, Long Fingers, was named for them.

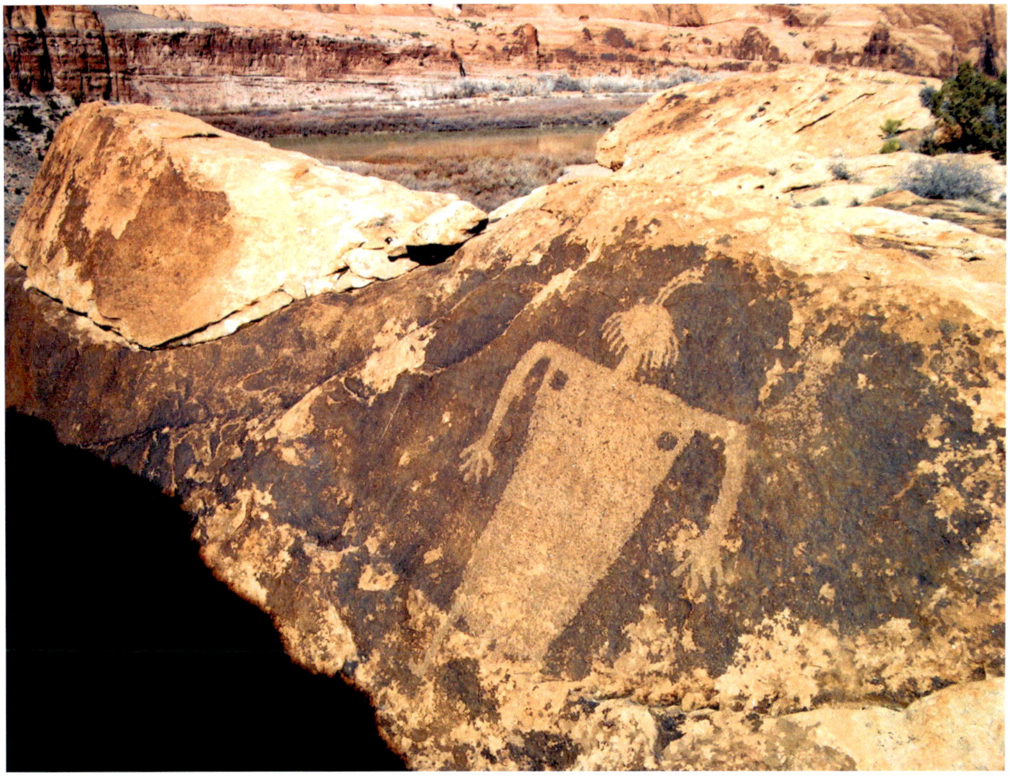

FIGURE 4.9. The Kane Creek Princess, an Ancestral Puebloan petroglyph near Moab.

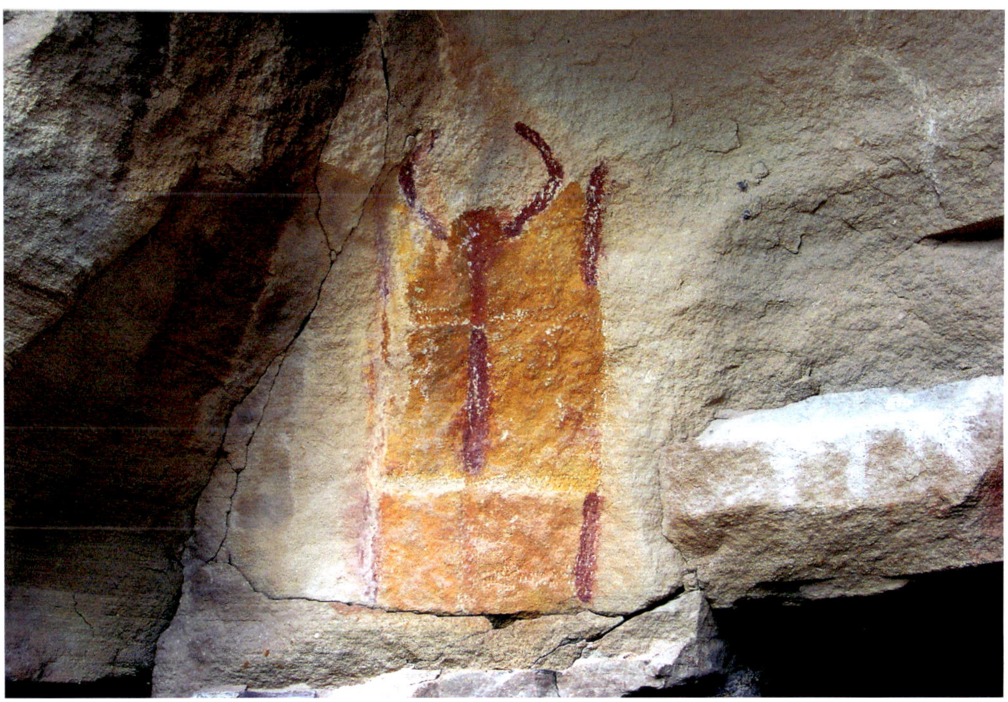

FIGURE 4.10. A Barrier Canyon–style pictograph in Range Creek Canyon. The anthropomorphic figure appears to be wearing a two-horned headdress.

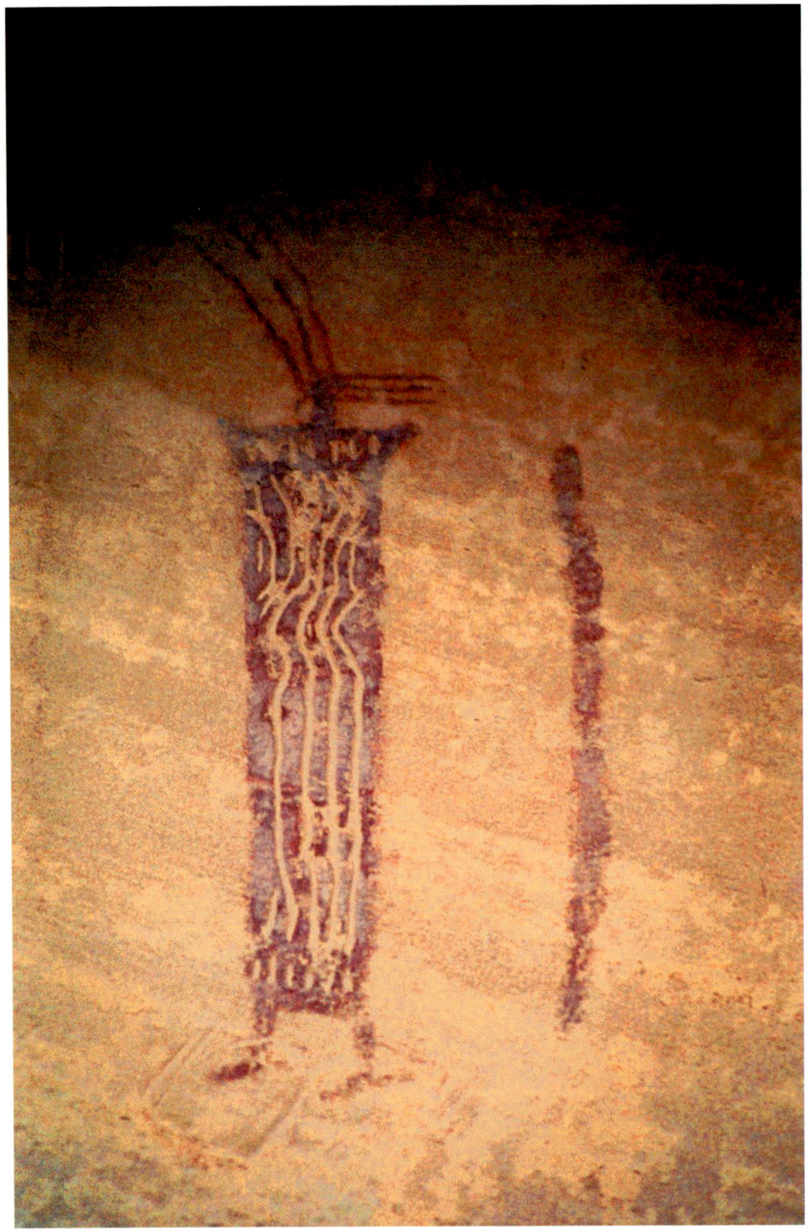

FIGURE 4.11. A horned Barrier Canyon–style anthropomorph in the San Rafael Reef.

5

UTAH: THE ROCK ART STATE

This op-ed essay appeared in the *Salt Lake Tribune* (in slightly different form) on March 6, 2017. Utah's state legislature passed the bill, later signed by the governor into law, designating Native American rock art as Utah's official works of art.

As you round the bend in the canyon and look ahead to see what lies beyond, your vision locks in on them. They command your attention. Their eyes bore into you like lasers from the distant past. Ghost-like, larger than life-size, they appear able to impose their will on you, yet these sentinels who have guarded this canyon for over a thousand years are mute. The fantastic painted figures, which to some resemble kings or spirits or shamans, are a direct connection to the artists who created them long, long ago. They are what we call Native American rock art: painted, pecked, etched, and carved into the sandstone cliffs and tumbled boulders, bearing testimony to the 10,000-year history of the people of our region. And Utah is home to some of the most impressive rock art in the world. Many thousands of sites bearing hundreds of thousands of images intrigue those who happen to see them, and to modern Native people, they may still live, speaking to those who can hear, telling of ancient lives, of truths forgotten, of the soul and spirit of people and cultures that came before.

Senator David P. Hinkins (R-Orangeville)—whose district includes Carbon, Emery, Grand, San Juan, Utah, and Wasatch counties—is the sponsor of Senate Bill 171, currently before the Utah legislature, which would designate Native American rock art as one of Utah's official state symbols. I cannot imagine a more appropriate symbol for our state. Utah takes its very name from the Utes, modern people whose ancestors were here long before Europeans arrived to draw borders and political boundaries. The artistic and cultural legacy of the Utes and other cultures that called and still call this state home is beautiful and awe-inspiring, and precisely captures the essence of the land, the country we call home.

Utah is well-known around the world for the beautiful and mysterious rock art that adorns our natural canvasses. We may well have the oldest single rock art panel in all of North America, near Bluff, in San Juan County, and we proudly boast of having the world's longest art gallery, Nine Mile Canyon, in Carbon County. The classic trapezoidal-bodied ambassadors of the Fremont culture that grace the cliff faces in the Uinta Basin and Capitol Reef stand powerful, threatening, and richly adorned. The imposing and mysterious figures of the Great Gallery in Canyonlands draw and inspire visitors from all continents. Spirals, mazes, horned snakes, bighorn sheep, headless elk, dancing deer, abstract designs, bewildering mythological creatures, corn and yucca plants, atlatls, hunting scenes, and handprints—hundreds of handprints, some reminiscent of the childhood handprints in plaster we brought home to our parents, reminding us of lives lived, of happy childhoods, of people saying, "I was here."

To view rock art, you must get out of your house and go where someone long ago created a work of lasting value on stone. To view it, you stand in the same spot as that artist did, in the very studio where the artistry was performed. You see the unchanged landscape, feel the kindred breeze, stand upon the selfsame soil as did that inspired painter or sculptor, and your appreciation of the creation is bolstered by the shared place. Visitors from far away can look at pictures online or in a book of Utah's rock art, and they do, but the allure goes beyond that: seeing the creations in their true environment is the preferred and optimal way to appreciate them. And it is the preferred and optimal way to appreciate Utah as well.

The rock art that adorns and enhances our state represents our past, but it also represents who we are: people who treasure our heritage, our diversity, the richness of culture, and incredible creativity. Please join me in supporting SB 171 and in thanking Senator Hinkins for sponsoring this truly meaningful initiative.

Note: A bill designating the Spiral Jetty as an official state symbol (HB 211) is also making its way through the legislature. The bills are not in opposition to each other, and both serve to recognize works of art important to Utahns. I urge support of both bills.

Utah Code 63G-1-601. State symbols.
(28)(29) Utah's state works of art are Native American rock art. Utah's state work of land art is the Spiral Jetty.

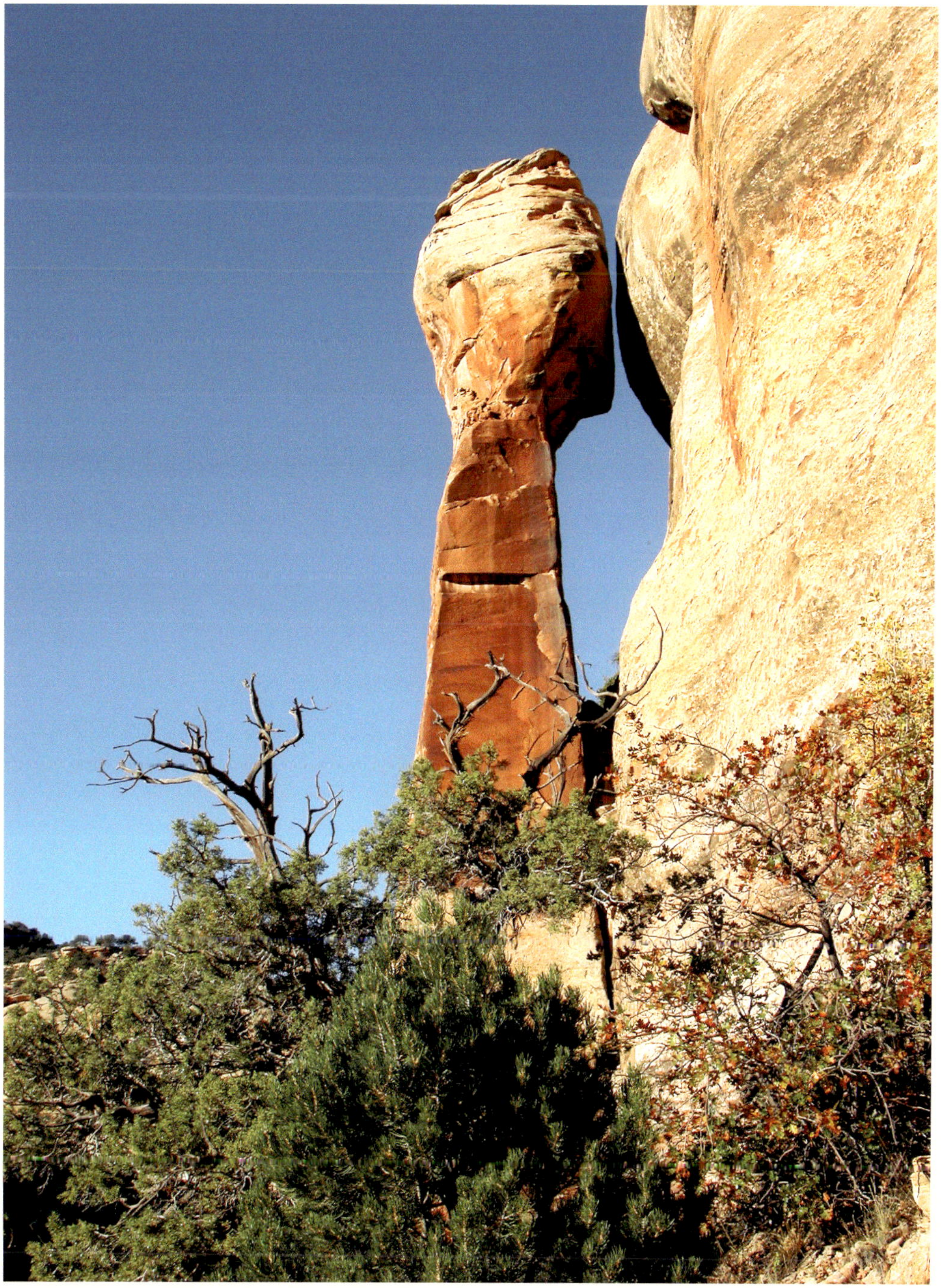

FIGURE 5.1. A balanced rock in Indian Creek, south of Moab.

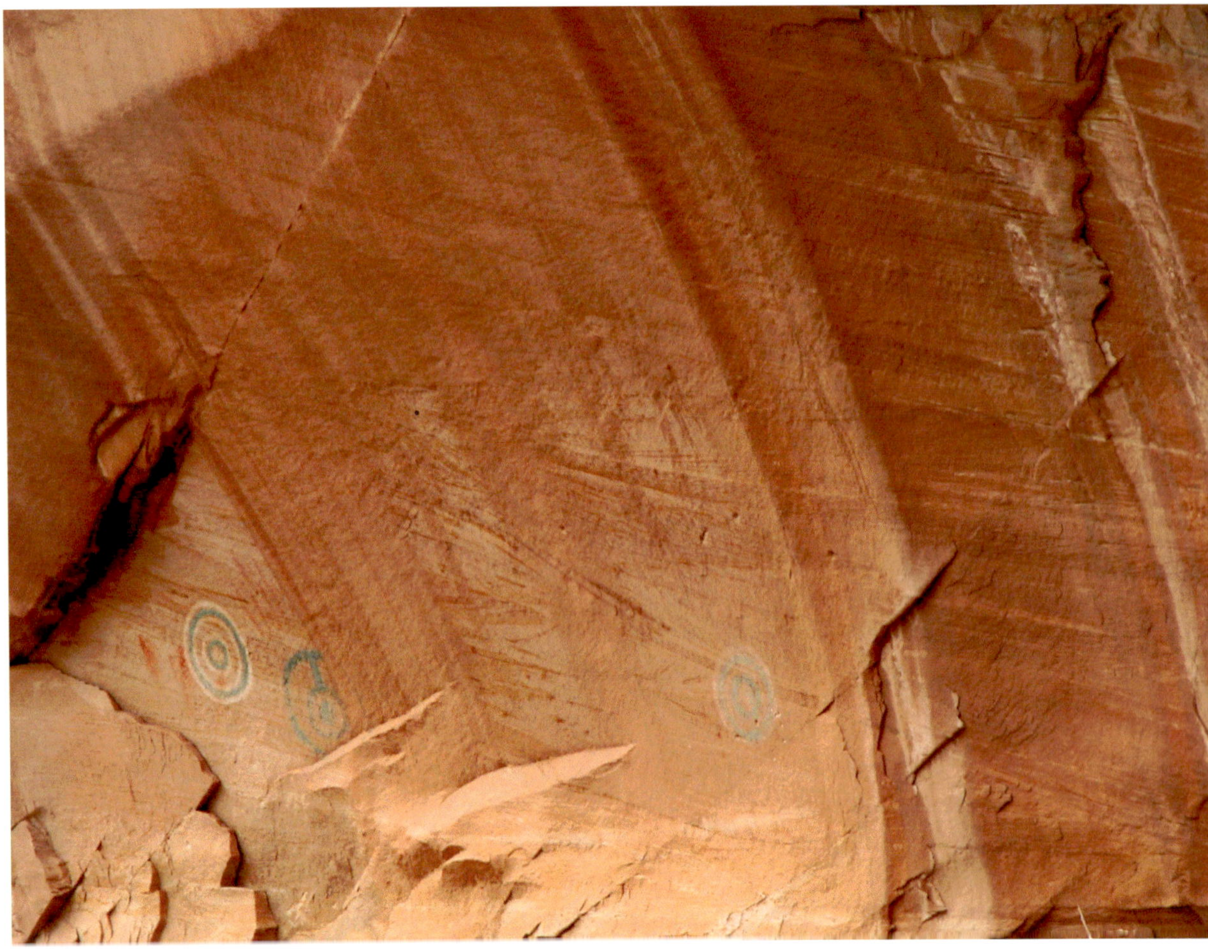

FIGURE 5.2. Concentric circle pictographs near the Ancestral Puebloan site Long Fingers in southern Utah (see figure 4.8, a photo of the pictographs for which the site was named). Their cultural affiliation is unknown. Circles and spirals were depicted in all time periods in Utah.

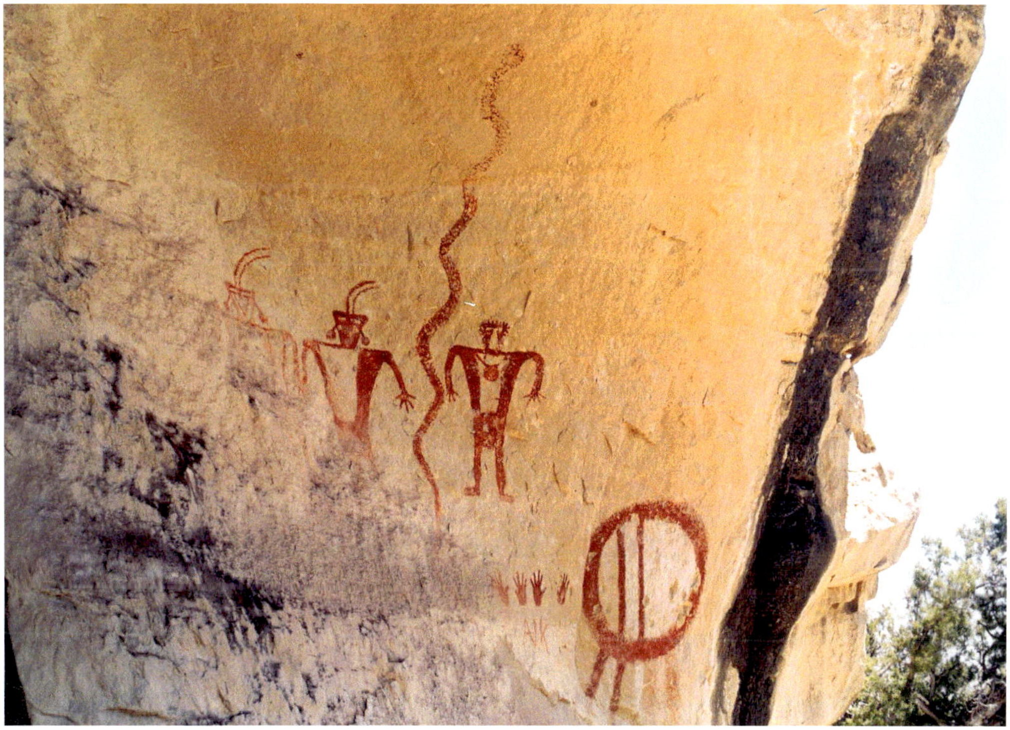

FIGURE 5.3. A large Fremont-style pictograph panel near Ivy Creek in eastern Utah.

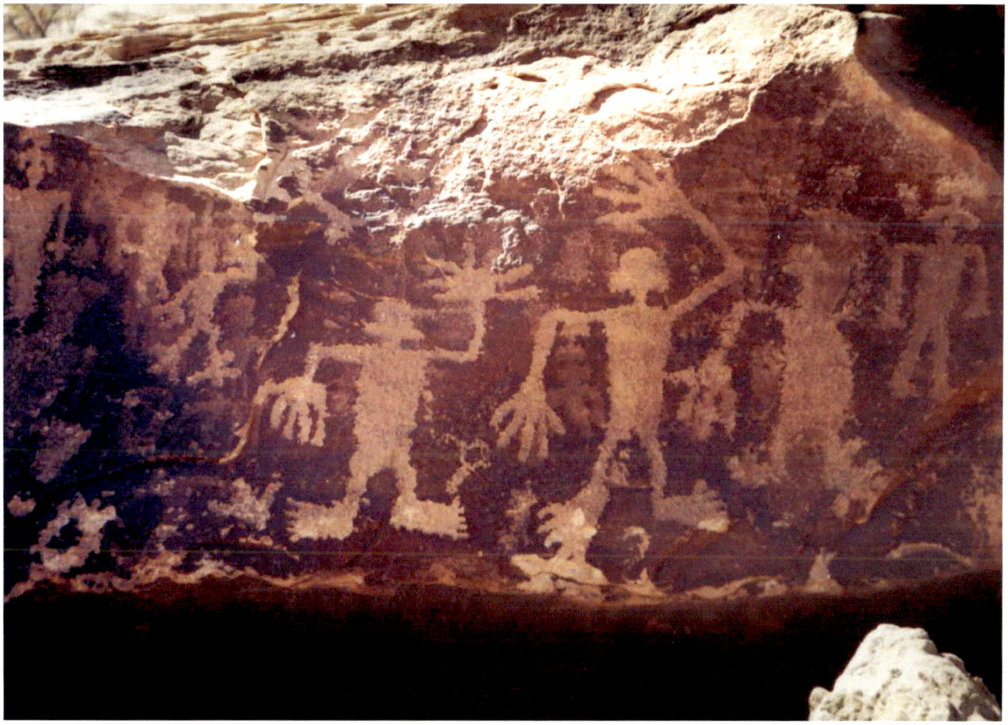

FIGURE 5.4. Basketmaker-style figures pecked into sandstone in McElmo Canyon, southwestern Colorado.

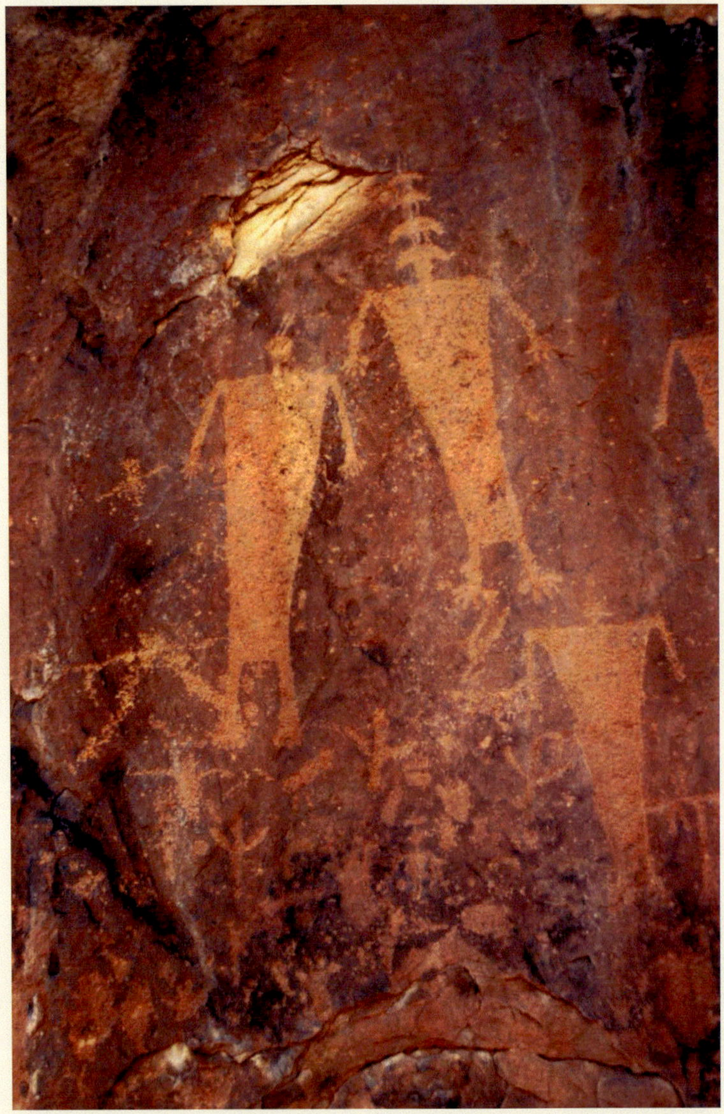

FIGURE 5.5. Part of a Basketmaker-style rock art panel in McElmo Canyon, southwestern Colorado.

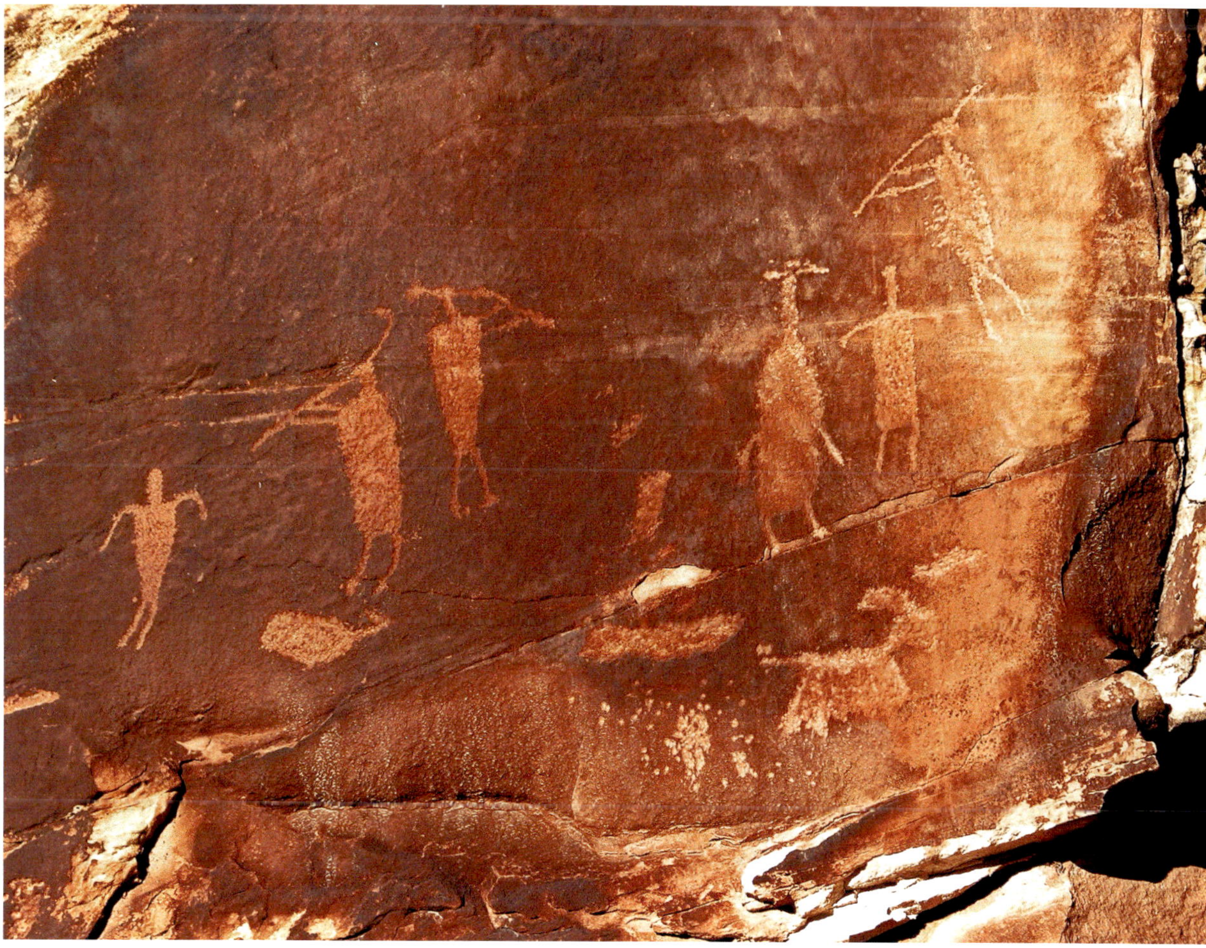

FIGURE 5.6. Three flute players performing for human and elk dancers on a rock art panel in Indian Creek Canyon, south of Moab.

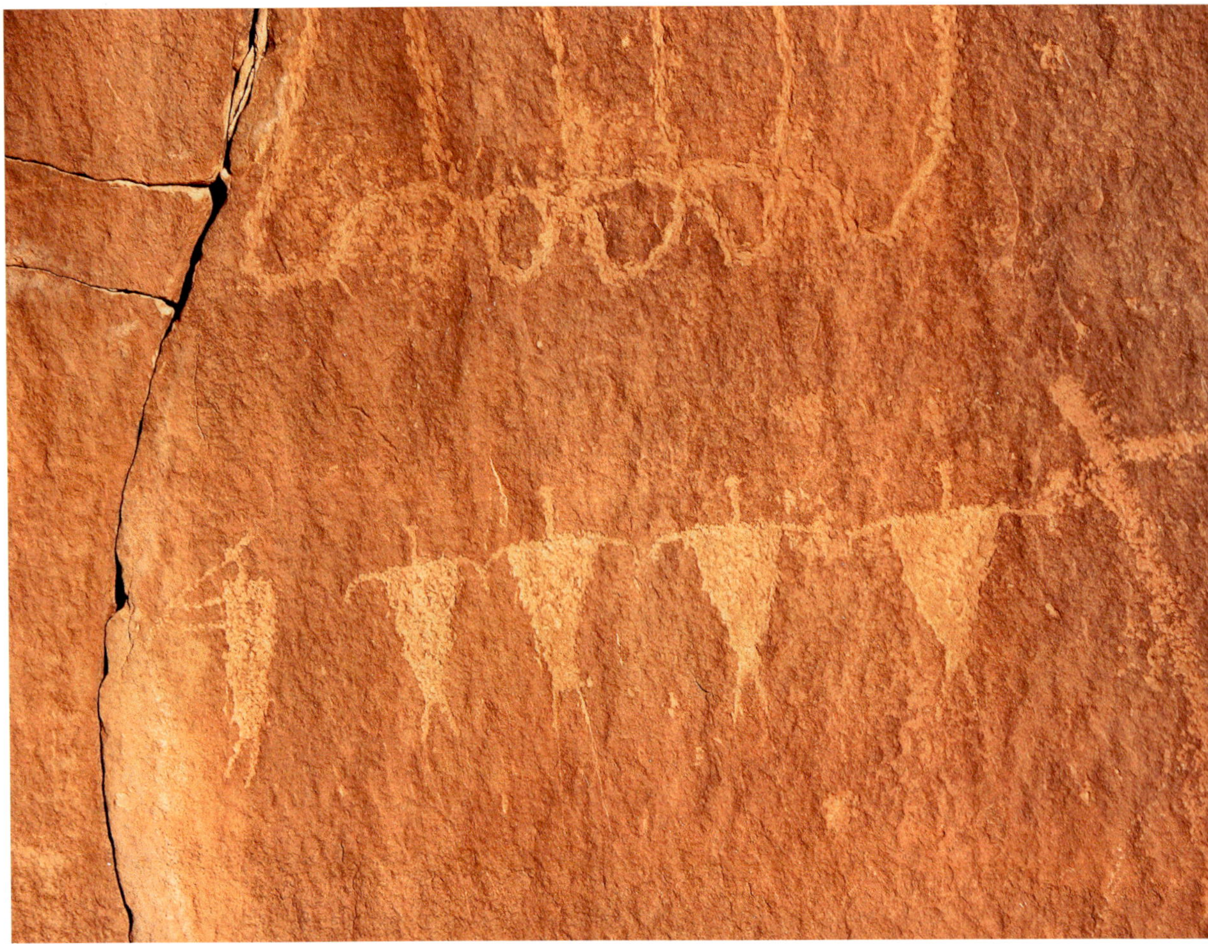

FIGURE 5.7. A flute player followed by a row of dancers in Indian Creek Canyon. These are probably affiliated with the Ancestral Puebloan culture.

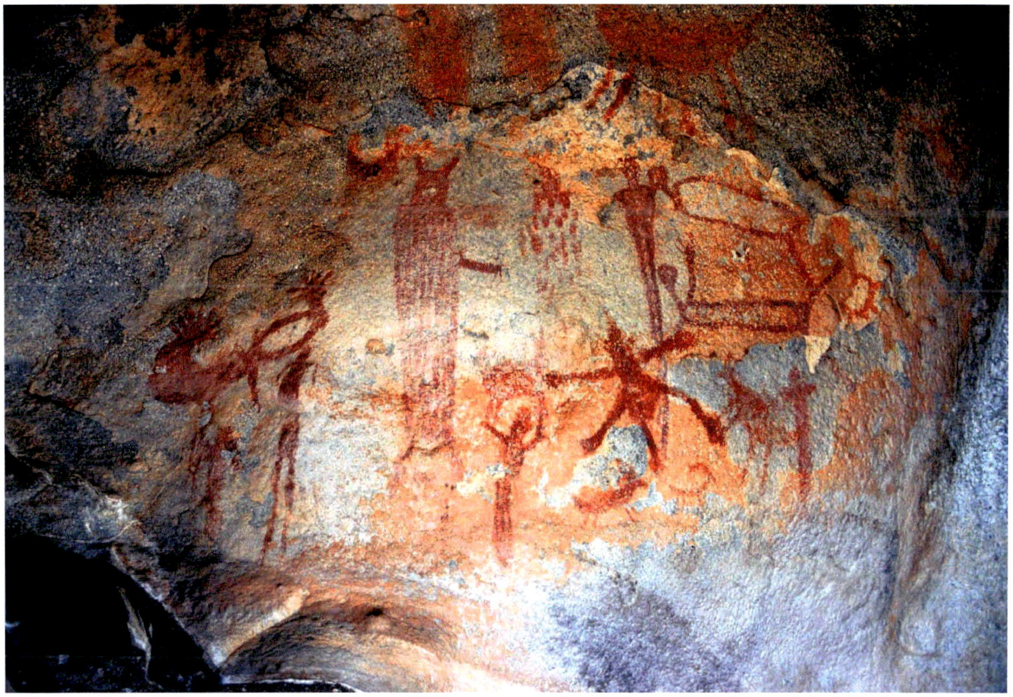

FIGURE 5.8. A magnificent Barrier Canyon–style pictograph near Hanksville, Utah.

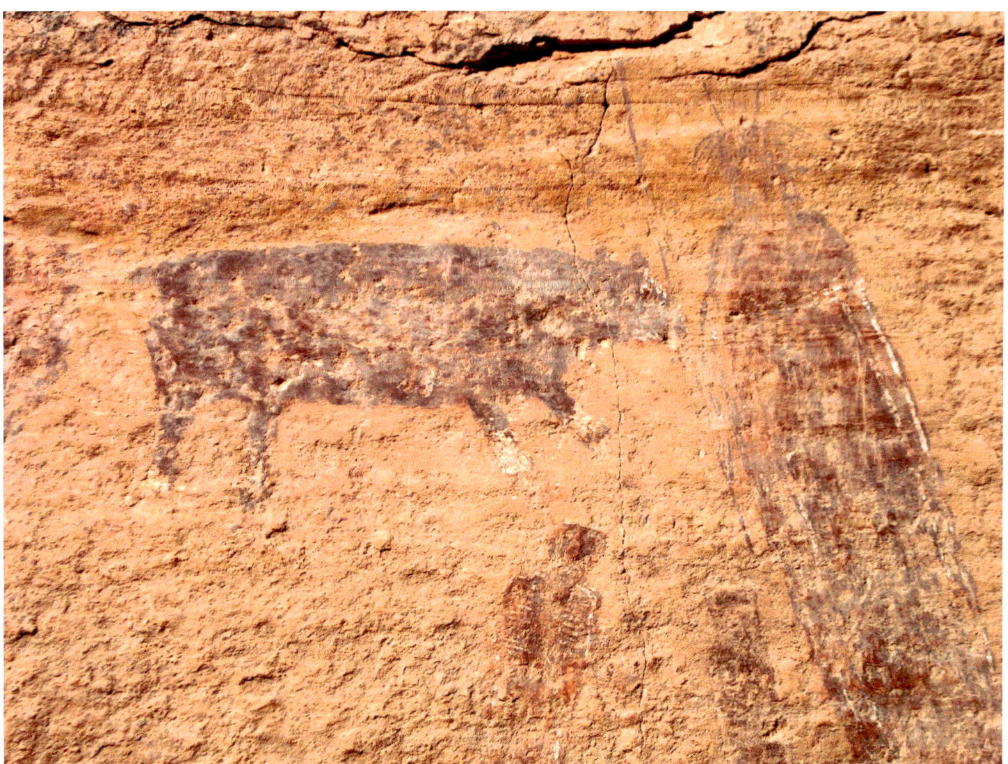

FIGURE 5.9. A painted bear-shaped figure next to an anthropomorph in the Maze District of Canyonlands National Park.

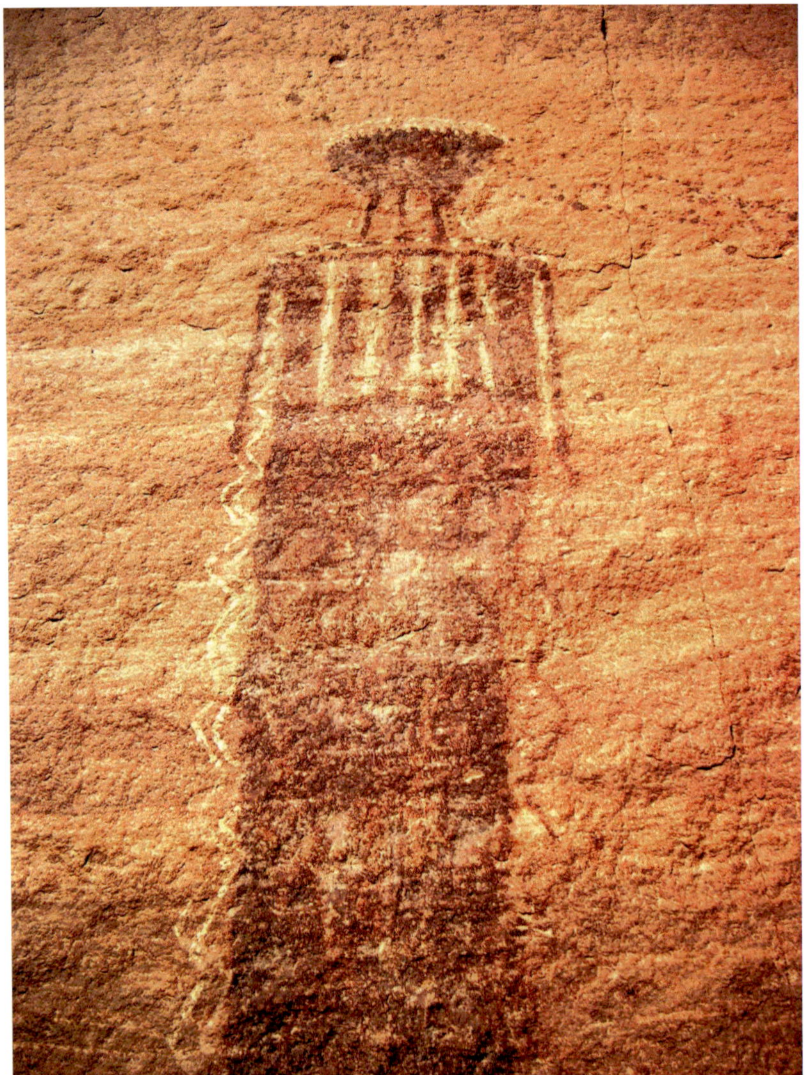

FIGURE 5.10. A finely executed Barrier Canyon–style anthropomorph in the Maze District of Canyonlands National Park.

6

ROCK ART CULTURE HISTORY

This part of the world—the Intermountain West—has been inhabited by people for over 10,000 years. Since cave art in Europe and Asia dates to well over 30,000 years ago, we know that the earliest inhabitants of this region were artistically creative and active. There are, however, very few verified examples of rock art in this area, or the New World in general, that date to 10,000 years ago. One reason is, of course, it is very unlikely that a rock art figure could survive for thousands of years. Think of an old building you have seen with the faded remnants of an advertisement painted on the side. Even with the relatively modern paints applied to the structure or sign, after just 75 or 100 years, it is weathered and sometimes barely legible. Think of how that sign will look in 500 or 1,000 years. Not very likely to survive, is it?

Surely early people created rock art, and no doubt some of it will be found and verified. For now, in the Intermountain West, by far most of the rock art we know of, and most of what is shown in this book, is likely from more recent times—say, the past 5,000 years. While the earliest people in this area were likely hunters of megafauna such as mammoths and giant ground sloths, those who came after were faced with environments not that different from current ones. They hunted and gathered, roamed widely, moved camp regularly, and left a light footprint on the land. It has only been in the past 2,000 years that residents of this area began doing some farming as part of their subsistence strategies.

The rock art in this book is primarily associated with three distinct traditions: one that we call the Barrier Canyon style, another associated with the Fremont and Anasazi/Ancestral Puebloan cultures, and the most recent from the tribes that were here when Europeans arrived, primarily the Utes and Navajos. These styles are reasonably distinct from one another, and most researchers have thought them to have been distinct in time. Barrier Canyon style is generally thought to date to the Archaic period, sometime prior to 2,000 years ago, and the Fremont and Anasazi styles to after 2,000 years ago, remaining dominant in the region until the arrival of historic groups, most likely within the last 1,000 years.

The prehistory of Utah and the surrounding area is generally divided into four relatively indistinct periods, each with certain kinds of rock art that seem to be associated.

Paleo-Indian Period, ca. 10,000–7000 BC

During the earliest occupation of the region, some of the now-extinct megafauna—including mammoths, giant ground sloths, saber-tooth cats, and short-faced bears—were present. A small number of rock art panels may depict now-extinct fauna and are thought to have been created during the Paleo-Indian period. No distinct styles have been noted or posited because of the extreme rarity of art from this period. Paleo-Indian people were certainly artistic and surely created many works, including rock art pieces, but the great amount of time that has passed has taken its toll on the creative work of those who lived so long ago.

Archaic Period, ca. 7000 BC–AD 1

This period is marked by a broad-based hunting and gathering economy, high mobility, the use of atlatls and darts for hunting, and the production of exquisite basketry. The rock art of this period may include a number of different styles and subjects. The most widely known and studied art likely from this period is the Barrier Canyon style, which includes large ghost-like anthropomorphs and a variety of animal- and bird-like figures.

Formative, or Fremont/Anasazi Period, ca. AD 1–1300

This period features greater sedentism, farming, and the introduction of ceramics and the bow and arrow. Rock art figures include distinctive anthropomorphs, zoomorphs, and many abstract designs and figures.

Late Prehistoric/Historic Period, ca. AD 1300–1900

Generally considered to be the art of the historic tribes of the area—notably the Ute, Shoshone, Goshute, Paiute, and Navajo—these rock art figures include depictions of bears and their pawprints, bison, abstract designs, and, for the historic period, horses, figures riding horses, buildings, trains, and boats. Historic European rock art is generally limited to names, dates, and brands, although carvings on aspen trees by European immigrants, particularly those by Basque sheepherders, are particularly artistic and intriguing.

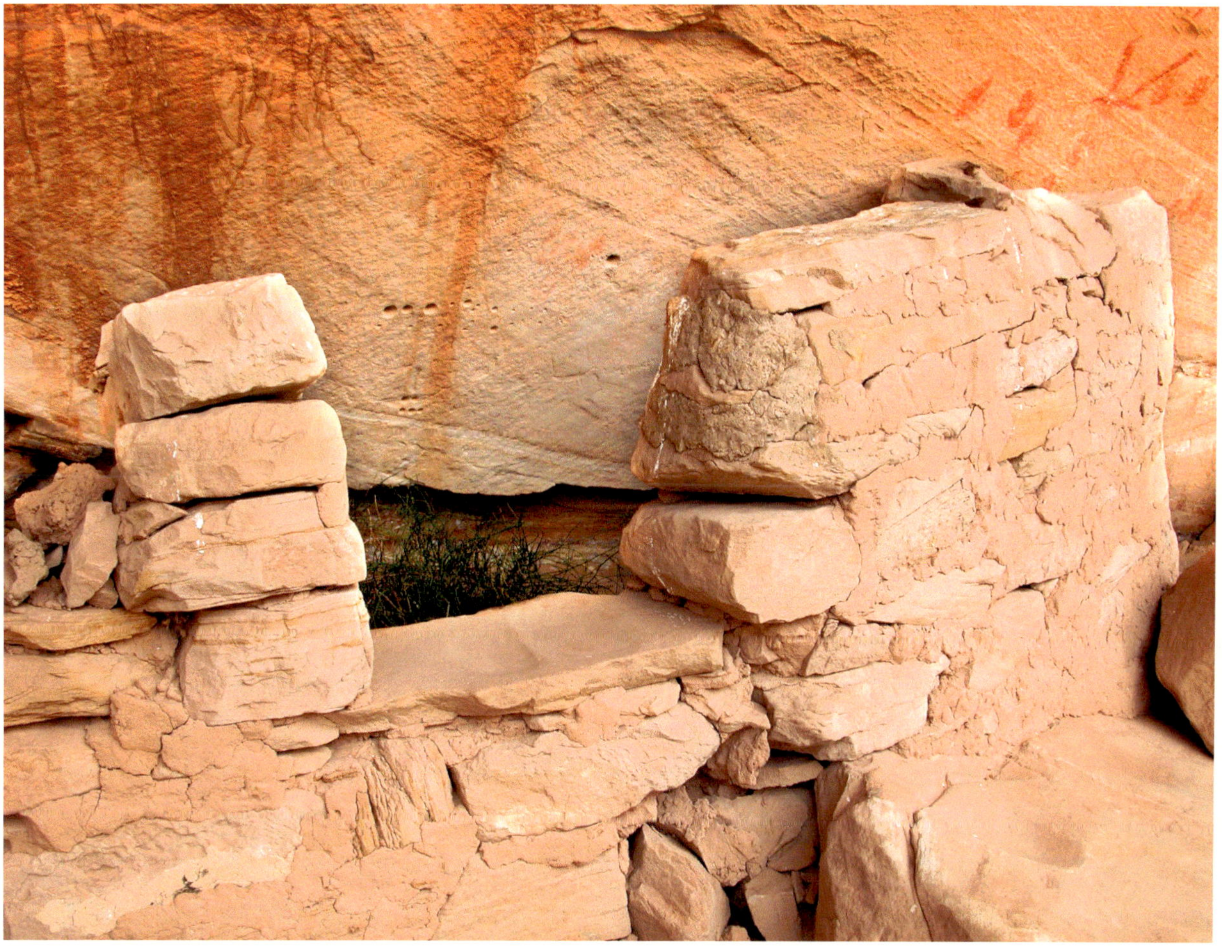

FIGURE 6.1. Rock and adobe structure in Nine Mile Canyon affiliated with the Fremont culture.

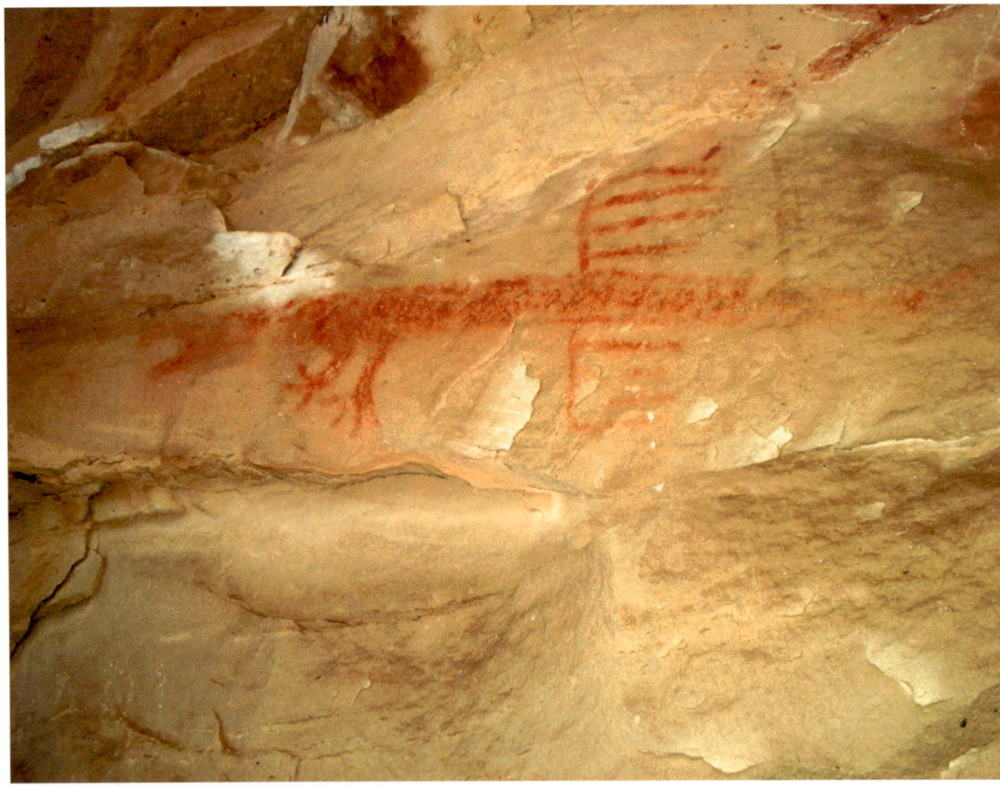

FIGURE 6.2. A fantastical creature in a small canyon in the San Rafael Swell.

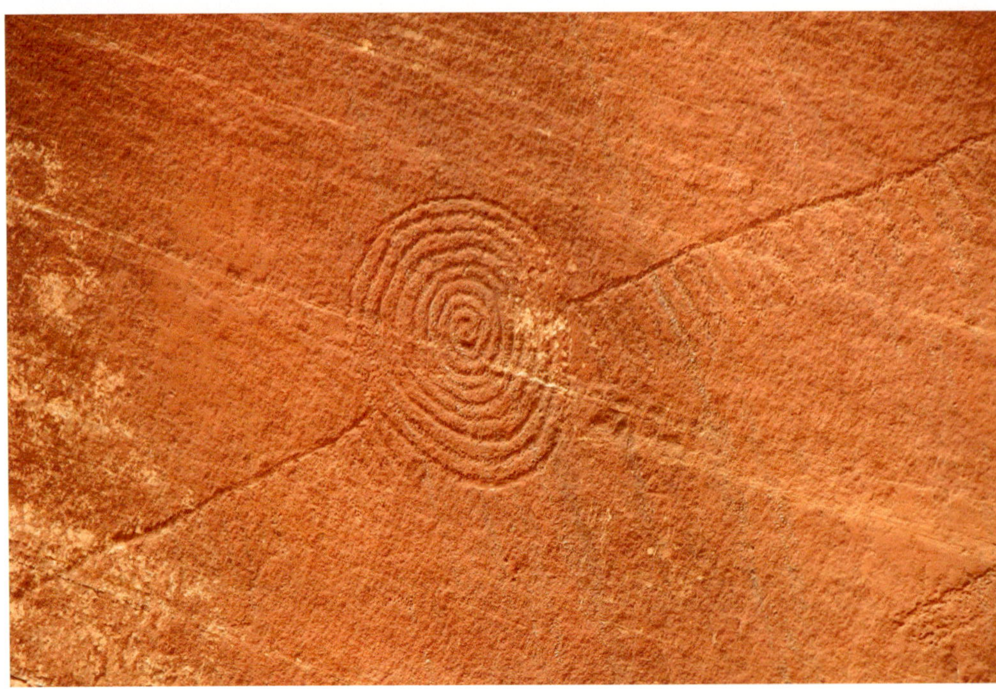

FIGURE 6.3. A spiral petroglyph near an archaeological site in southern Utah. The cultural affiliation is unknown.

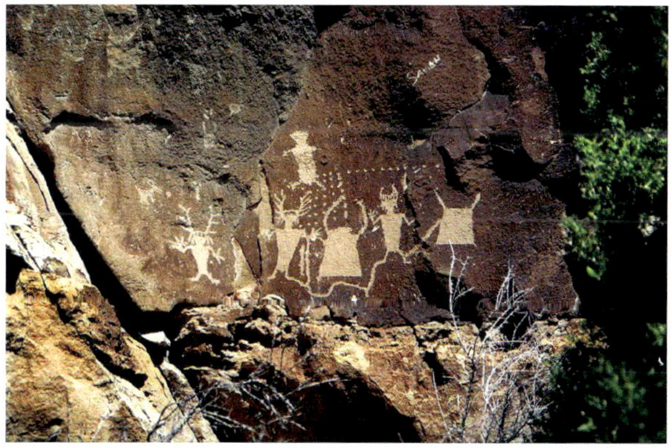

FIGURE 6.4. A Fremont-style petroglyph panel in Horsecorn Canyon near the Green River. It was recorded in 1931 by the Claflin-Emerson Expedition.

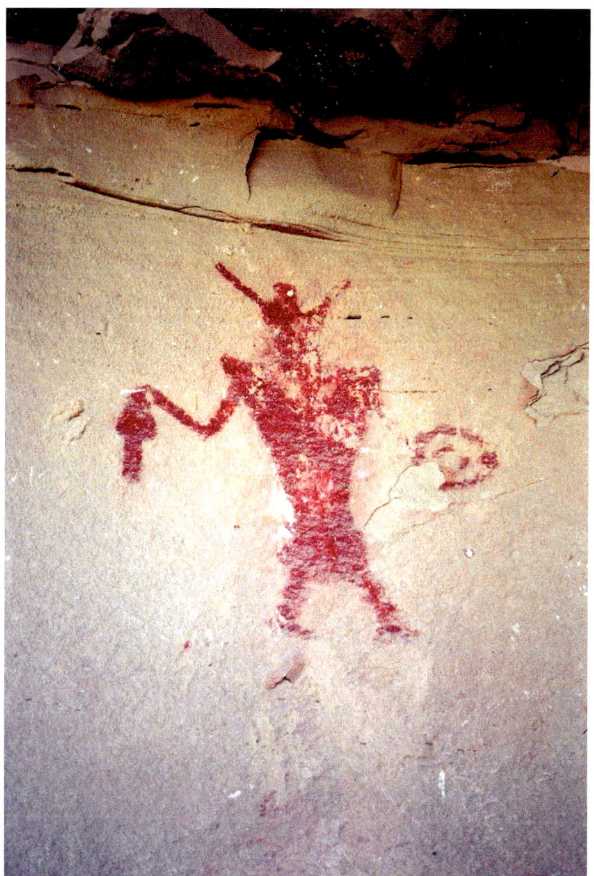

FIGURE 6.5. A Fremont-style pictograph in Gordon Creek Canyon in eastern Utah. It is similar to anthropomorphs in in the Vernal area that appear to be holding shields and stylized human heads.

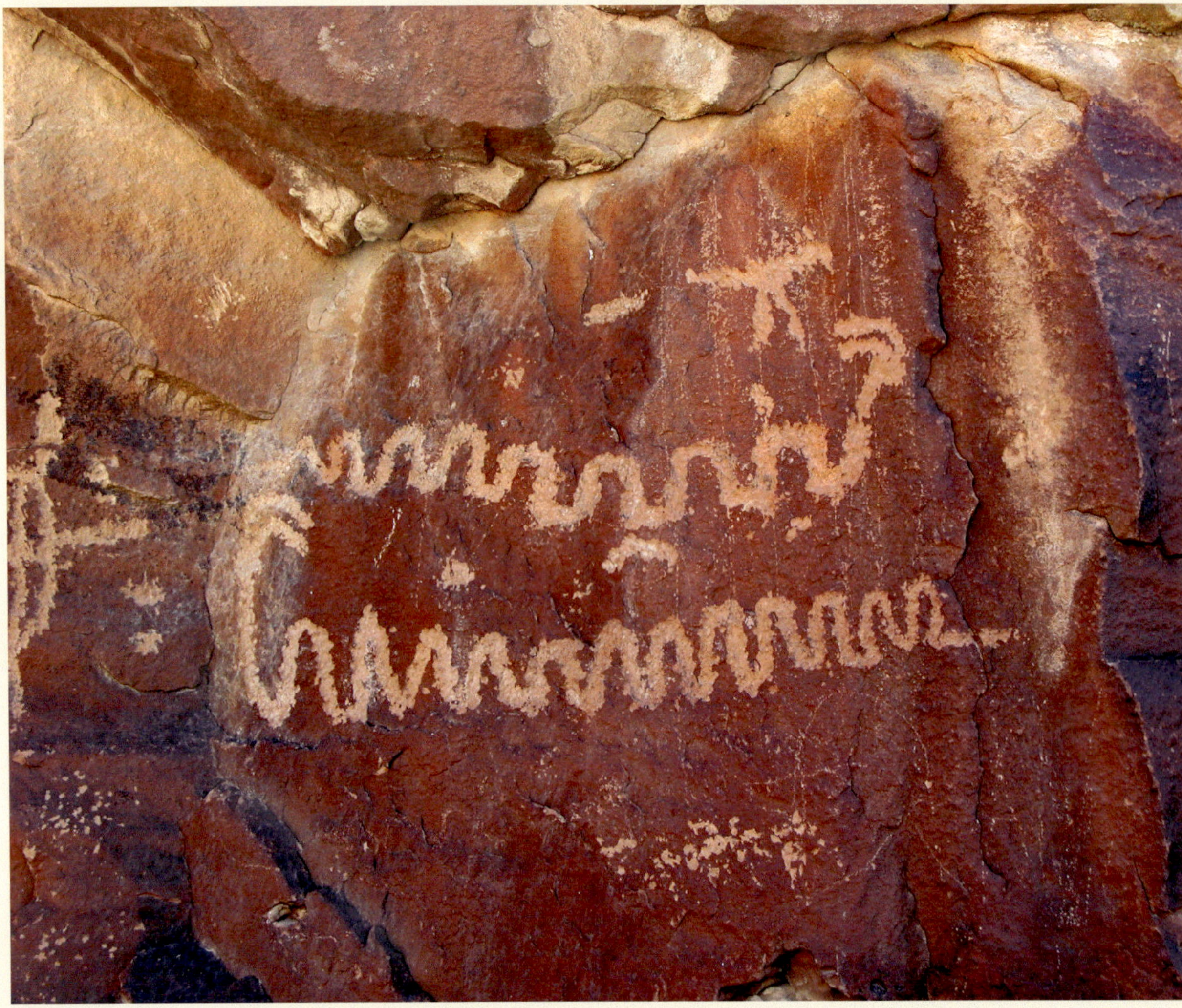

FIGURE 6.6. A Fremont-style horned or feathered snake petroglyph panel in Nine Mile Canyon.

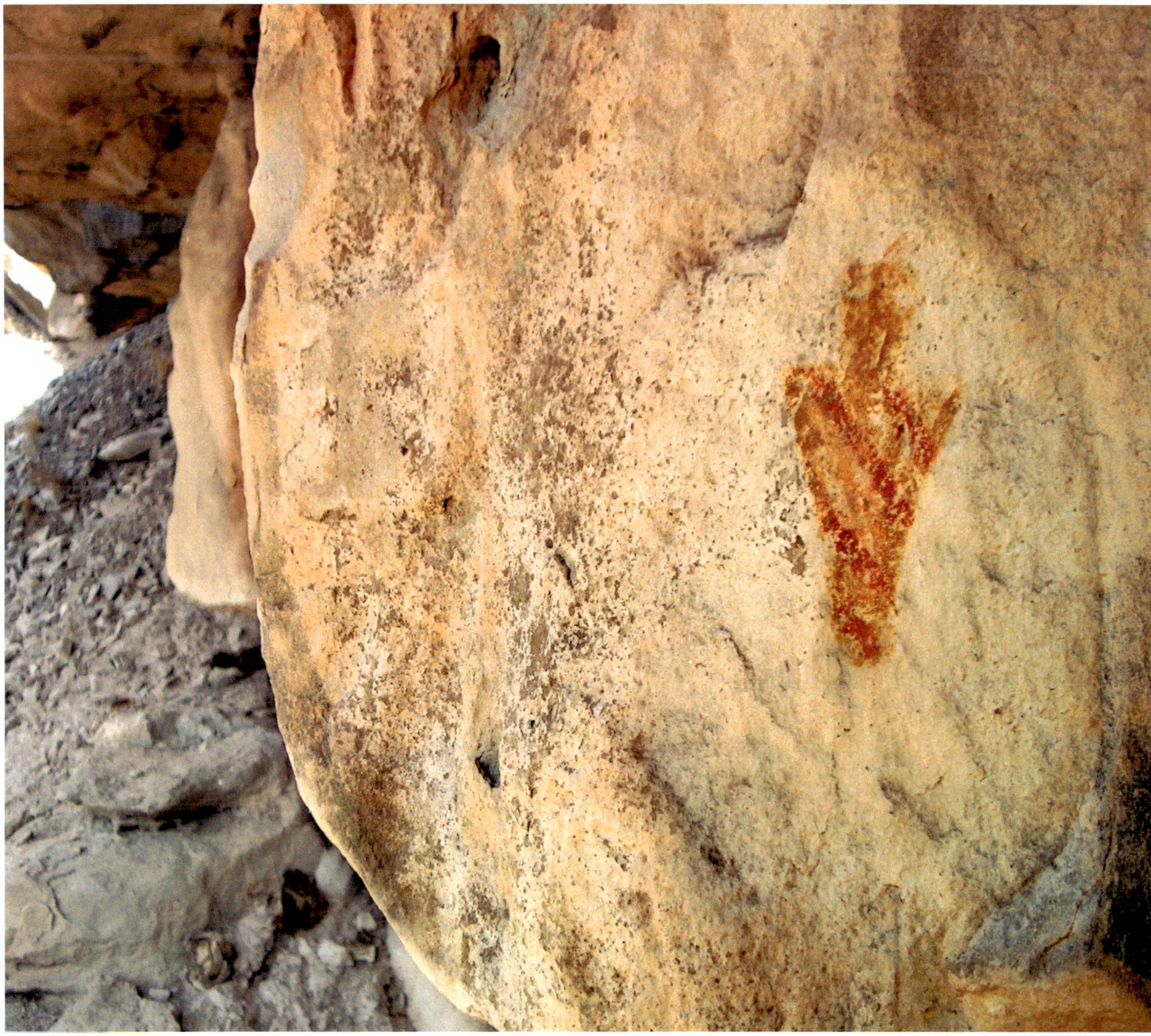

FIGURE 6.7. An unusual Fremont-style anthropomorph in Range Creek Canyon painted with gold pigment.

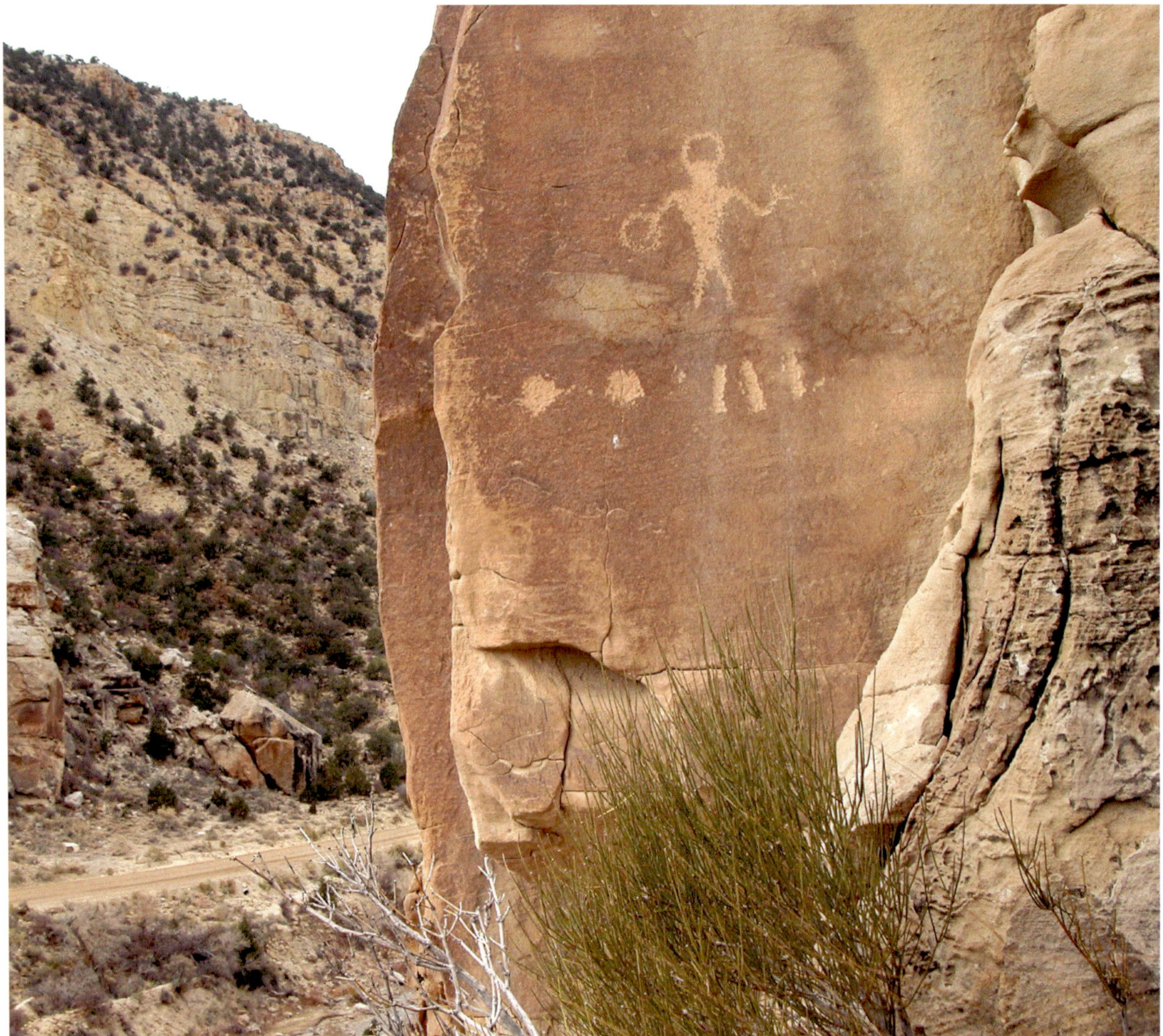

FIGURE 6.8. A Fremont-style anthropomorph in Ferron Canyon, eastern Utah.

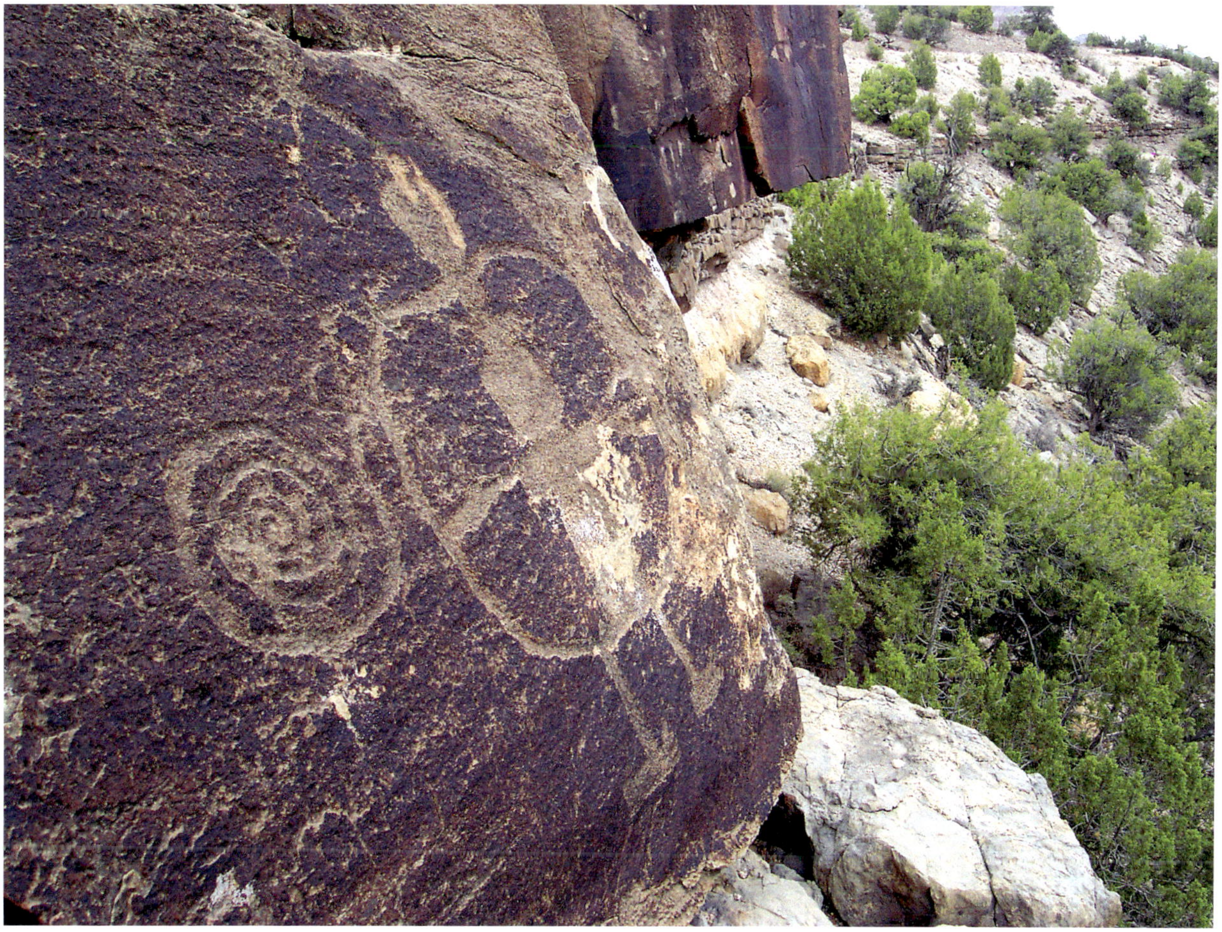

FIGURE 6.9. A Fremont-style shield figure high above the road in Range Creek Canyon.

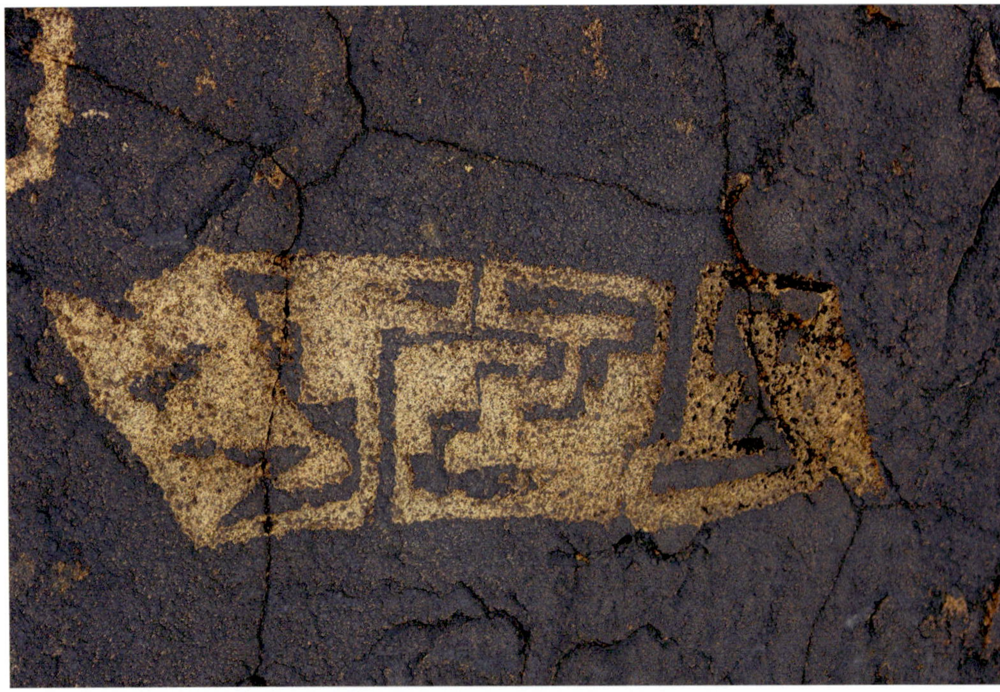

FIGURE 6.10. An unusual petroglyph in Santa Clara Canyon, southwestern Utah. The style is thought to be Ancestral Puebloan.

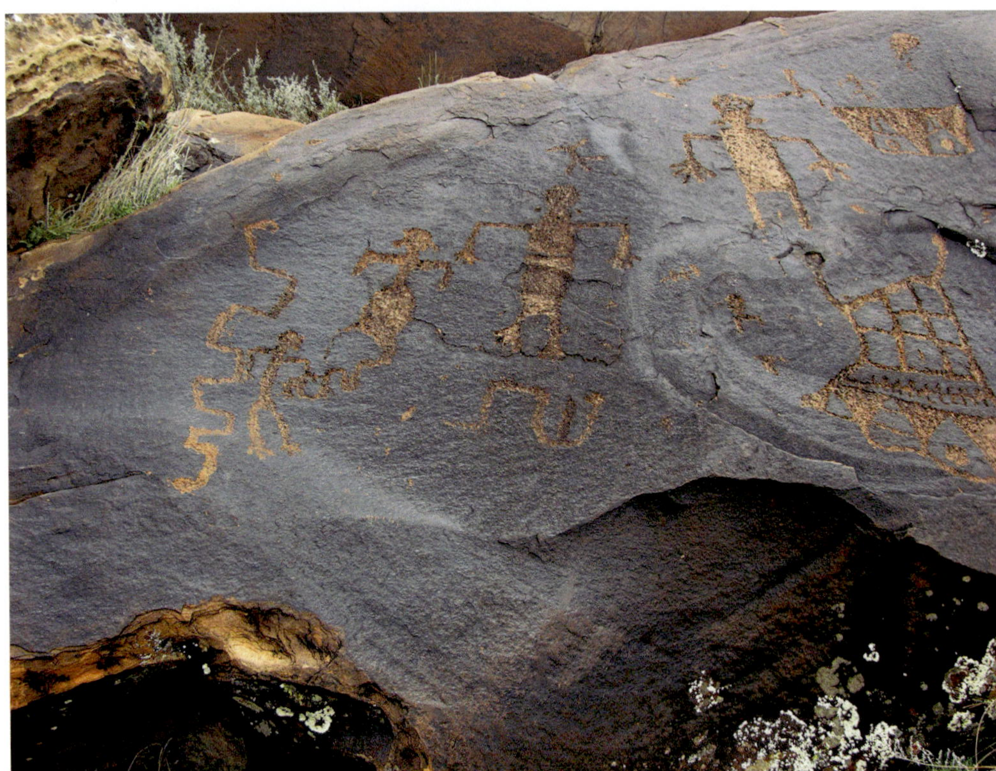

FIGURE 6.11. An Ancestral Puebloan–style petroglyph panel in Santa Clara Canyon, southwestern Utah.

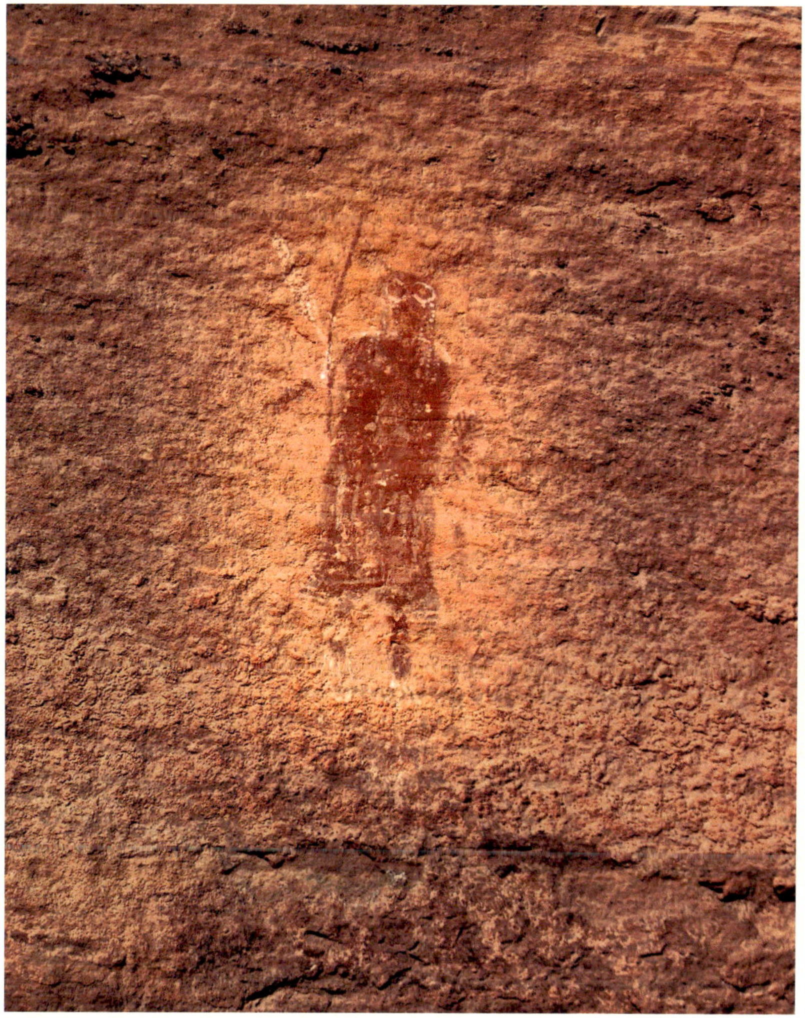

FIGURE 6.12. A Barrier Canyon–style pictograph in the Horseshoe Canyon area of southern Utah.

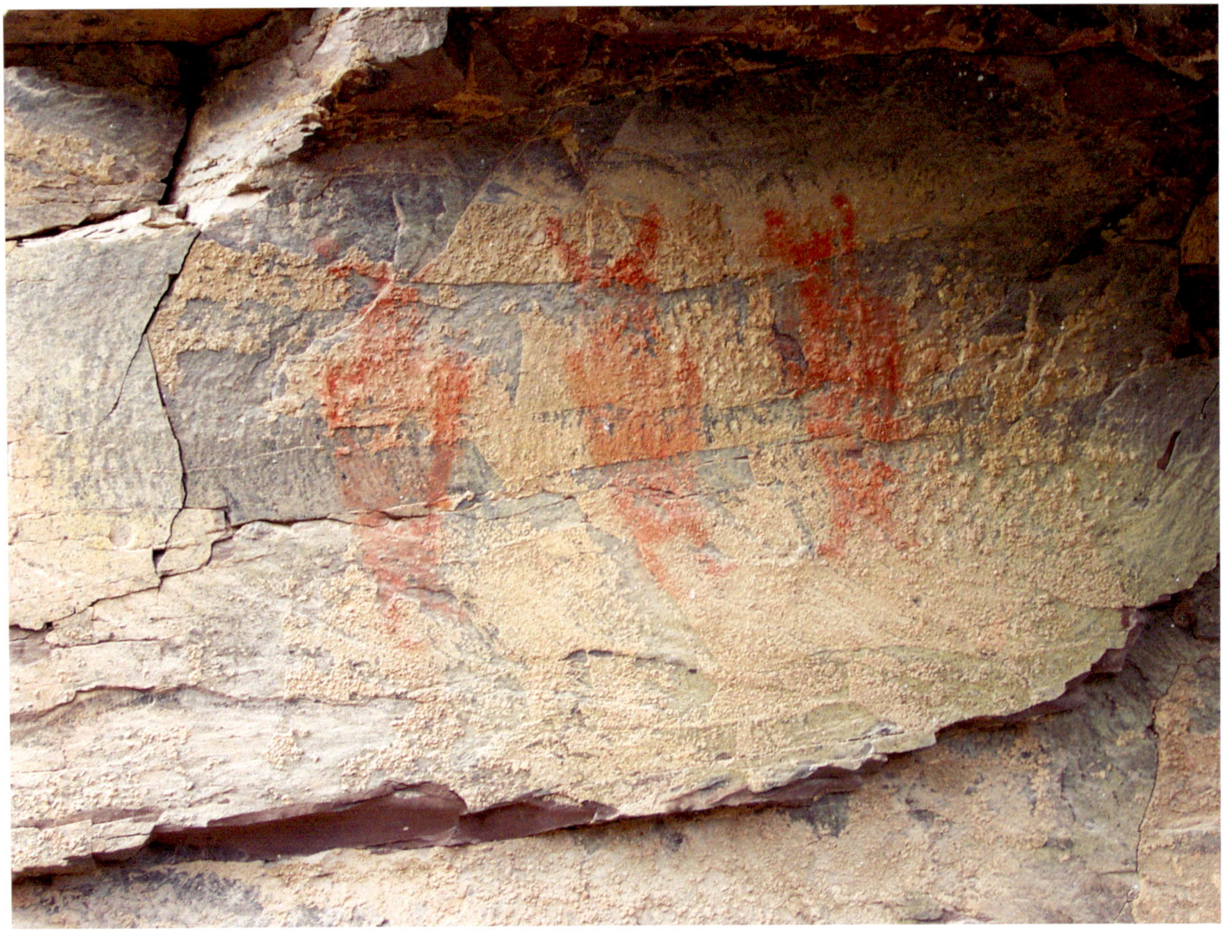

FIGURE 6.13. Fremont-style anthropomorphs adorning a sandstone wall.

7

IMAGES ON STONE MARK THE PASSAGE OF TIME

Placing rock art in time poses a bit of a problem for archaeologists. First, the art is generally pecked or abraded on stone, and unless some regular change has taken place—such as weathering, patination, or vegetative growth (for example, lichen or moss)—most rock art is difficult to date. These agents and processes do occur and would be valuable for dating except for the fact that they are all very dependent on conditions such as exposure to sunlight and moisture, variables that can differ greatly within the space of only a few feet. Generally, differing degrees of change after their creation are useful primarily for relative dating (identifying that some figures were made before others), and then only in a very restricted area, such as on a single panel.

Painted works provide greater opportunities for dating, although several considerations limit the possible application of dating techniques to the art itself. First, in order for radiocarbon dating to be applied, the pigment or other medium used to create it must be derived from a living thing that was contemporary with the art. A painting done with plant-derived pigments such as ground seeds or berries would be a candidate for radiocarbon dating, as would one painted with plant juices, animal fat, or blood. Any pigments made with an inorganic material such as a mineral or media such as water would not be dateable using the radiocarbon method. Even when organic materials were used, the applicability of radiocarbon dating is limited. Most notably, since it is the art itself that would have to be sampled, and the sample would be destroyed in the dating process, few researchers or stewards are willing to damage the art in order to date it. Some dates have been obtained from pieces of pigment that have naturally flaked or spalled off from the art itself. This occurrence is rare, and even when it does occur, the amount of material available for dating is often scant and may not be enough to yield a reliable date.

Some limiting dates have been obtained by using radiocarbon or other methods to date sediments that have been deposited over a rock art panel. Such a date provides information about the latest date the art could have been created (before the overlying sediments were deposited), but not how long before.

Another tool used by archaeologists to date artifacts is unfortunately not very applicable to rock art, yet, interestingly, it is the tool most often used to date or assign cultural affiliation to art. That tool is association. Archaeologists date many things that are themselves not conducive to metric dating (such as stone tools and ceramic sherds) by dating the sediments in which they are found. Artifacts found in a stratigraphic layer that was deposited 500 years ago can be assumed to be 500 years old. Since rock art is generally not found buried in dated stratigraphic contexts, it is generally not able to be precisely dated by association and is not itself very useful in determining dates of buried deposits.

However, since typical dating techniques are not very useful in dating rock art, much of the work on placing rock art in time and place has been by somewhat loose association. Over time, researchers noted that certain styles of rock art tended to be found near sites of certain ages, and the affiliation between the style of art and the cultural period was posited.

As discussed in chapter 4, some elements contained in the art itself may be useful in determining when it was created. A depiction of an extinct animal such as a mastodon could tell us that the art was created when those animals still existed. Comparing motifs in rock art with those found on artifacts such as pottery and architectural murals is a very productive way to order and understand rock art and its cultural affiliations. Likewise, depictions of elements that are known to date to only a certain time period—such as the bow and arrow, horses, and railroads—allow estimates of when the work might have been created.

Overall, we have only a very general notion of the age of different rock art styles, and we urge great caution in using these classifications in any but the most general and classificatory way.

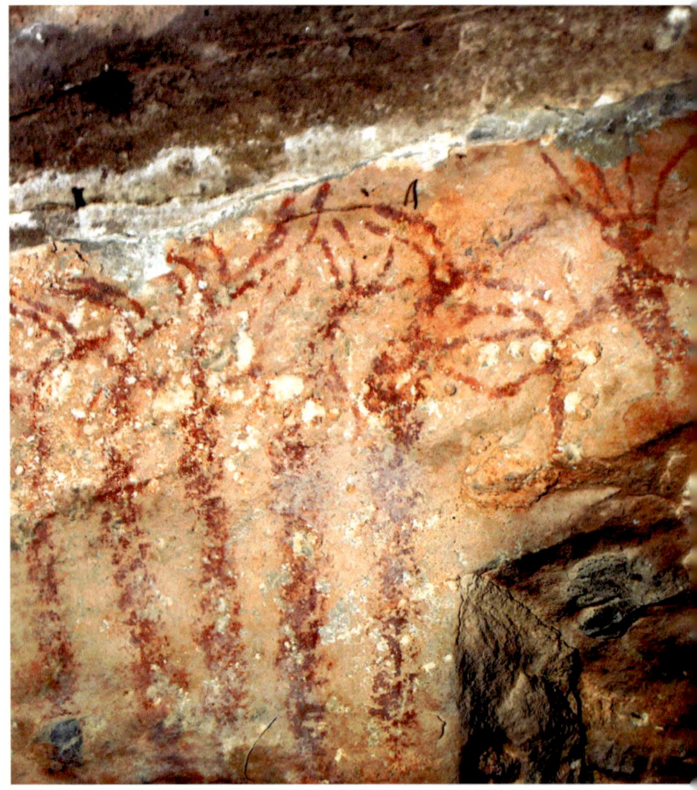

FIGURE 7.1. Unusual anthropomorphs on a small Barrier Canyon–style pictograph panel at the northern end of the San Rafael Swell.

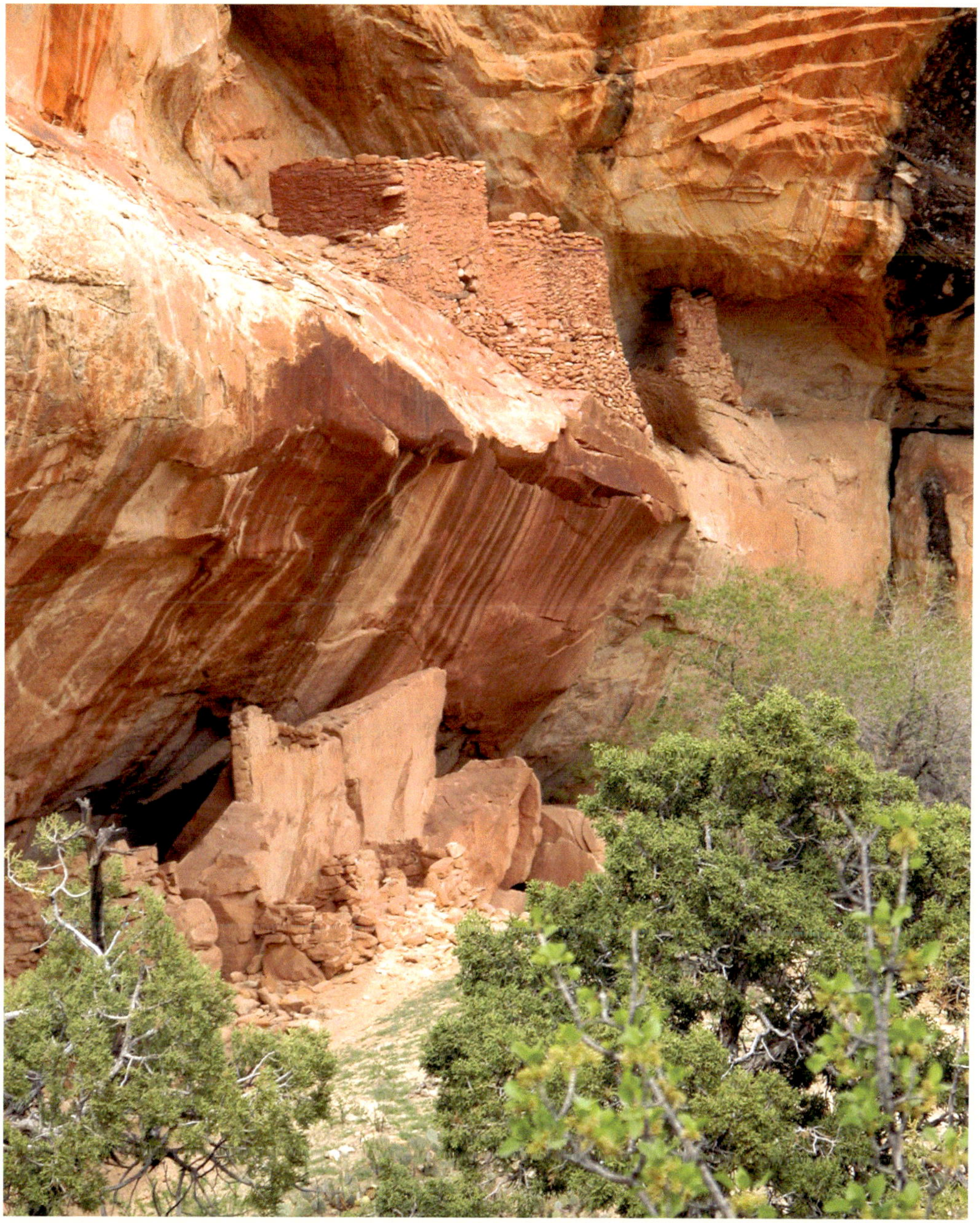

FIGURE 7.2. A habitation site with partial walls of stone and adobe tucked into a sandstone alcove in southern Utah. It is associated with the Ancestral Puebloan culture.

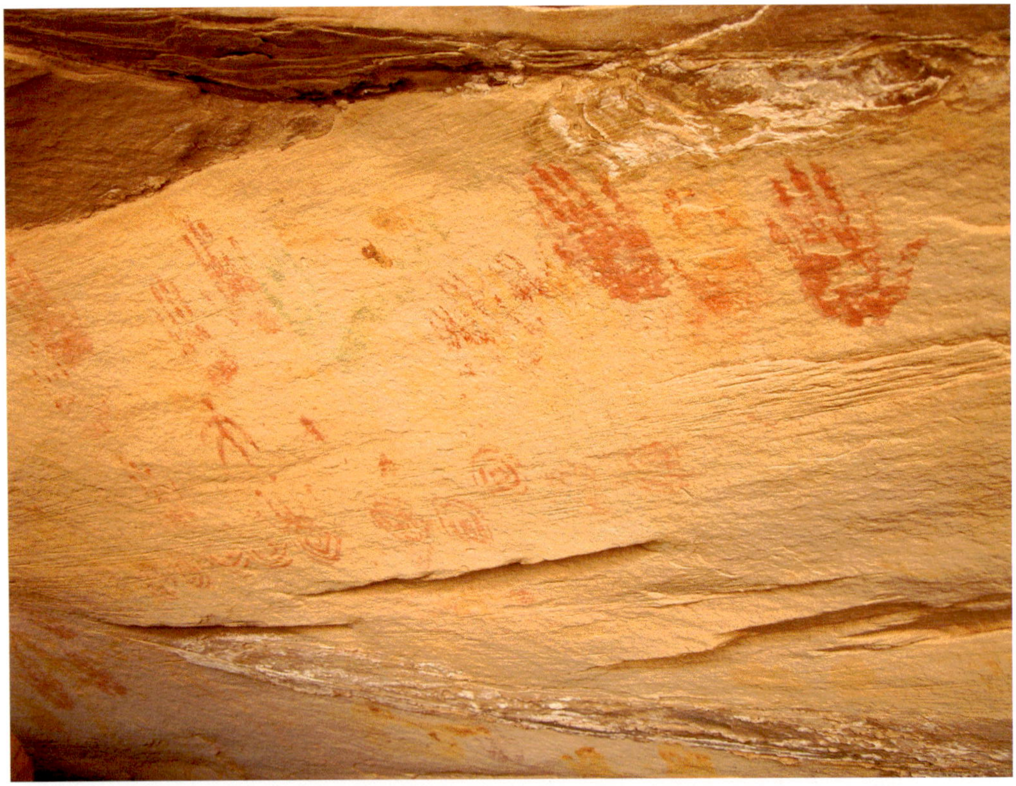

FIGURE 7.3. Positive handprints, spirals, and an anthropomorph in a large alcove in southern Utah.

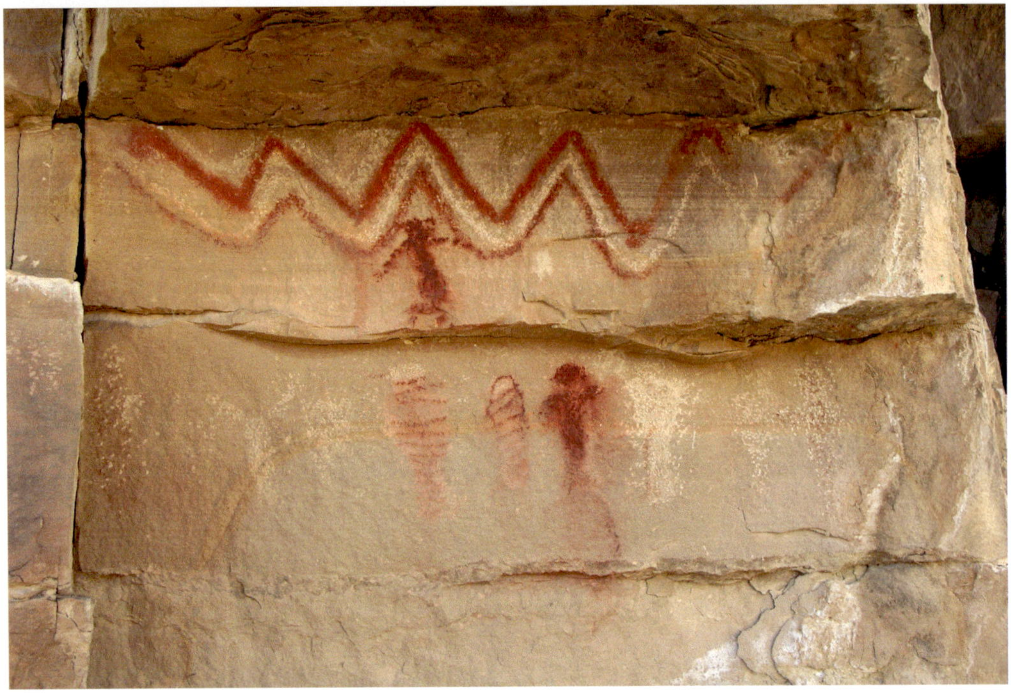

FIGURE 7.4. Wavy lines and anthropomorphs painted on a wall in Ferron Box, eastern Utah.

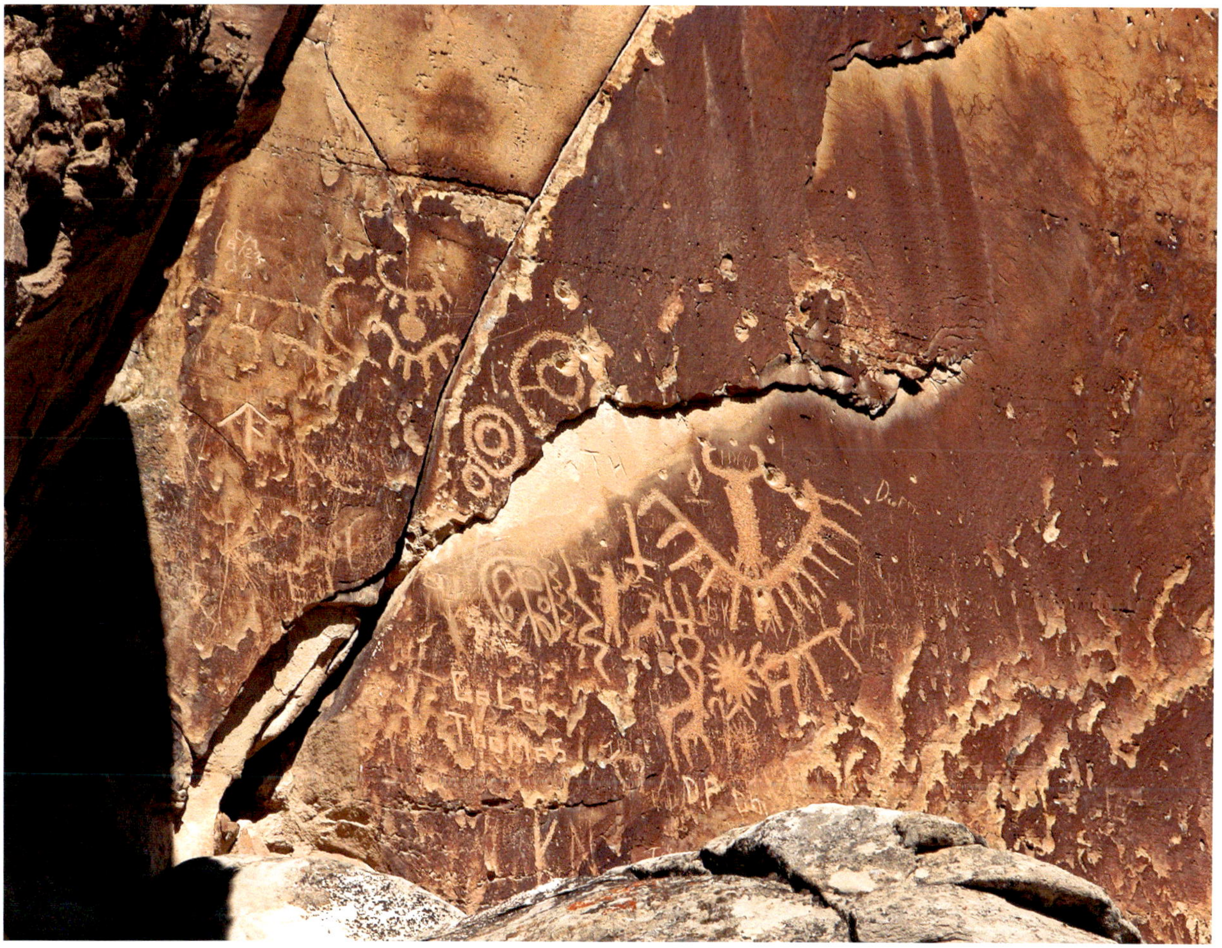

FIGURE 7.5. A large petroglyph panel located in Ferron Canyon, eastern Utah, with Fremont-style figures, among others.

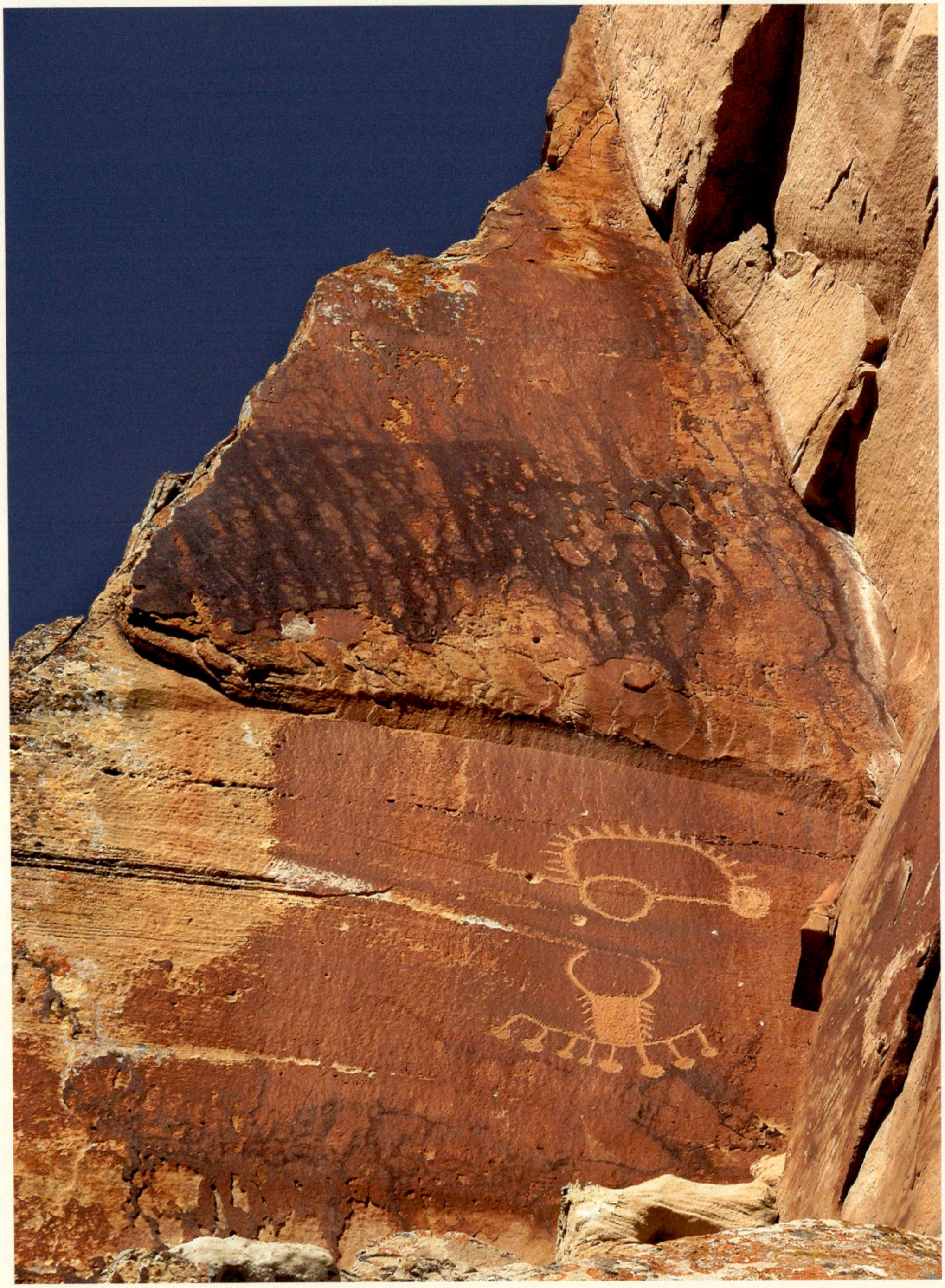

FIGURE 7.6. Fremont-style petroglyphs in Ferron Canyon, eastern Utah.

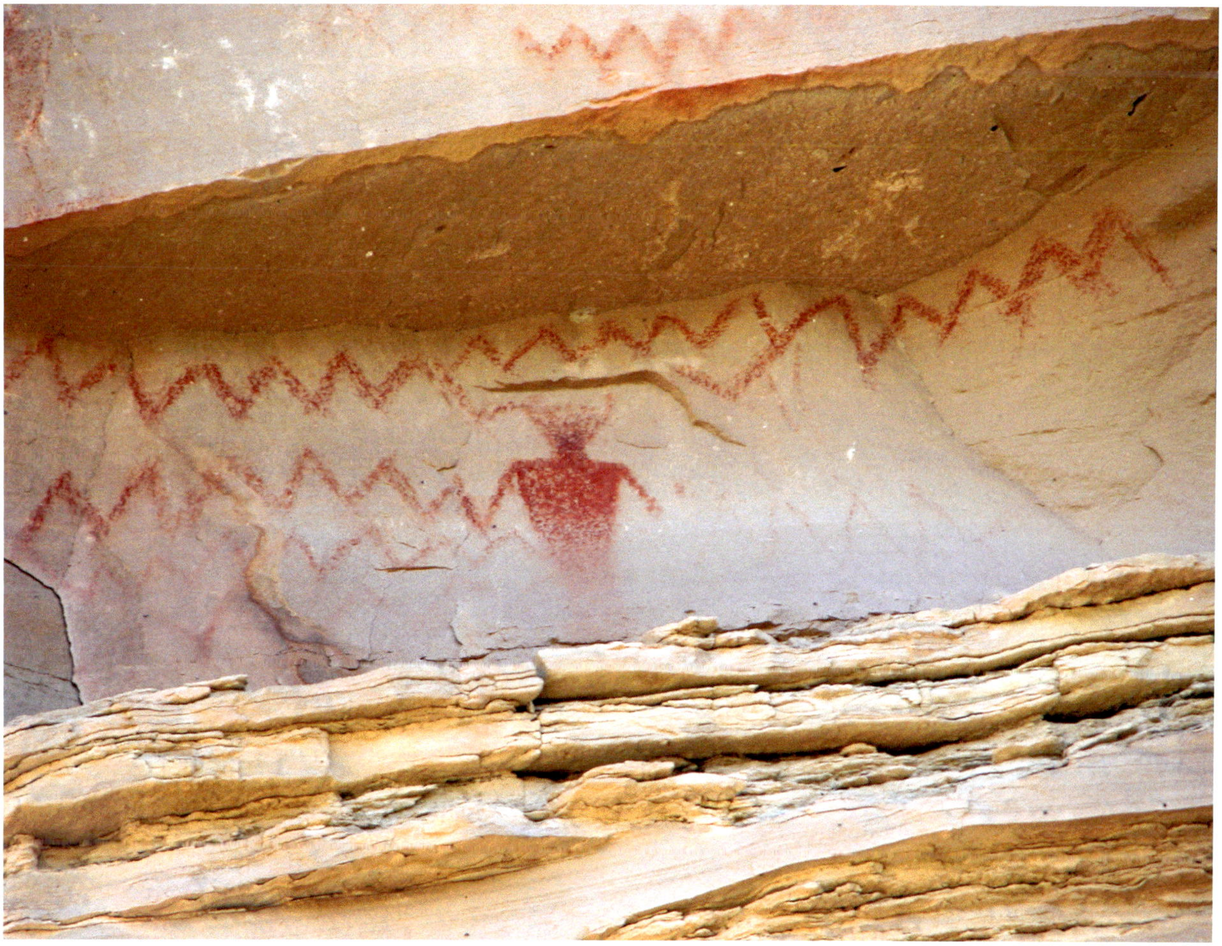

FIGURE 7.7. A Fremont-style anthropomorph and wavy lines painted in Ferron Box, eastern Utah.

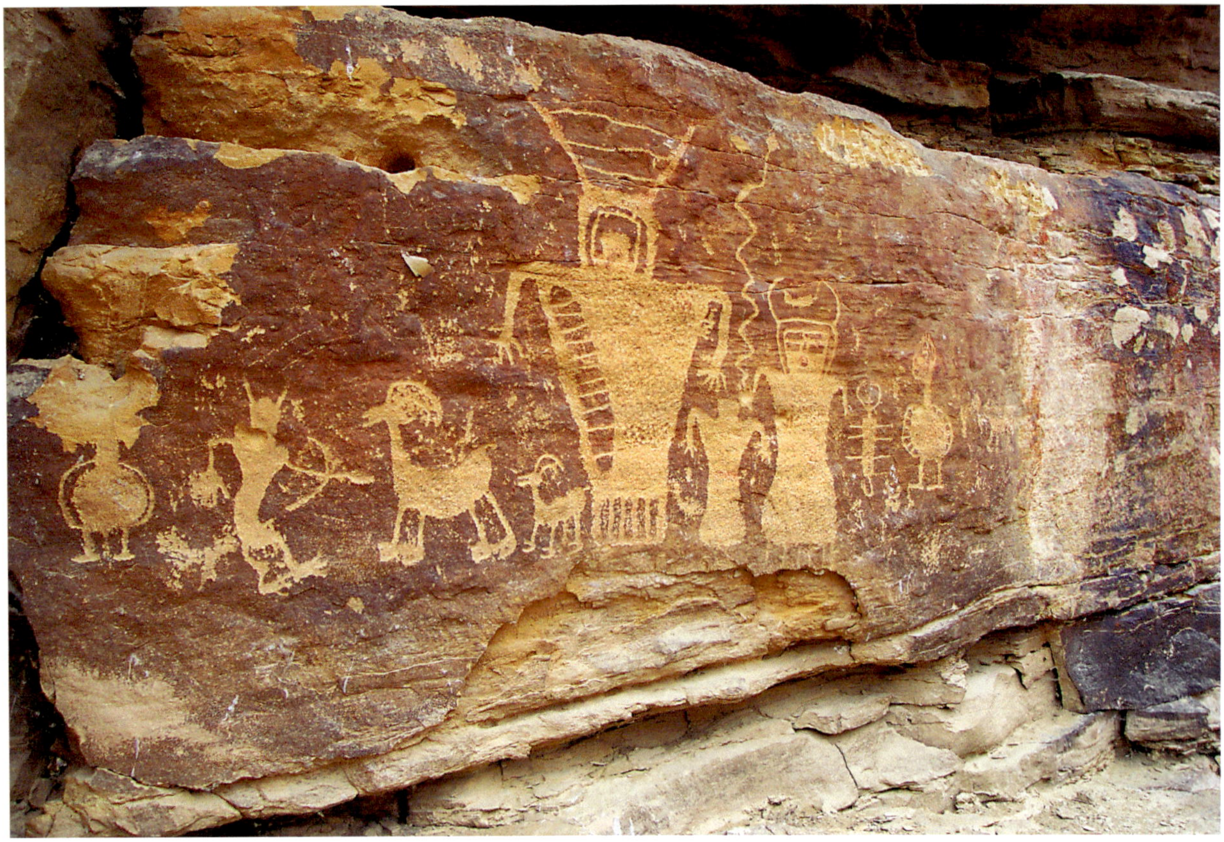

FIGURE 7.8. Fremont-style petroglyphs in Nine Mile Canyon on what is sometimes referred to as the Family Panel.

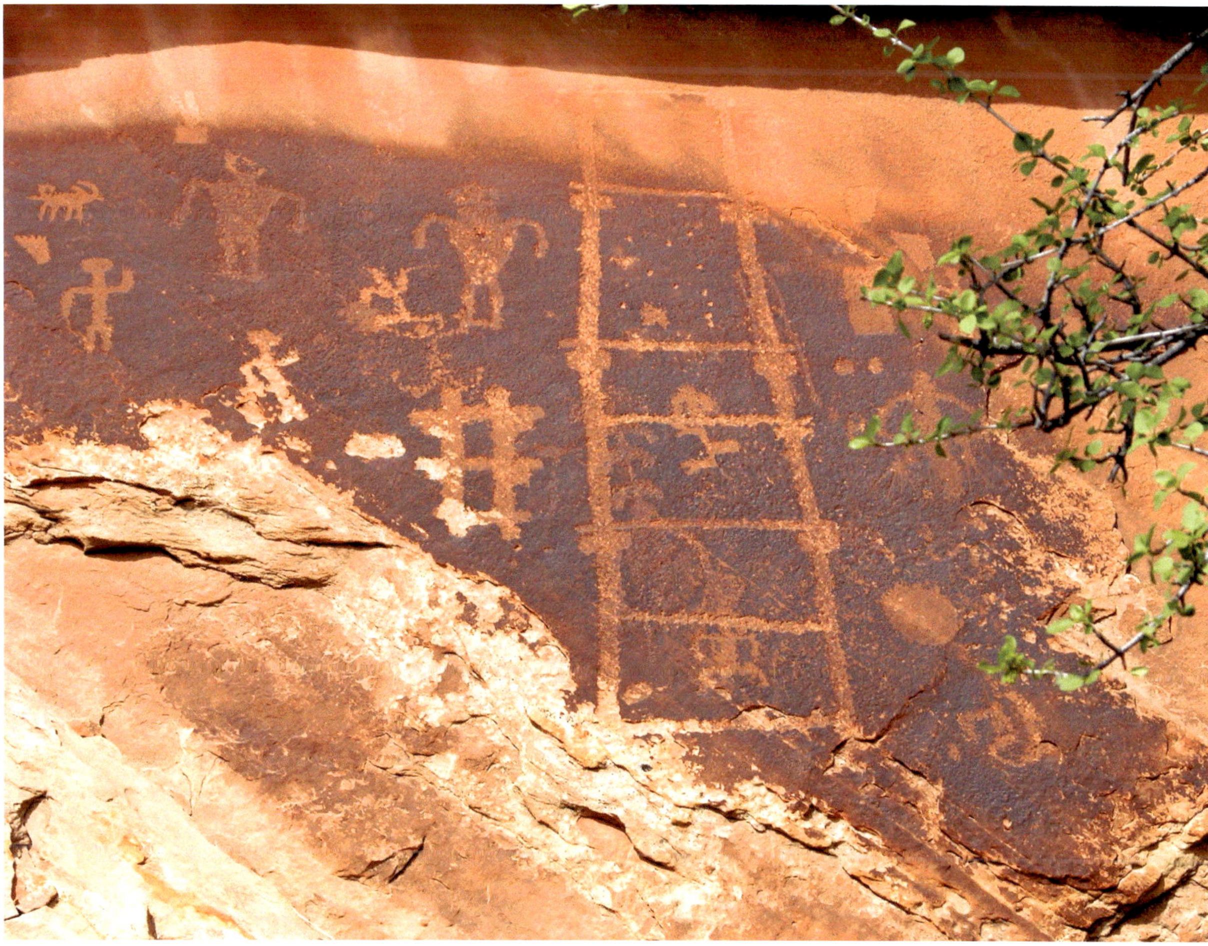

FIGURE 7.9. A petroglyph in southern Utah that possibly depicts a wooden ladder. The figure is similar to those found at Ancestral Puebloan sites.

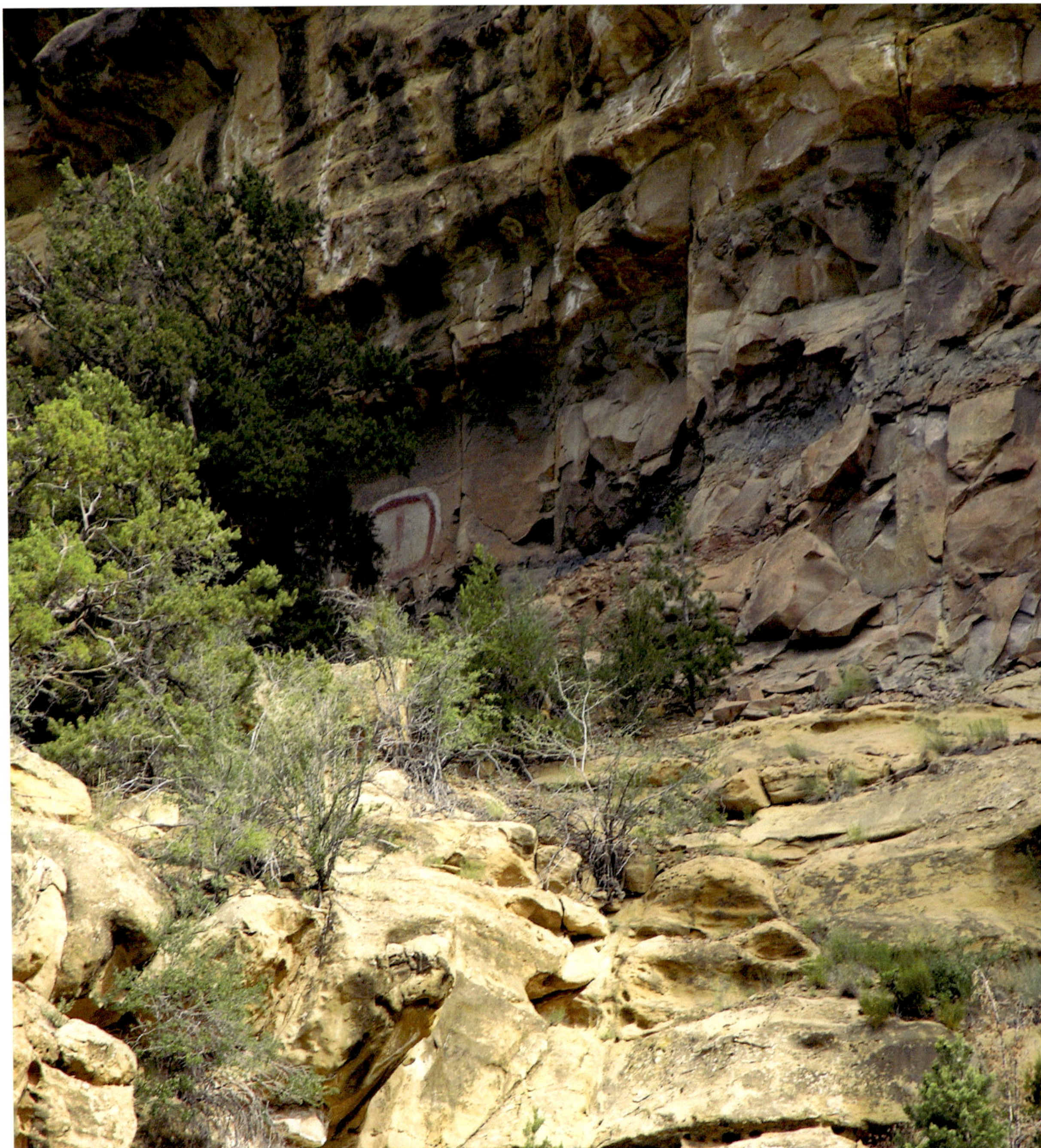

FIGURE 7.10. A red and white shield-like motif on a cliff in Range Creek Canyon.

8

GHOST FIGURES

The often large, legless, somewhat anthropomorphic figures that frequently dominate works of Barrier Canyon style rock art are sometimes referred to as "ghost figures" (see, for example, figures 2.1, 3.1, 4.11, 5.10, 8.1, 8.2, and 8.3). I think it is an interesting and telling characterization, one that speaks as much about the Western culture that has described the art as it does about the art itself.

The figures are certainly fantastic representations of somewhat human-reminiscent forms. They generally have an upright body with a human-like head, shoulders, and a rectangular to trapezoidal body that often tapers or truncates footless at the bottom. Arms, feet, and legs are sometimes but not always present. The figures may have intricate interior designs, but the shape is likely what gave rise to the term *ghost figure*. To some people, they appear to be draped in a robe or cape that sometimes covers the arms and obscures the legs and feet. "Ghost figure" is probably more mysterious, if less descriptive, than "robe or costume figures."

The figures certainly are mysterious, at least to an outside observer. To the artists they may have been straightforward depictions of something quite mundane, such as persons engaged in everyday activities, but that seems unlikely to me. If we take a minute to compare the way human-like forms are portrayed in Barrier Canyon style rock art with those of the Fremont or later Ute and Paiute figures, several observations leap to mind.

Fremont and Late Prehistoric anthropomorphs are usually recognizable as representations of humans. They generally have heads, arms, legs, hands, feet, and torsos in roughly the correct positions and proportions (e.g., figures 9.4 and 9.10). They range from simple figures, perhaps holding a bow and arrow, to complex and awe-inspiring figures with elaborate hats and head adornment, clothing, jewelry, weapons, shields, and even severed human heads in their hands (e.g., figures 6.5 and 9.9). The figures can be outlandish and frightening, but they are rather clearly depictions of people. Heroic, legendary, extraordinary people, but people nonetheless.

Likewise, depictions of non-human animals in Fremont and Late Prehistoric art tend toward the realistic. Bighorn sheep are common, followed by deer and elk, bears, mountain lions, lizards, snakes, various birds, and occasional insect-like forms (e.g., figures 10.5, 11.6, and 11.9). Animal depictions are most often relatively straightforward, with little embellishment. They appear to be depictions of the actual animal. Sometimes those animals appear in unrealistic poses, or with parts embellished or missing, but they generally tend toward realism. An exception might be snakes, which in some areas are depicted with horns—usually like those seen on bighorn sheep (e.g., figures 6.6 and 9.2). These pictures clearly represent something extraordinary, as horned snakes do not exist naturally in the region—that I know of.

With some exceptions, Fremont and Late Prehistoric art tends toward realistic representations of humans and the natural world. The figures can be exaggerated and highly embellished, but they tend to depict recognizable things, things that look the same today as they did in the past. However, the many incredibly complex and artistic abstract, geometric, ethereal, and grand artistic expressions are another matter, as the rich world that they appear to connect to is inaccessible to modern interpretation.

The ghost figures in Barrier Canyon style art clearly reference stylistic and symbolic worlds alien to modern viewers. Barrier Canyon style depictions of non-human animals are likewise fantastic and fluid. Animals are often not entirely recognizable, as they, like the anthropomorphs, are stylized and may represent animal-like things that do not exist in the natural world. Non-human animal forms are also often seen in interaction with the human-like forms—perhaps implying that they communicated with each other and worked with, or against, each other (e.g., figures 8.1 and 8.9). Western culture has only occasional references to human-animal communication, except for children's stories, which are full of talking animals and animals that help, and harm, little humans.

Viewing and making sense of a Barrier Canyon style artwork may be difficult for an average product of modern Western culture. Whereas in modern Western culture we have a rich spiritual tradition, Western religions generally do not have references to human variants that may have some human and some superhuman or distinctly extra-human characteristics. God or gods are typically considered to be basically human in form. Modern Western depictions of the Judeo-Christian God typically show an older, bearded white man. Extra-human forms are generally restricted to angels or devils, and depictions of one form of God, the Holy Ghost, are usually lacking. In addition, animal forms in Western culture tend toward the realistic, with variants restricted for the most part to creatures from folklore, such as werewolves.

So it is understandable that we call Barrier Canyon style anthropomorphs ghost figures as we have no other readily available and widely understood language to describe images of things that fall outside our religious and folkloric traditions. The figures and designs in ancient art represented specific characters and icons, entire stories and beliefs that made up the culture of the artists. These stories embodied their beliefs, their worldview, their history, their sense of who they were. We can see that for the artists who created Barrier Canyon style art and the later Fremont and Late Prehistoric art, their cultures had wildly more diverse stories and belief systems than we Westerners have today. How I wish I could know the stories referenced by the various figures of the Great Gallery. But that is not possible. We can, however, know that the stories were undoubtedly fantastic, rich, and thrilling, as are the pictures left on the walls for us to gaze upon and ponder.

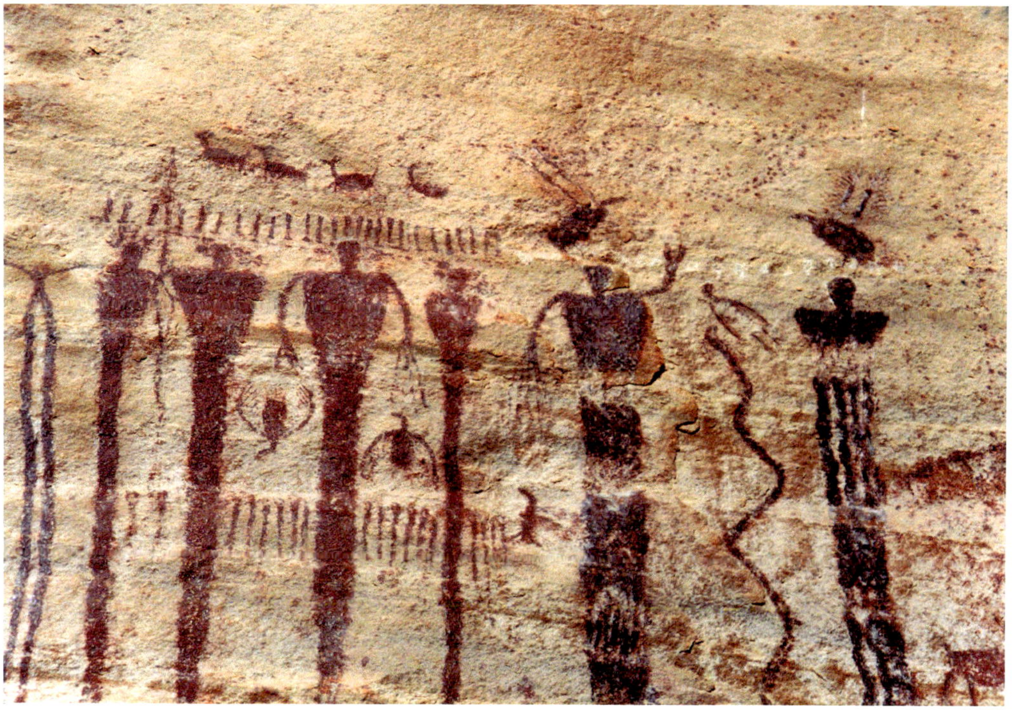

FIGURE 8.1. Barrier Canyon–style anthropomorphs on a pictograph panel in Buckhorn Wash in the San Rafael Swell, with birds flying around them and bighorn sheep walking above.

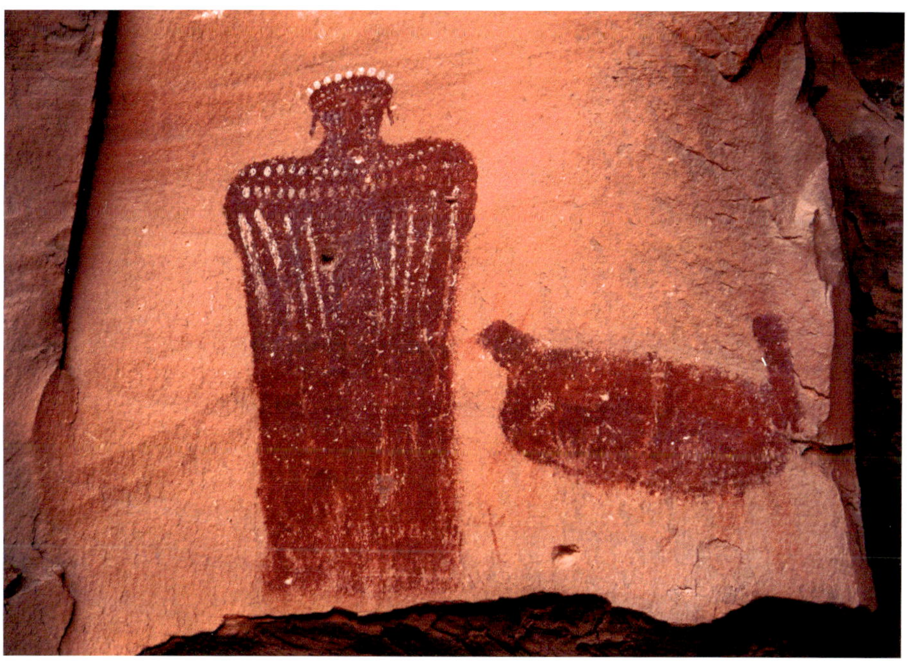

FIGURE 8.2. A Barrier Canyon–style pictograph known as the Moqui Queen or Cleopatra, with a crown of dots, earbobs, and interior body paint.

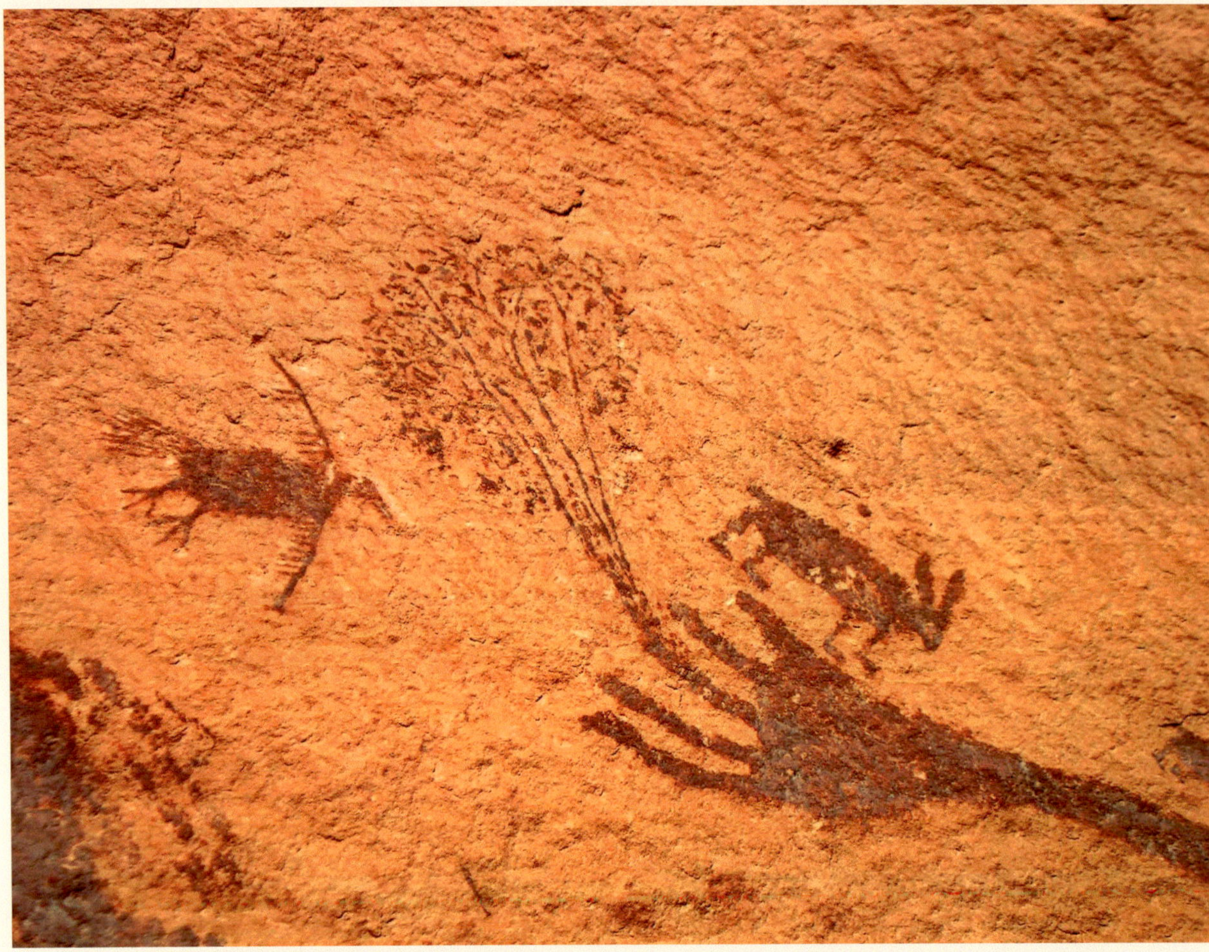

FIGURE 8.3. A detailed Barrier Canyon–style image of what appears to be Indian ricegrass, an important food for regional foragers, coming out of the middle finger of an anthropomorph in the Maze District of Canyonlands National Park.

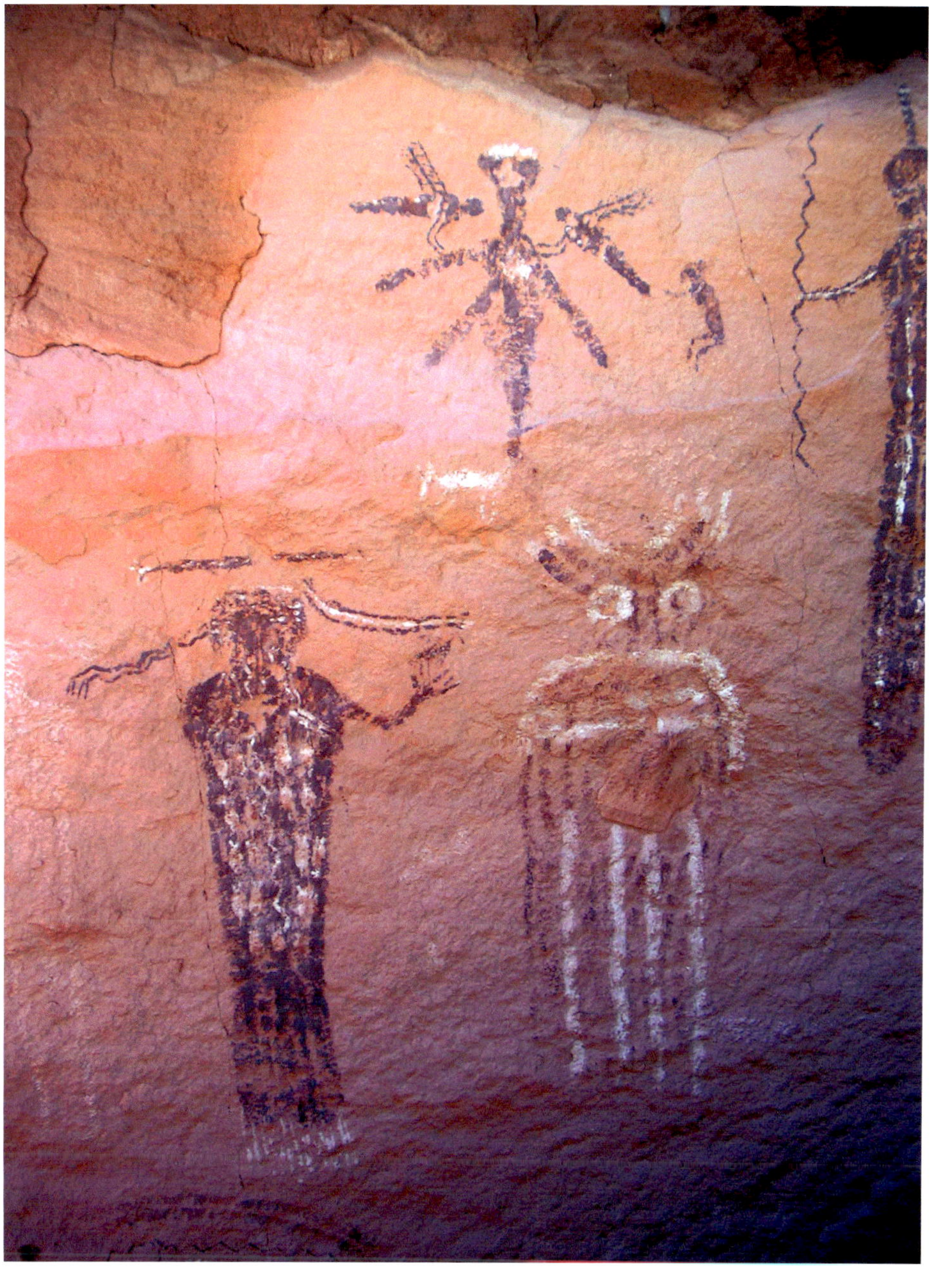

FIGURE 8.4. A Barrier Canyon–style pictograph with what appear to be dragonflies, an infrequent but not rare motif in Southwestern rock art.

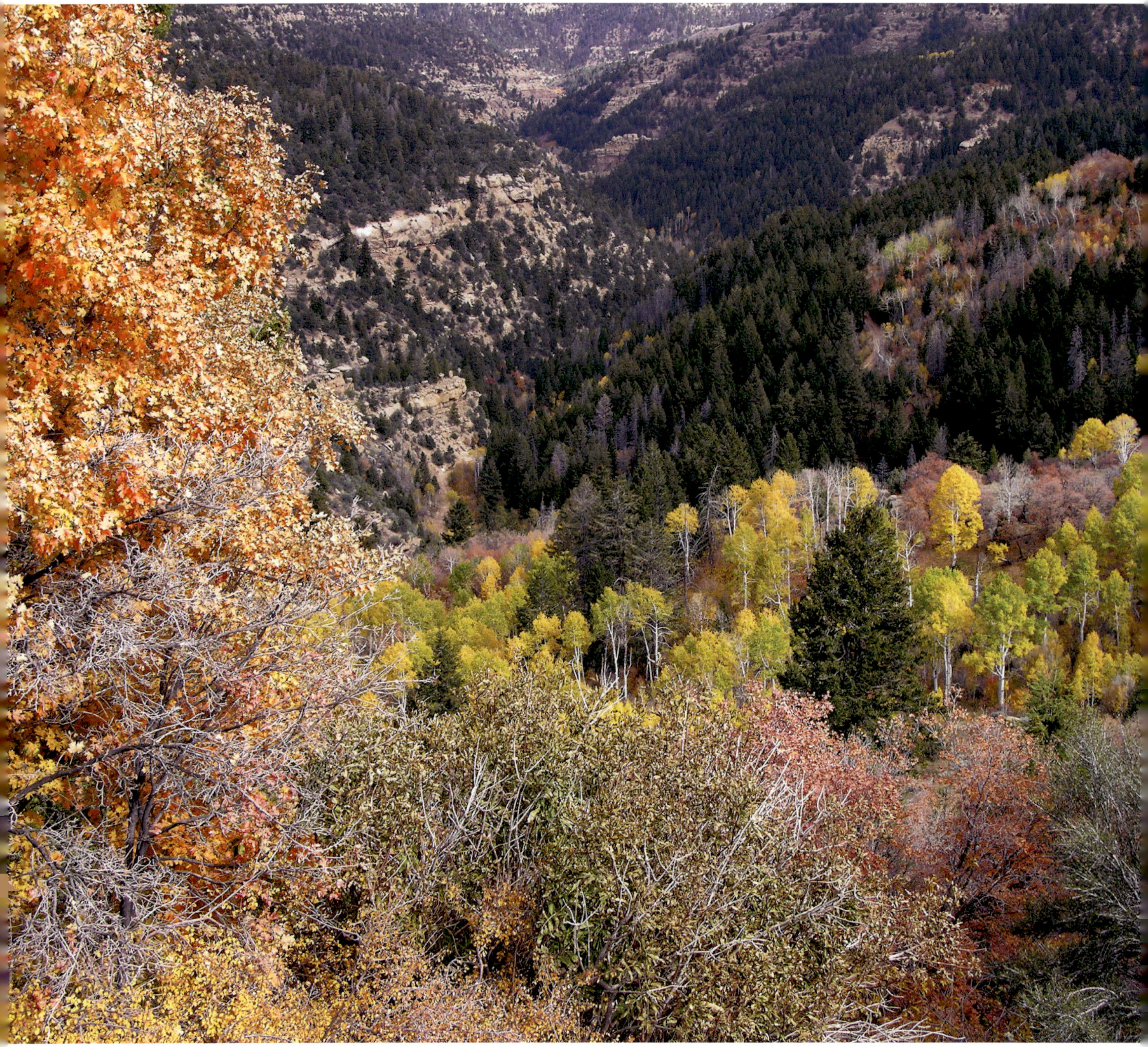

FIGURE 8.5. Fine fall foliage in Range Creek Canyon.

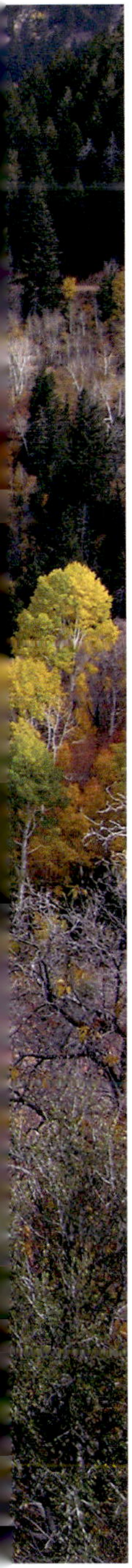

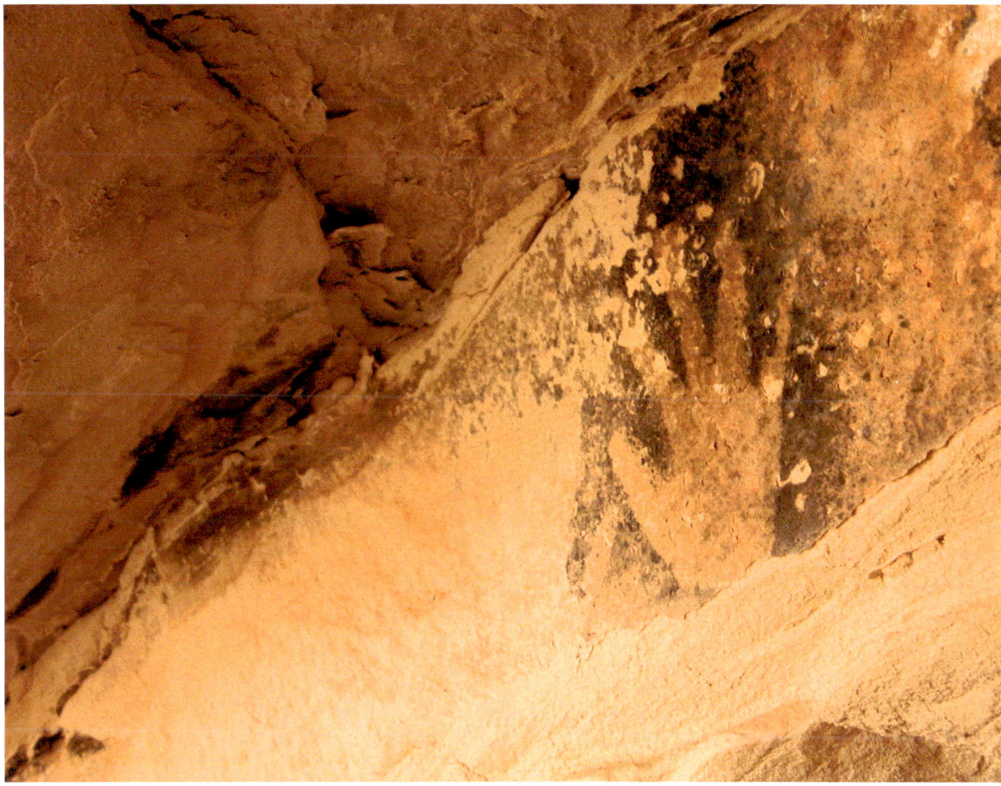

FIGURE 8.6. Negative (stenciled or outlined) handprint pictographs in southern Utah. The cultural affiliation is unknown.

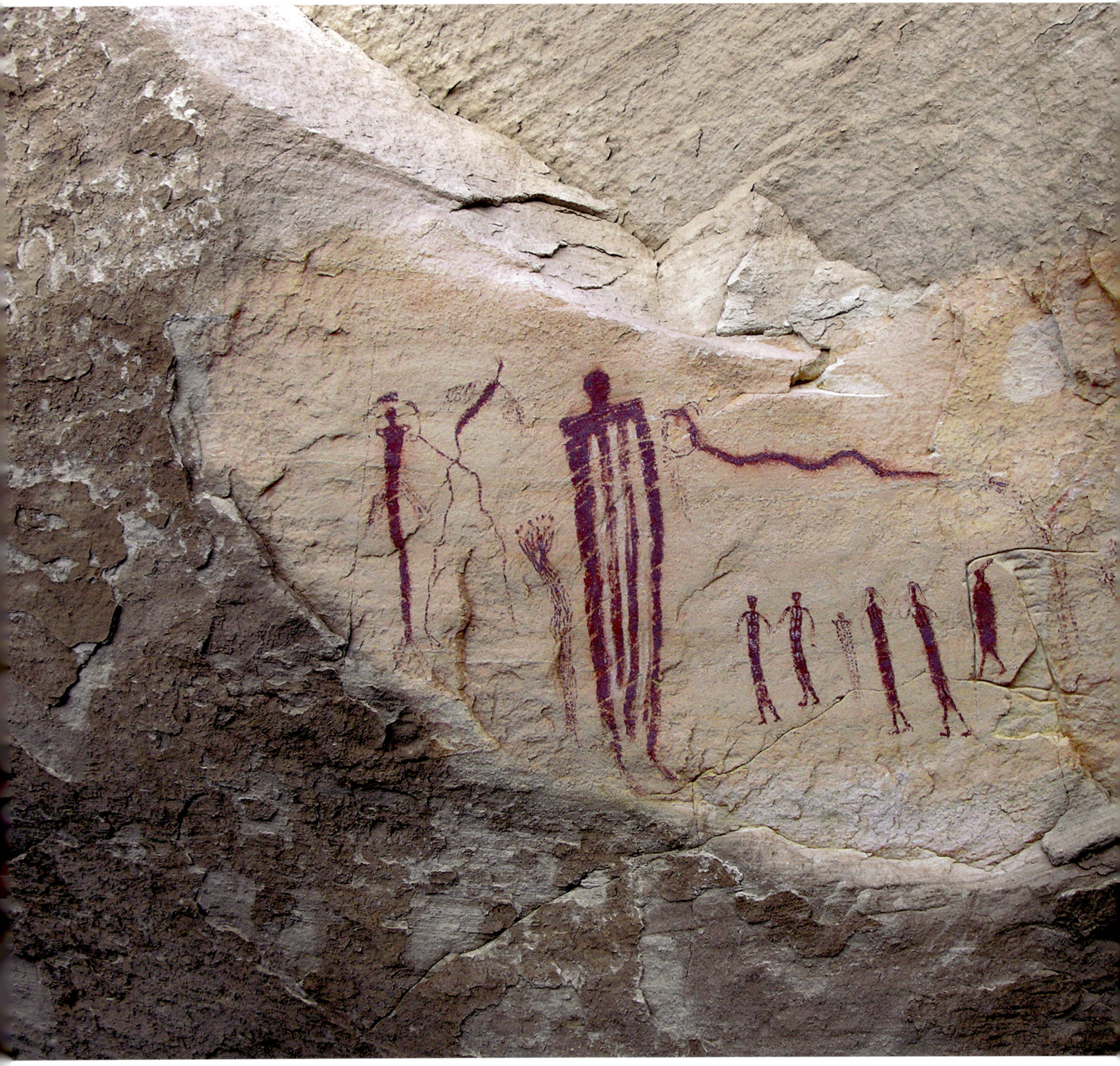

FIGURE 8.7. A Barrier Canyon–style pictograph panel with numerous anthropomorphs in the San Rafael Swell area.

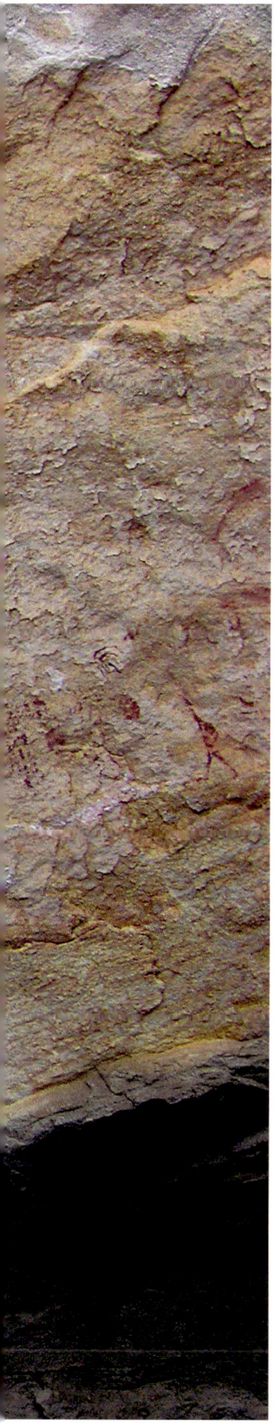

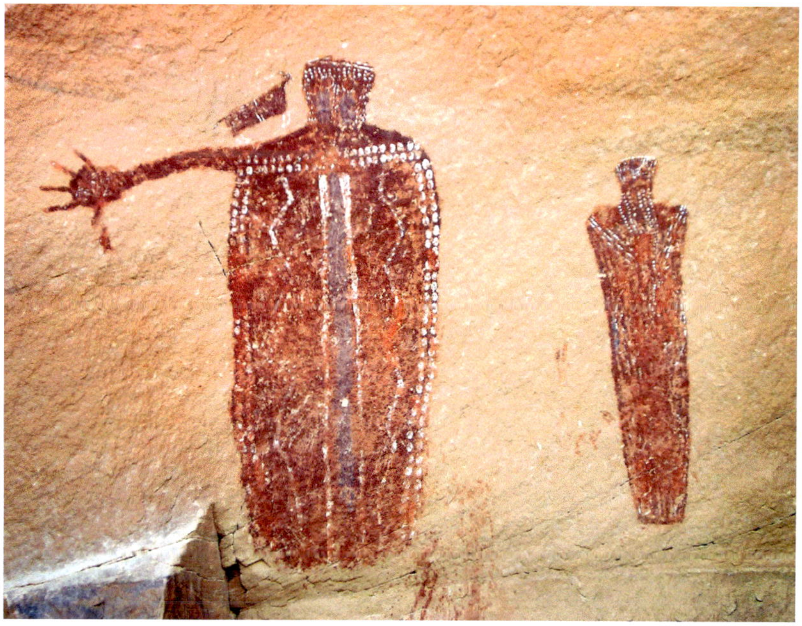

FIGURE 8.8. Exquisitely detailed pictographs in the Vermilion Cliffs area of southern Utah on what is commonly known as the Perfect Panel.

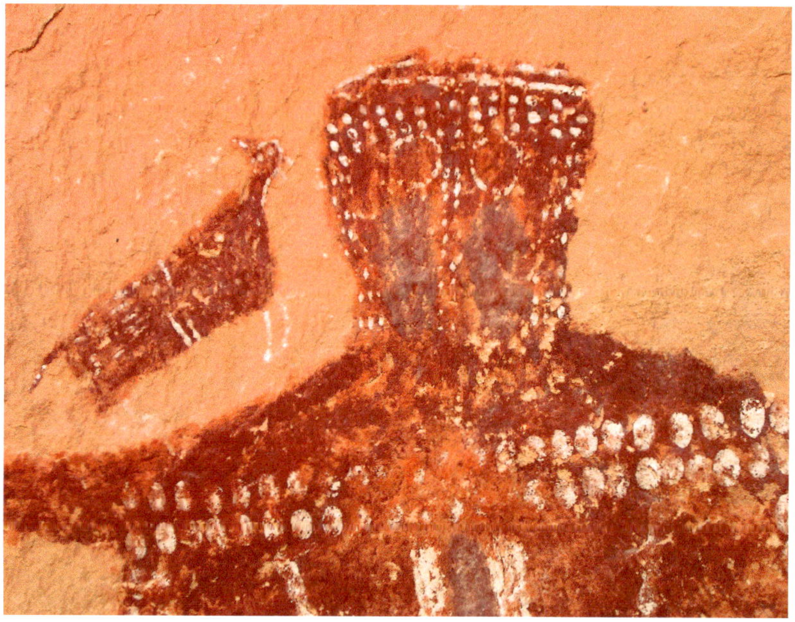

FIGURE 8.9. Detail of a pictograph on the Perfect Panel in the Vermilion Cliffs area of southern Utah (see figure 8.8). The Barrier Canyon–style anthropomorph appears to have a zoomorph perched on its shoulder.

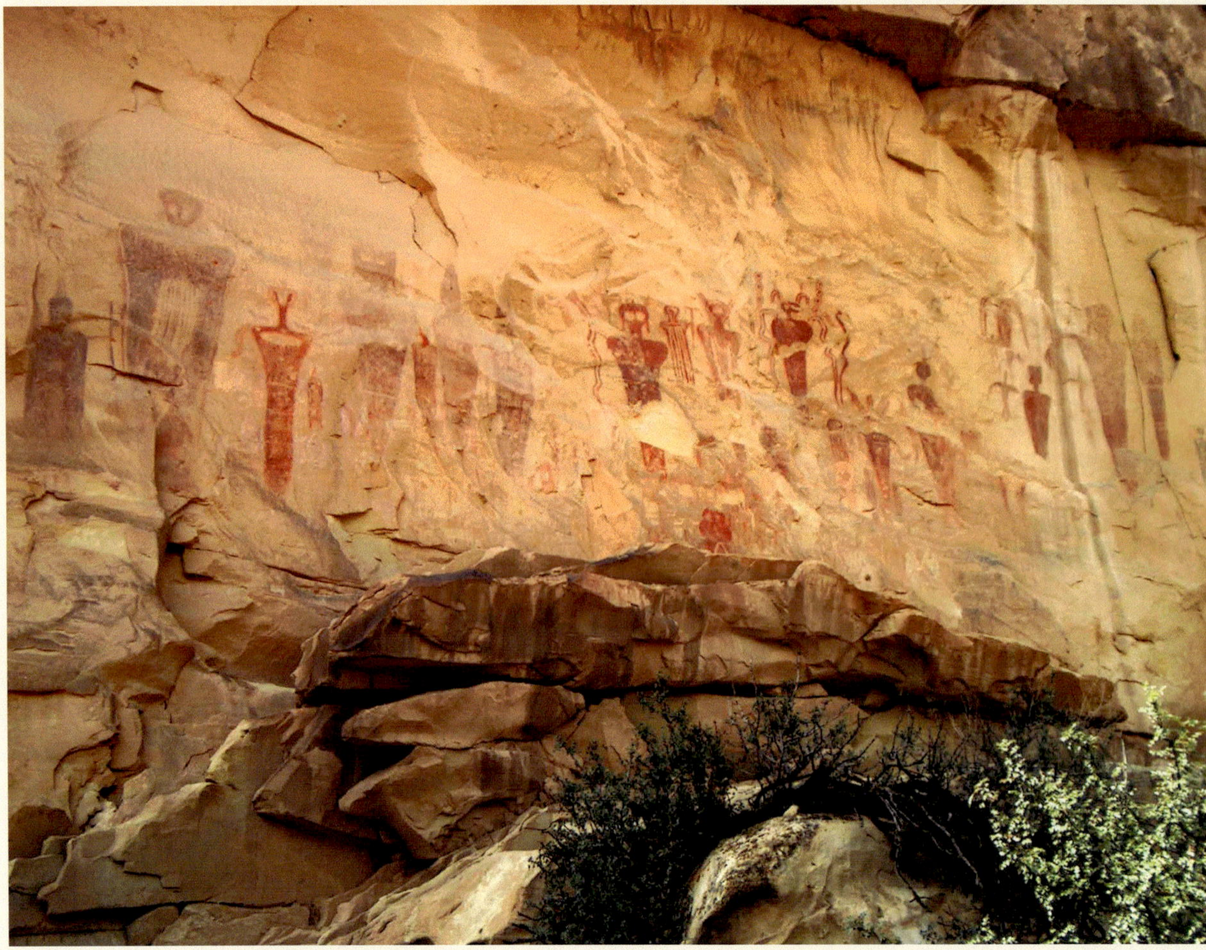

FIGURE 8.10. A Barrier Canyon–style panel with numerous anthropomorphs in Sego Canyon in the Book Cliffs.

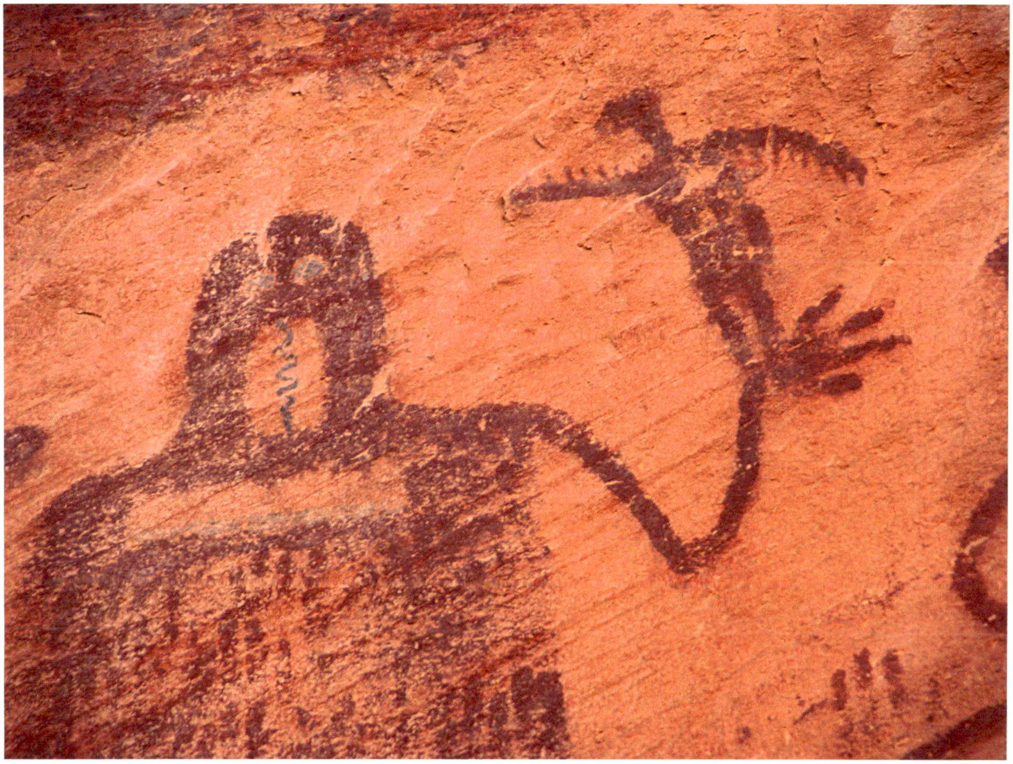

FIGURE 8.11. Detail of a Barrier Canyon–style anthropomorph with bluish-gray pupils and what appear to be a bluish-gray snake in its mouth and a bird-like figure on its wrist.

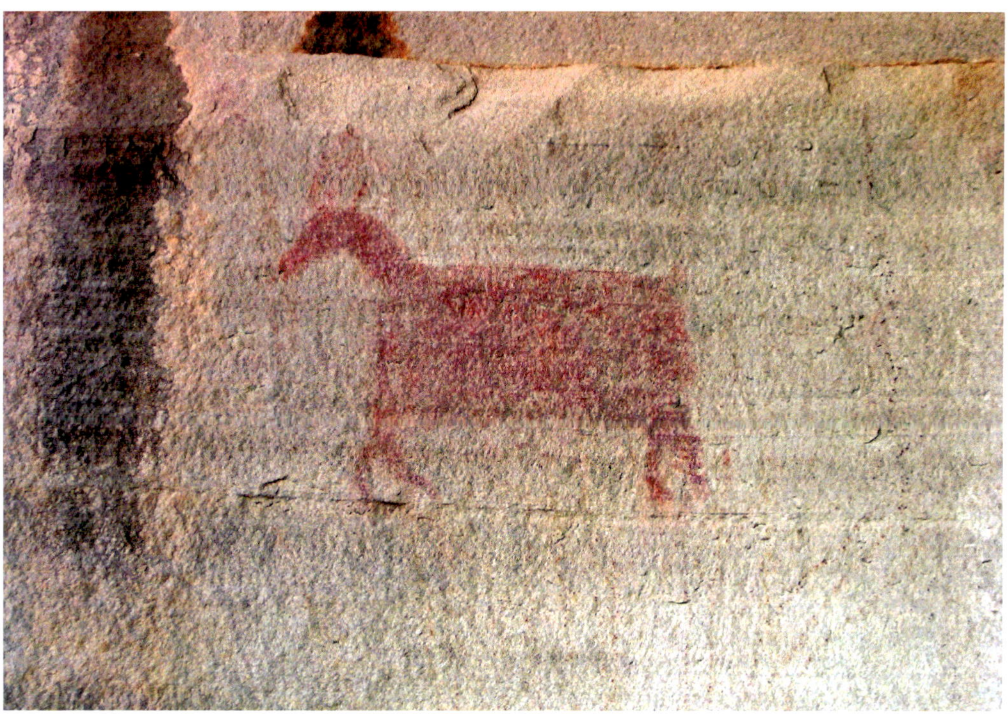

FIGURE 8.12. A graceful zoomorph pictograph thought to be Barrier Canyon–style high above Range Creek in eastern Utah.

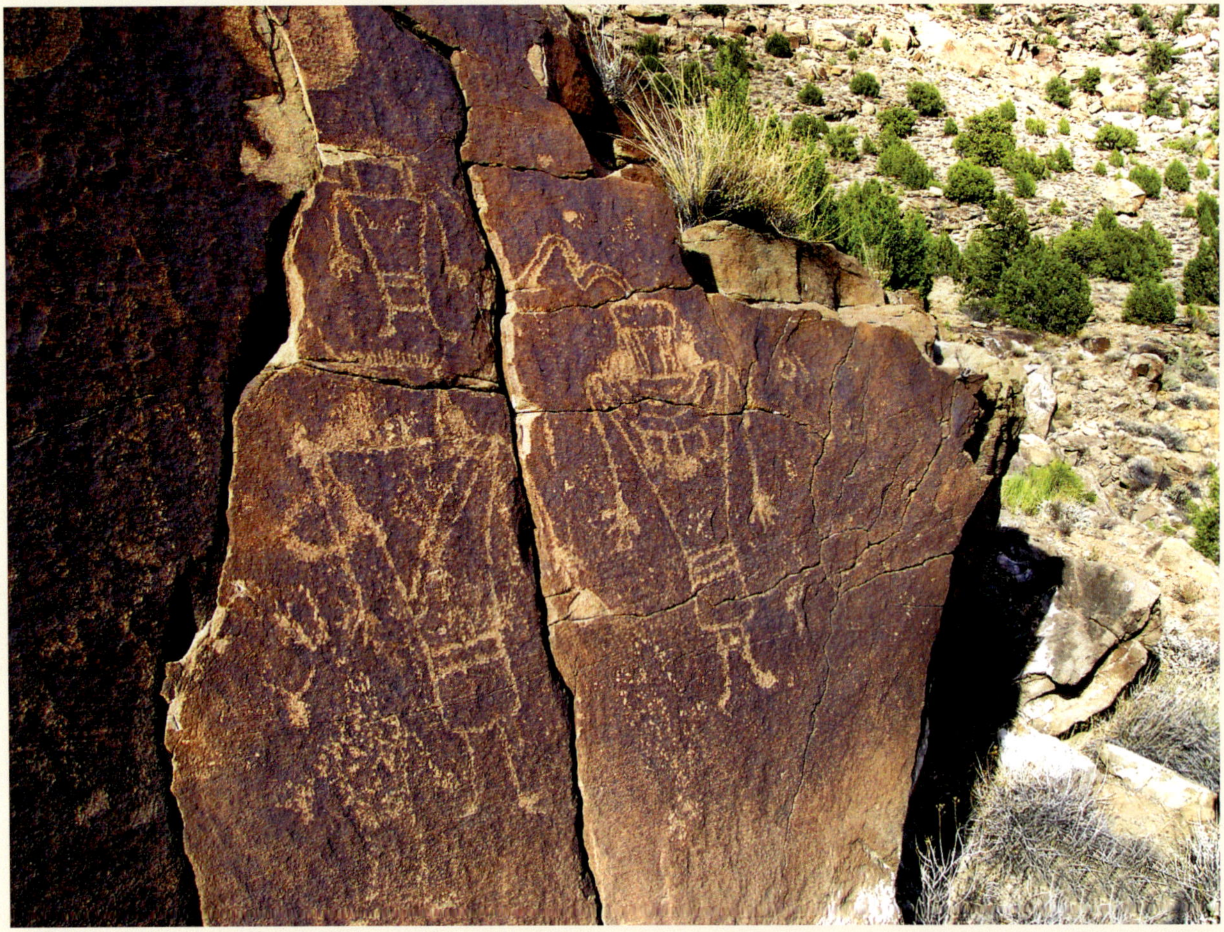

FIGURE 9.1. A prominent Range Creek Canyon panel that seems to greet visitors. It is similar to Fremont-style panels in Capitol Reef National Park and is reminiscent of the Pilling figurines found in Range Creek and now in the USU Eastern Prehistoric Museum in Price.

9

THE FREMONT TRADITION

Rock art from the Fremont period is rich and diverse, and contains a great variety of stylized and abstract designs, as well as zoomorphic and anthropomorphic figures. A striking element that is particularly emblematic of the rock art of the Uinta Basin and Capitol Reef areas is the trapezoidal-bodied anthropomorph commonly referred to as a Classic Fremont style figure (e.g., figure 4.6).

These representations are indeed recognizable, as their broad-shouldered countenances are bold and proudly executed, often dominating a panel or group of designs. They can be large, sometimes life-size, and they often display ornamentation across the chest area reminiscent of sizeable or extravagant necklaces. Some brandish what appear to be weapons or shields, and some even appear to be holding war trophies: a number of panels appear to depict warriors holding severed human heads (e.g., figures 6.5 and 9.9).

Some appear to be depictions of the small clay figurines occasionally found in Fremont sites (e.g., figure 9.1). Some figures have legs and large feet, but they are rarely depicted as engaged in activities other than posing for the artist. But not all anthropomorphic figures in Fremont rock art conform to the classic design, and some may be seen engaging in activities such as hunting or fighting (e.g., figure 11.11). They may also be depicted in some sort of relationship with zoomorphic figures, most commonly bighorn sheep, such as stalking them or merely standing among them (e.g., figure 10.1).

In contrast to the ghost figures of the Barrier Canyon style, Fremont anthropomorphs are rarely shown in apparent communication with or interacting with other figures. While Barrier Canyon style rock art often depicts anthropomorphic figures with birds or abstract creatures surrounding them, hovering over them, or otherwise interacting with them, that is rarely the case with Fremont style figures.

For this reason, I am fairly confident that the cultural/spiritual/religious background from which the rock art imagery was drawn was strikingly different between the people who created the earlier Barrier Canyon style and those who created the Fremont style. Barrier Canyon style figures are extra-natural and appear to commune with spirits and creatures. Fremont figures are warriors who stand alone. No ghost-like figures appear in dominant positions in Fremont rock art, but they are ubiquitous in Barrier Canyon style panels. Some scholars see an overlap of the styles in some areas of the San Rafael Swell and Tavaputs Plateau (e.g., figure 12.7), but for the most part the styles appear to be distinct. We would expect some melding of styles, however isolated, even if there were a significant population replacement, depending on the timing and nature of the culture change.

I do not know how these observations relate to the spiritual/cultural content of the art, but I am certain that those who made the Barrier Canyon style rock art and those who made the Fremont style were from very different cultural traditions. In my opinion, they were likely different peoples.

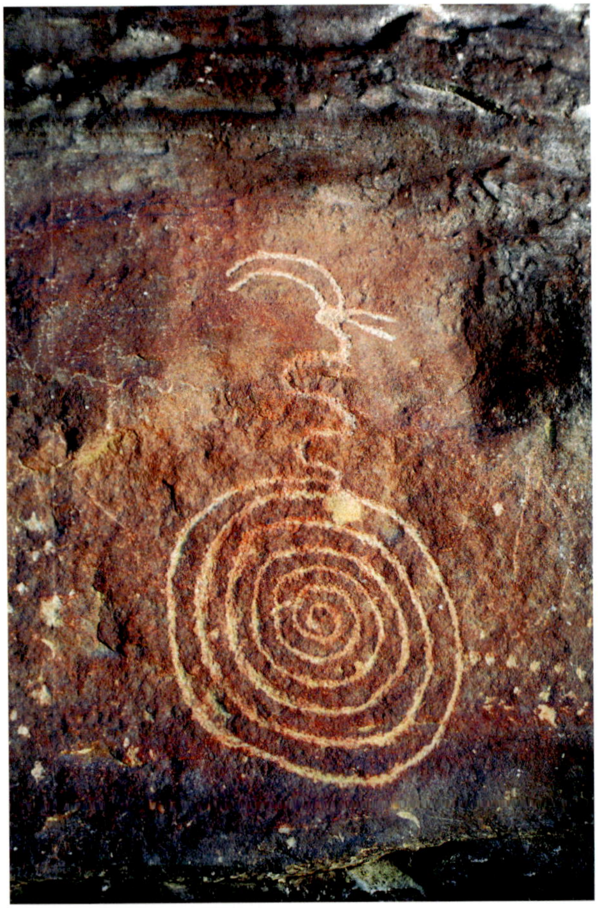

FIGURE 9.2. A Fremont-style coiled snake, one of many horned or feathered snake figures in Nine Mile Canyon. This one is at once graphic and graceful.

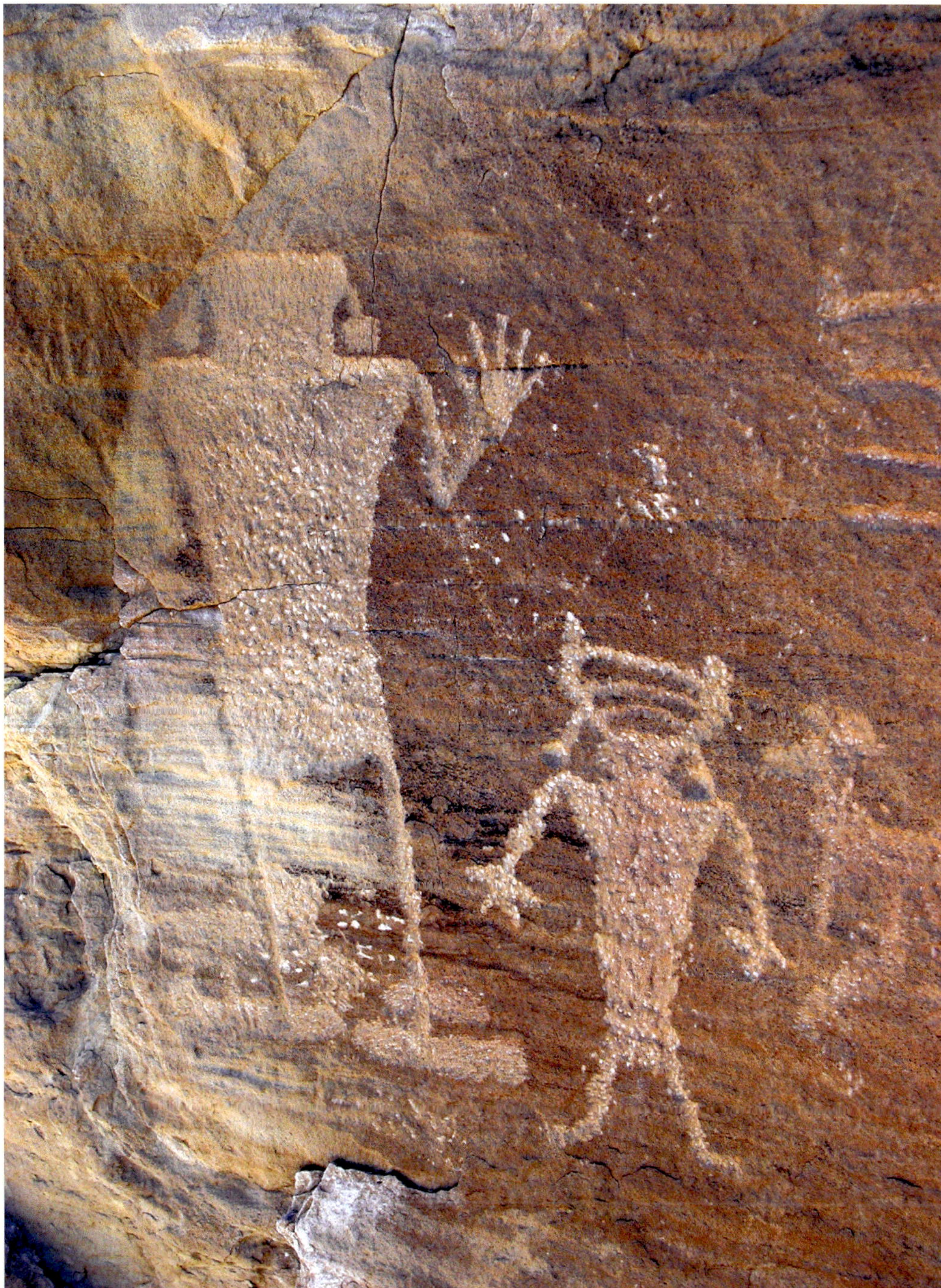

FIGURE 9.3. Fremont-style petroglyphs in Dry Canyon, a tributary of Nine Mile Canyon, which drains into the Green River.

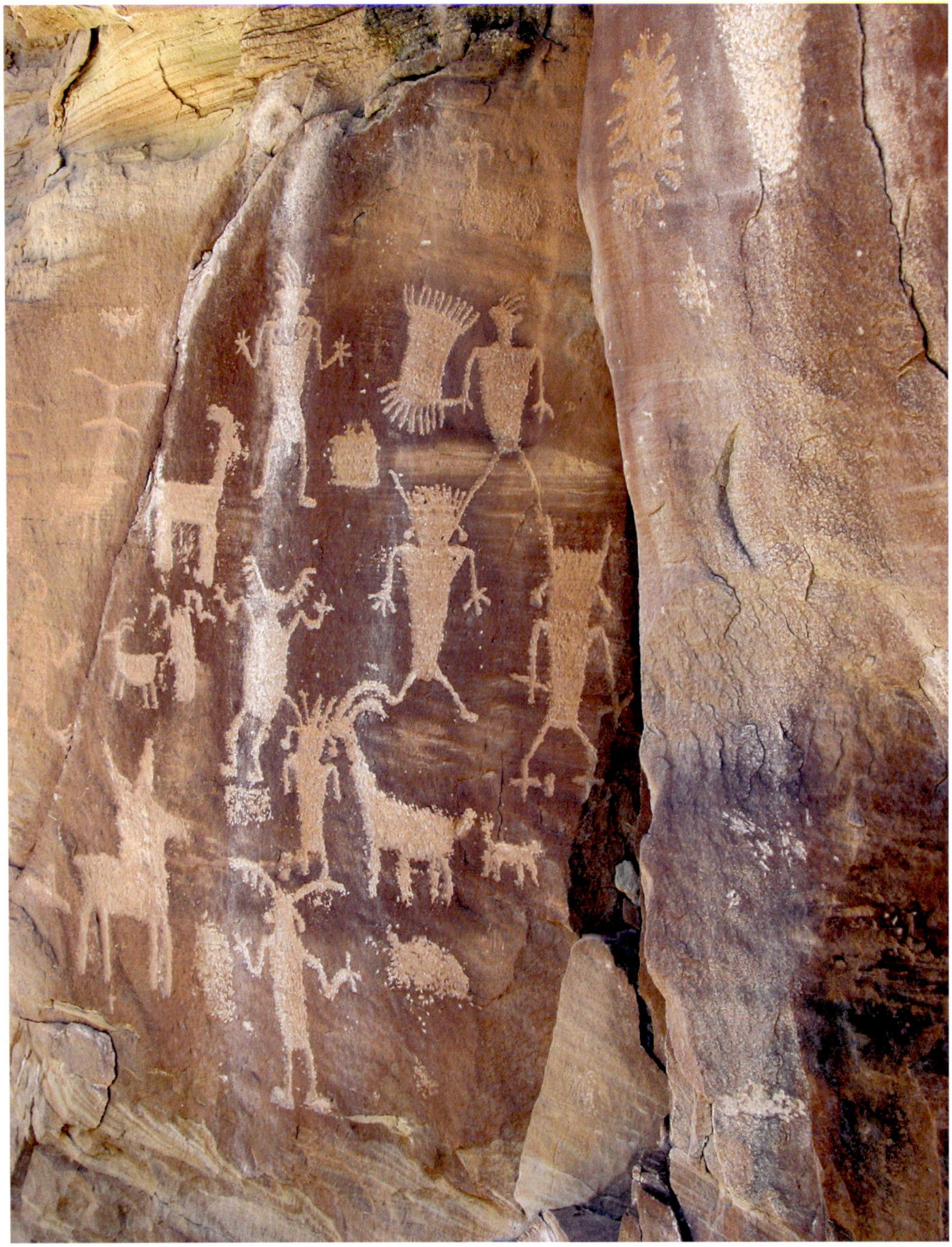

FIGURE 9.4. Fremont-style figures on a petroglyph panel in Dry Canyon.

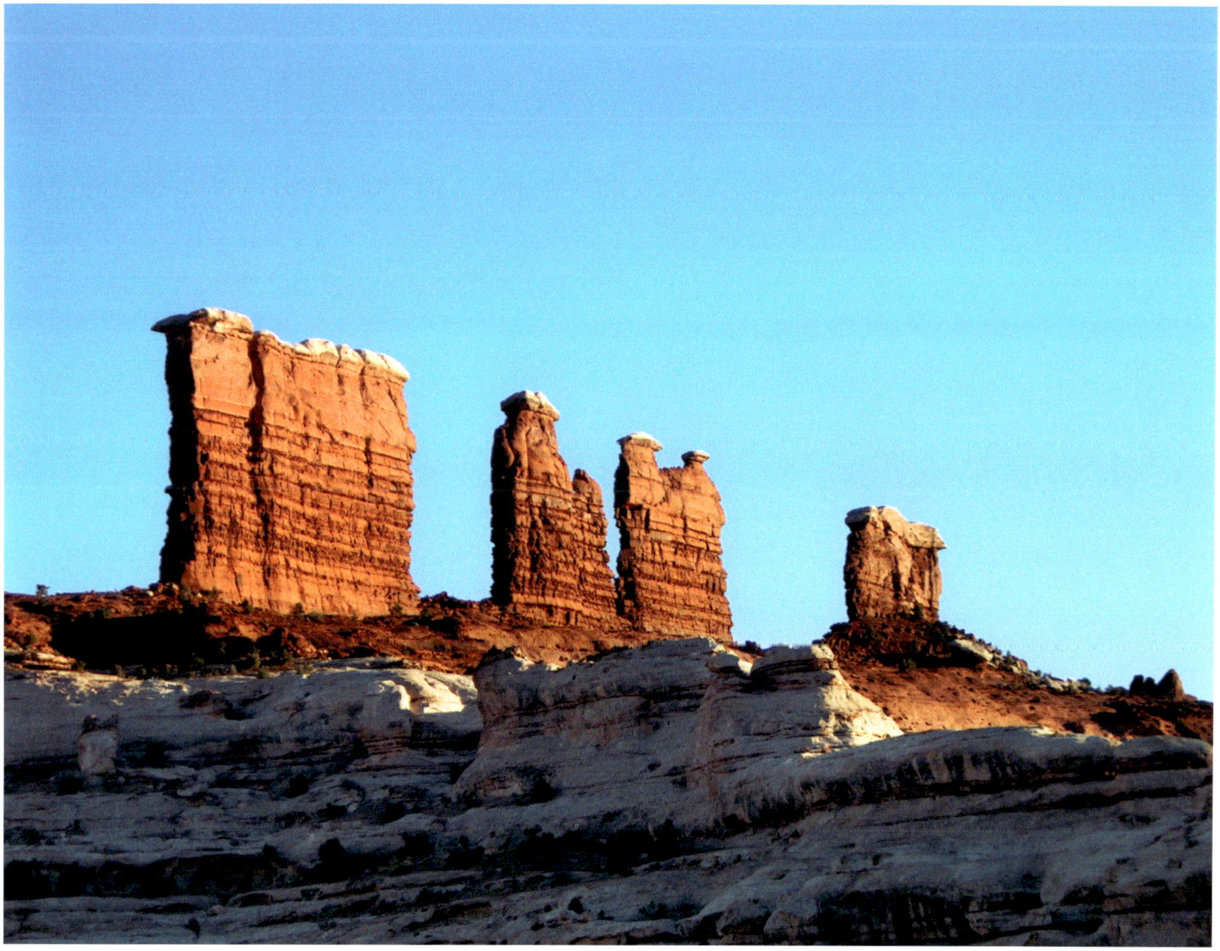

FIGURE 9.5. The formation known as the Chocolate Drops, which seem to be the guardians of the Maze District of Canyonlands National Park.

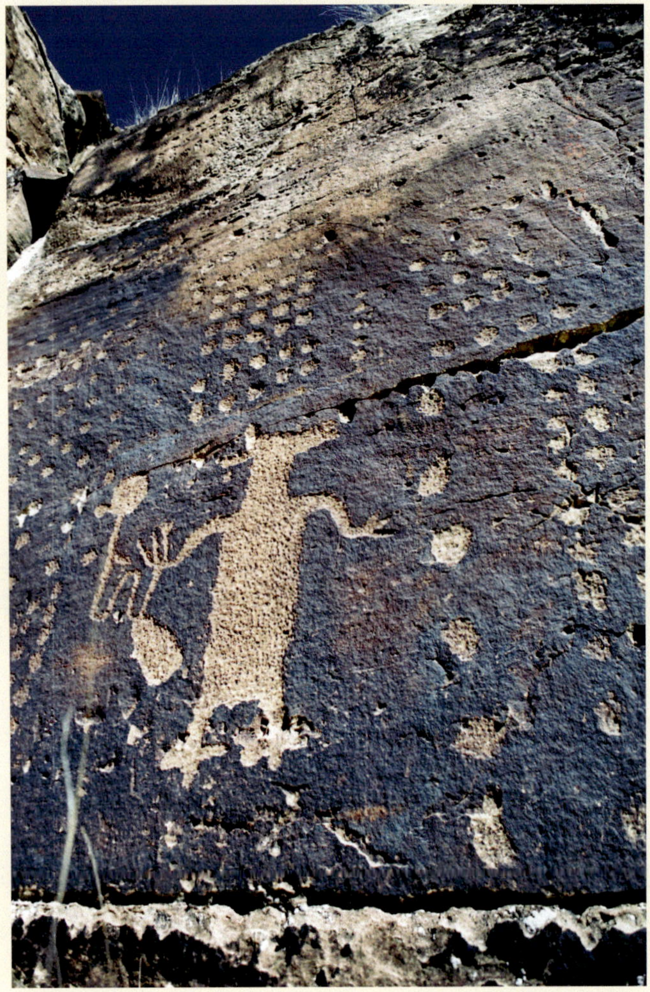

FIGURE 9.6. A Fremont-style panel in Nine Mile Canyon. To some people it appears to illustrate Pueblo and Navajo stories about how Coyote helped the Creator place the stars in the sky.

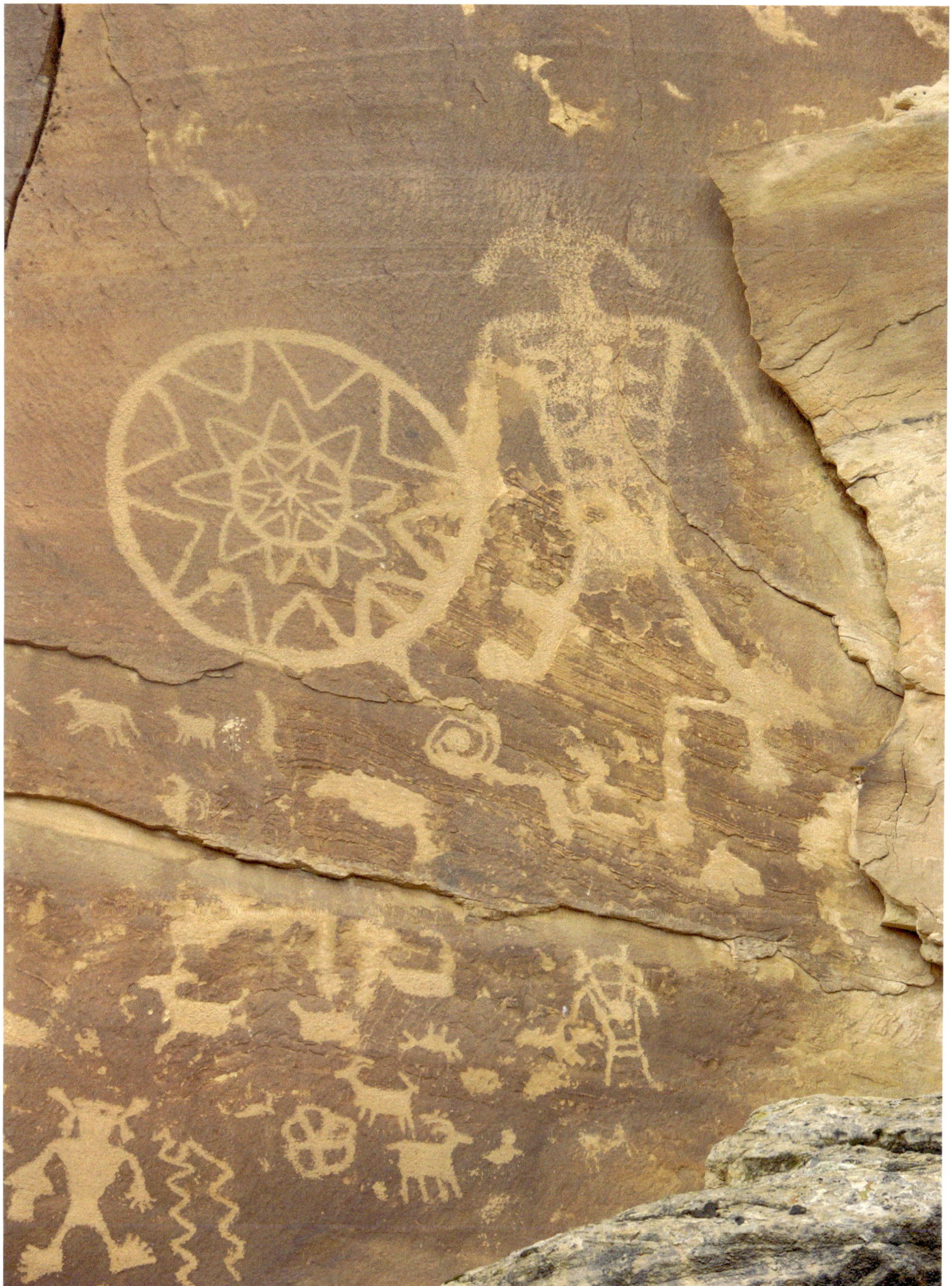

FIGURE 9.7. A large panel in Ashley Creek Canyon with Fremont-style anthropomorphs, as well as shields, a spiral, and several zoomorphs.

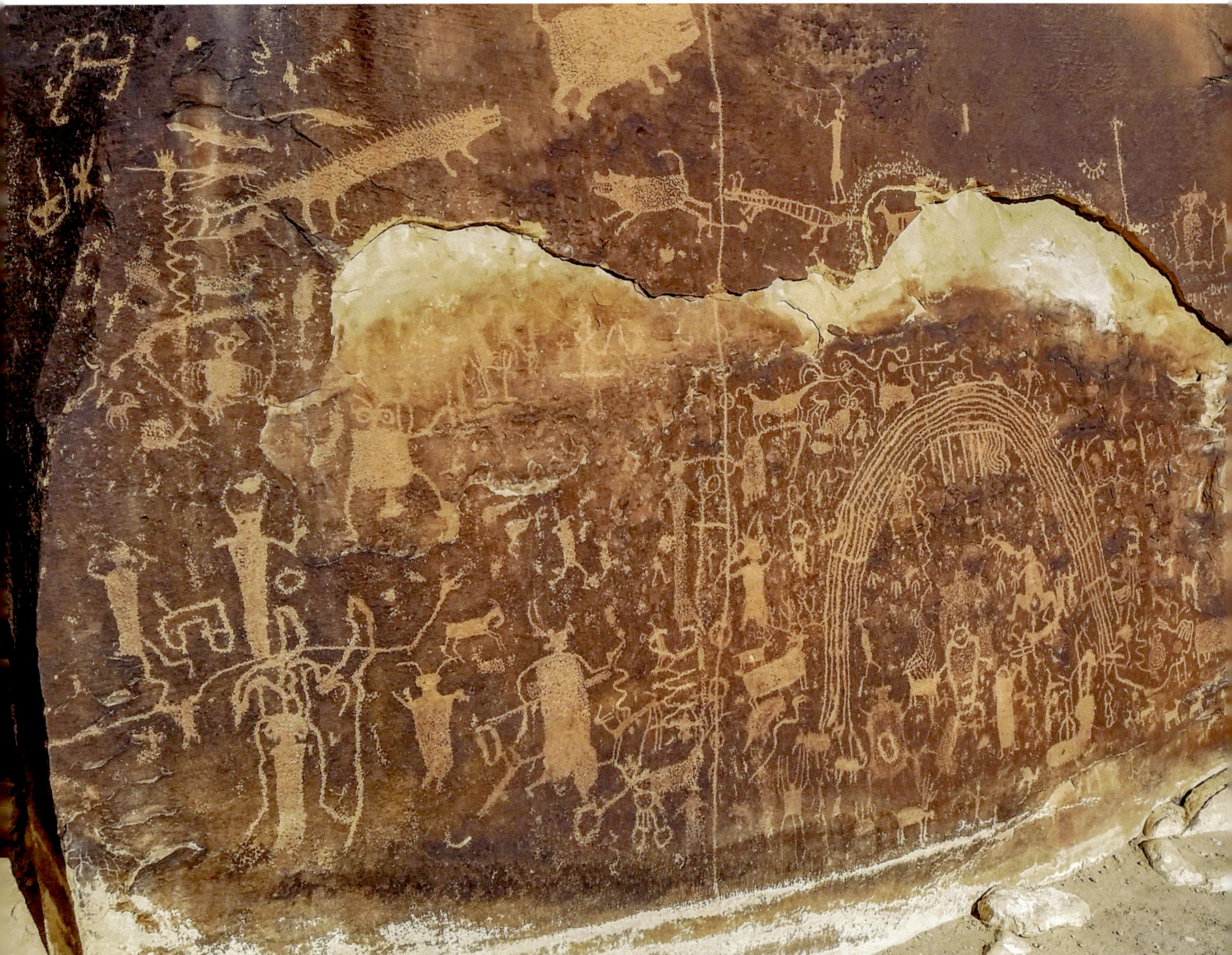

FIGURE 9.8. A wonderfully detailed petroglyph panel on a rocky point in Rochester Creek Canyon, eastern Utah, with fantastic creatures and anthropomorphs.

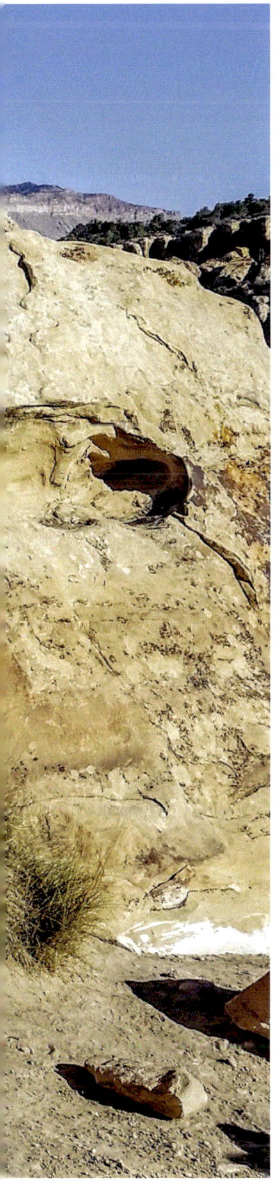

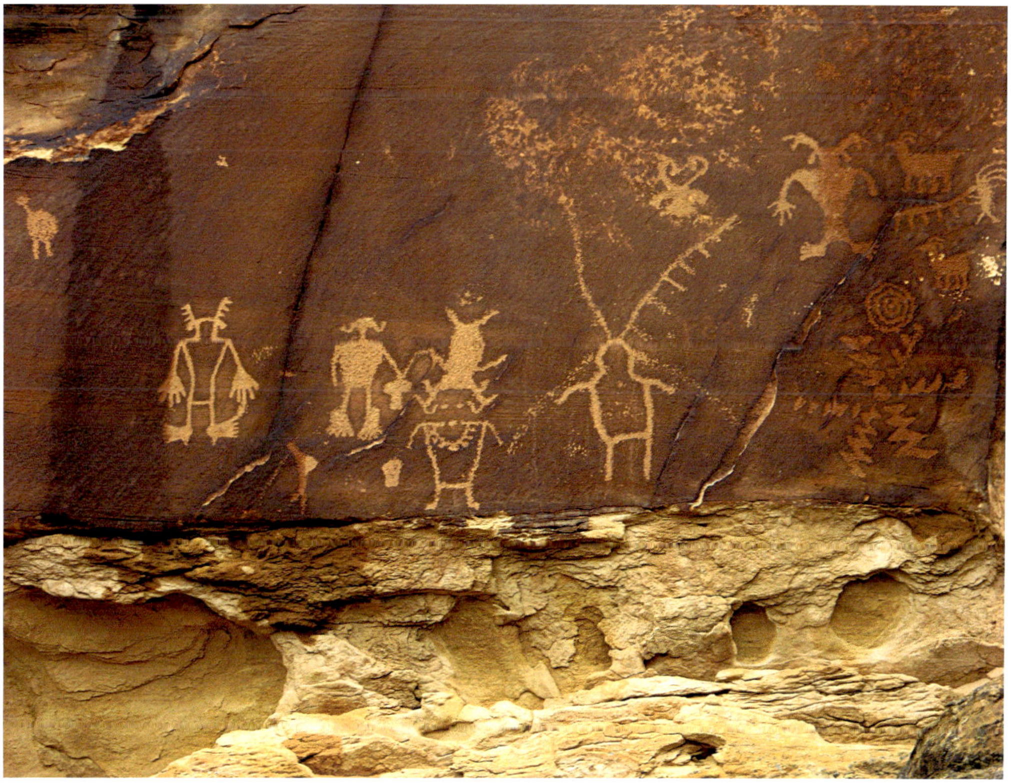

FIGURE 9.9. Fremont-style figures in Ashley Creek Canyon, northeastern Utah. This panel has a diversity of figures, including some with large hands and feet. It may also depict figures holding severed human heads.

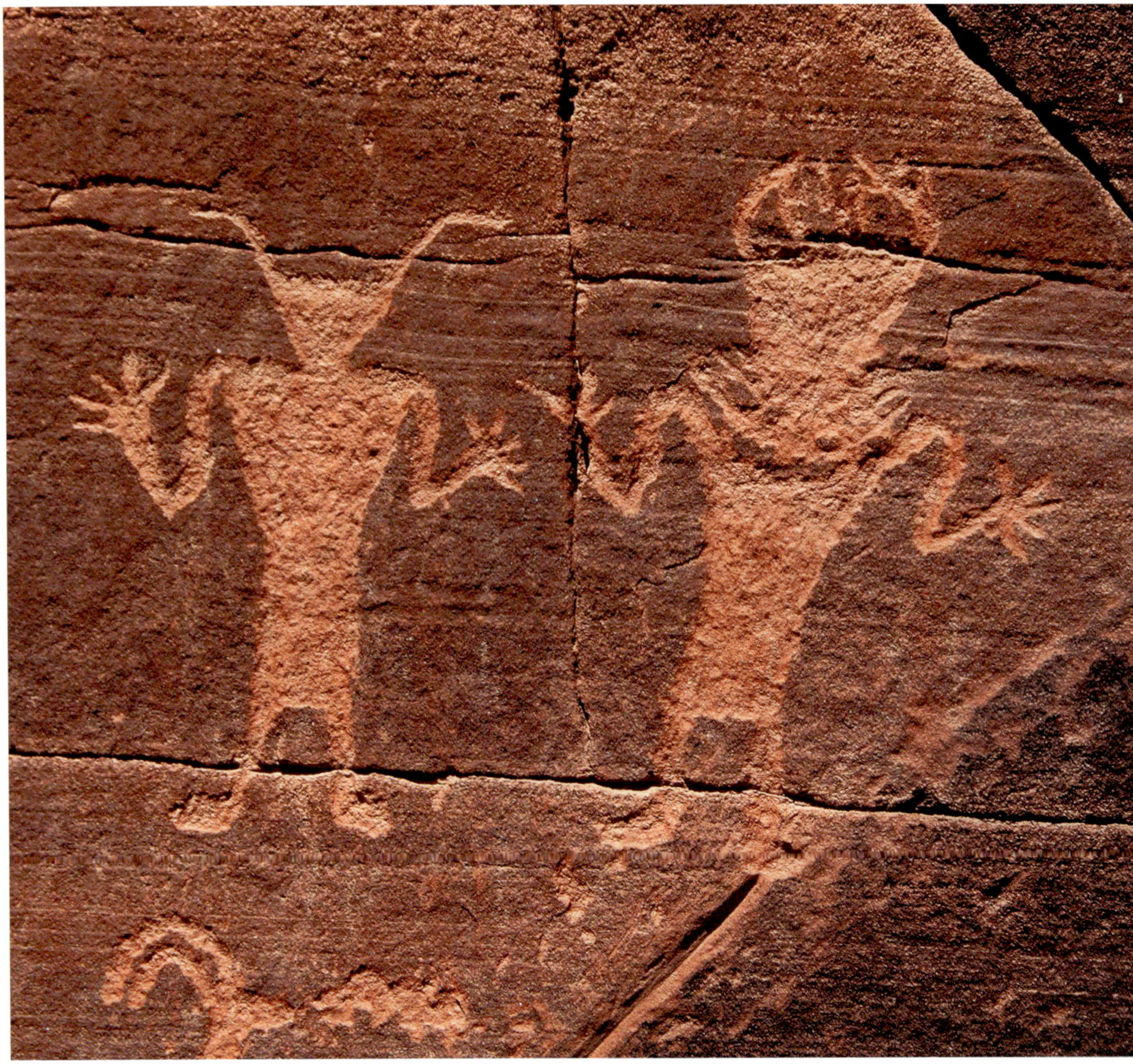

FIGURE 9.10. A Fremont-style petroglyph panel in Dry Canyon, a tributary of Nine Mile Canyon.

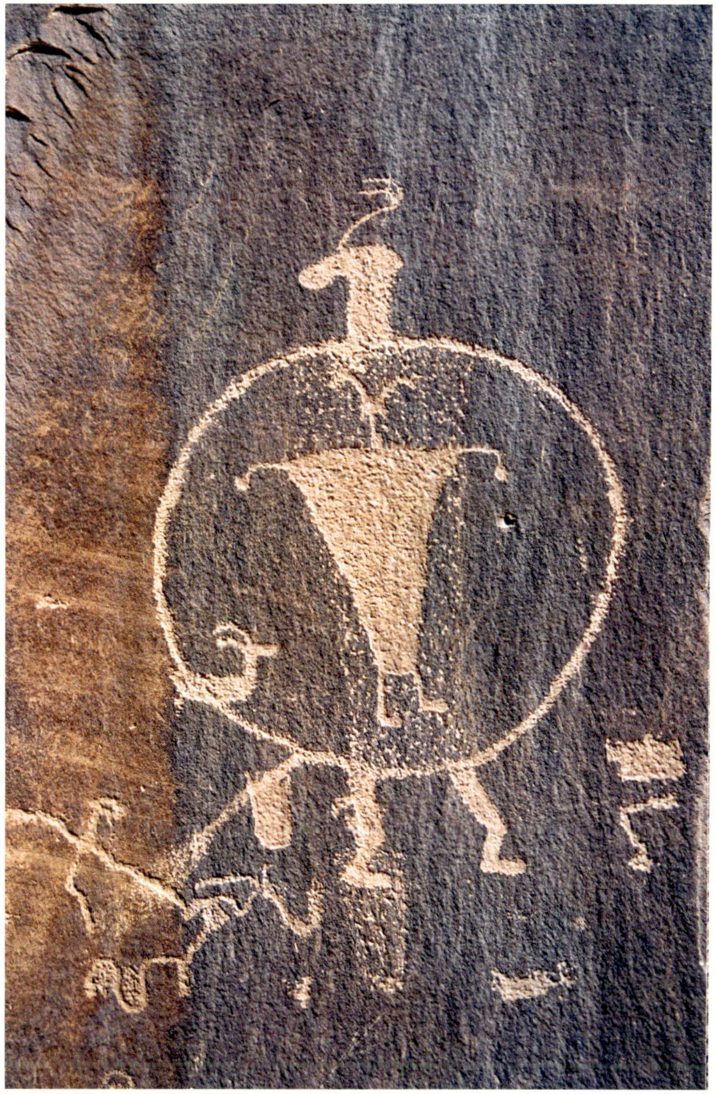

FIGURE 9.11. A Nine Mile Canyon anthropomorph that appears to be standing behind a shield that bears the image of another anthropomorph.

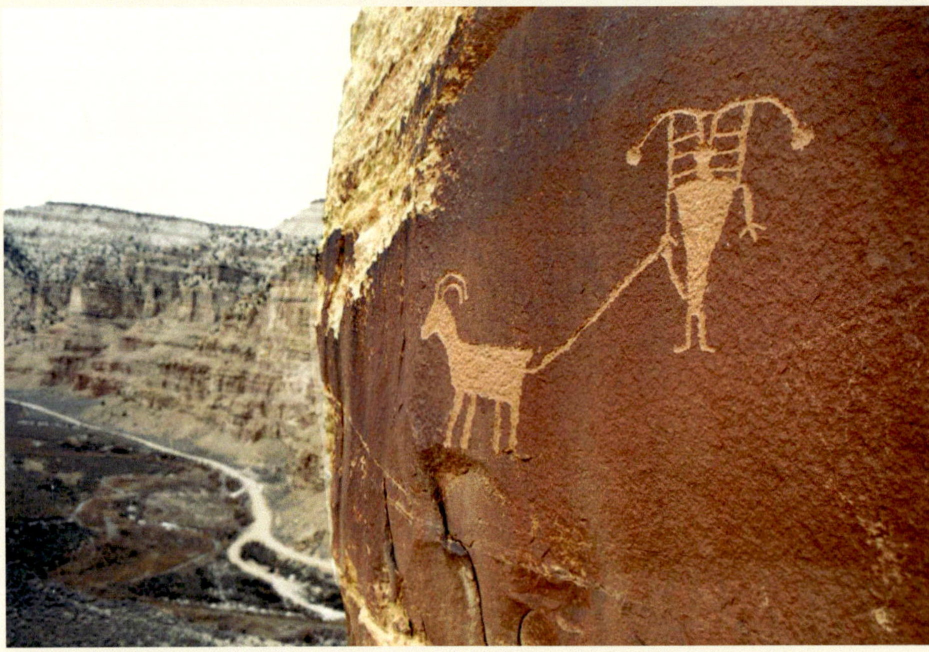

FIGURE 10.1. A Fremont-style petroglyph above Nine Mile Canyon featuring an anthropomorph with a "backpack" and a leashed bighorn sheep.

10

BIGHORN SHEEP

Bighorn sheep are commonly depicted in the rock art of this region (e.g., figures 10.1-10.7). Other animals that appear to be represented include snakes, lizards, birds of various kinds, insects, bear, deer, elk, and bison (e.g., figures 3.7, 8.3, 8.4, 8.11, 13.6, 13.9, and 14.1). Some images appear to denote other mammals but lack specific characteristics to enable more precise identification. They could represent dogs, wolves, coyotes, bobcats, mountain lions, or any number of other candidates (e.g., figures 9.8., 11.5, 11.6). A couple of panels that I know of have images of what appear to be fish, and some have images that may represent now-extinct mammals, such as mammoths or ground sloths.

Bighorn sheep seem to be the most commonly depicted animals in this area. In some places they are represented as often as all other animals combined. Perhaps they were the most abundant larger animal and were desired for food and other resources they provided. We know that they were widely hunted for thousands of years and that they were likely much more common in prehistoric times than they are now since modern weapons decimated their numbers. The introduction of domestic sheep also brought diseases and parasites that significantly reduced bighorn populations.

Some rock art panels may portray hunting scenes. Hunters with weapons sometimes appear to stalk their prey (e.g., figure 10.2). This is the easiest kind of panel to classify because they seem to represent something relatively universal: hunters and their prey. Other images of bighorns are not as straightforward. Single animals may be depicted in a panel without apparent association with other images, but on some panels they are connected by lines to other animals or to human-like images (e.g., figure 10.1). Sometimes they appear in complex arrangements with a great number of other images and designs (e.g., figure 9.8). The more complex the image and number of elements, the more difficult making an attempt at interpretation becomes.

The great number of bighorn images may signify that it played a larger role in the imagery of prehistoric artists than simply a prey animal. It seems likely to me that the bighorn figured prominently in the stories, beliefs, and teachings of

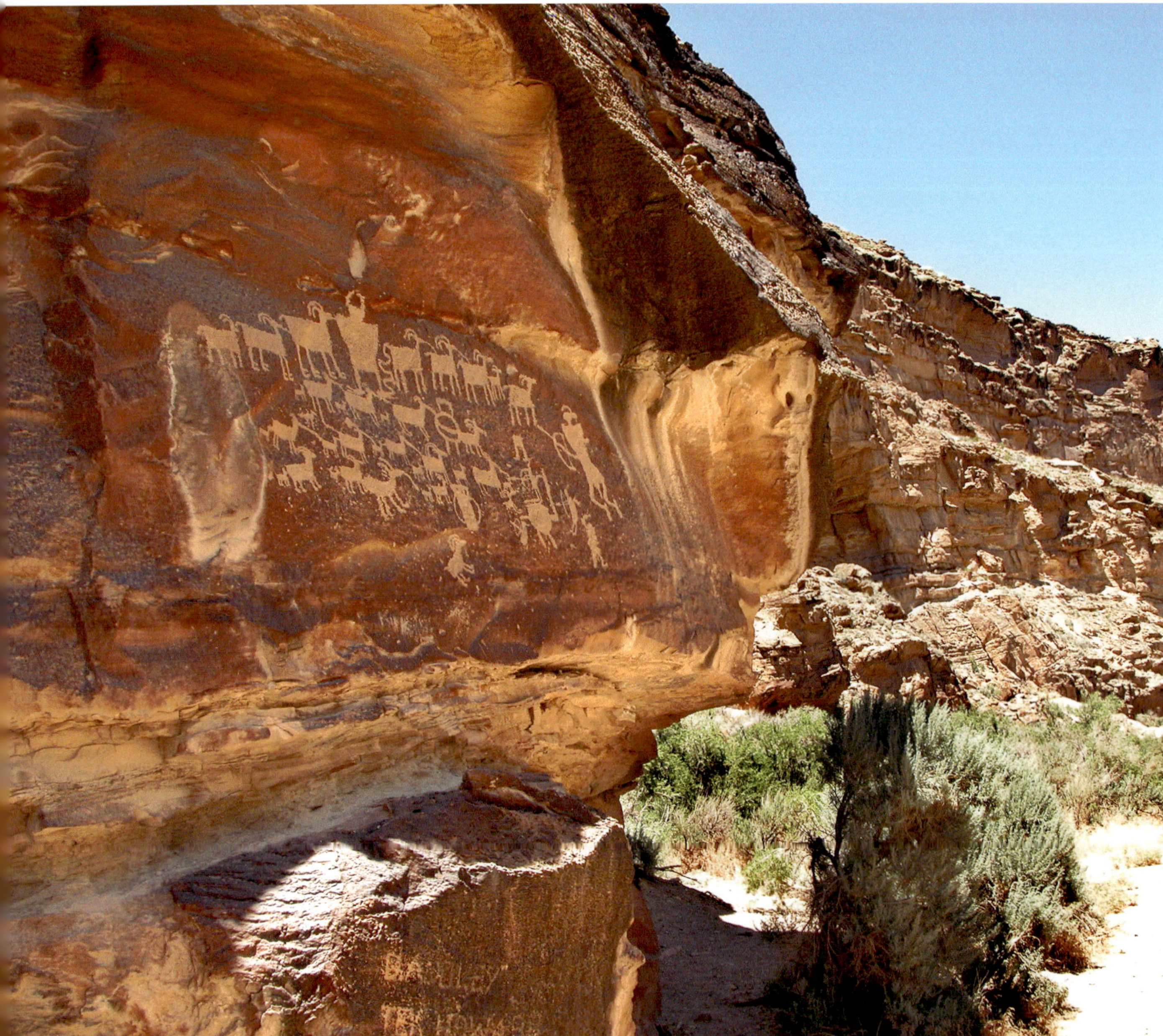

FIGURE 10.2. A Fremont-style petroglyph panel known as the Great Hunt. This image illustrates the danger this famous Nine Mile Canyon panel faced before the road was moved a distance away from it.

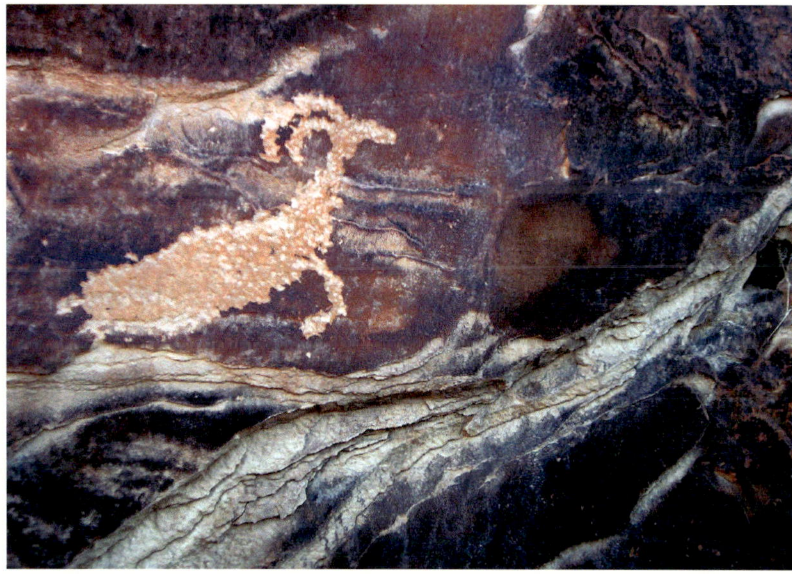

FIGURE 10.3. A Fremont-style jumping bighorn sheep in Cottonwood Canyon, a tributary of Nine Mile Canyon.

the artists of the region. While some panels appear to illustrate an actual scene or event, others may illustrate a story or legend and, in doing so, may represent things not at all related to hunting or bighorn sheep, despite the use of bighorn images.

I recently saw an image promoting an upcoming intercollegiate football game. The artwork depicted a bighorn ram and a bison charging toward each other at great speed, about to collide head-on. If someone viewing that artwork did not know that the ram represents Colorado State University and the bison (or buffalo) the University of Colorado, and that teams of students from the universities were about to engage in a sports contest, they would have no way of knowing what was being depicted. Bighorns and buffalos do not engage in sports, and they do not generally charge and butt each other, yet taken out of context, that is what the image might appear to depict. A thousand years from now, however, if the symbolism of the images is not understood to the viewer, a sheep versus bison fight could be the most reasonable interpretation.

Clearly, context—the cultural context of an image's creation—is paramount in interpreting and understanding art. As years and cultural change separate the creators from the viewers, the context is lost—irretrievably. We will never know what the bighorn meant to a Fremont artist. We can, however, infer a few things. First, we can be assured that people are not always literal interpreters of the world around them. By that I mean that human-created art is always rich with symbolism. It depicts things real and imaginary in contexts based in story, myth, legend, belief, historical knowledge, fantasy, hallucination, trance, comedy, sexuality, and more. All of those things that make us human, all of those thoughts and associations that inhabit our minds, can and do wind up in our creative expression. And that is what we see in the rock art captured in the photographs of Layne Miller. Second, we know that people are sometimes literal interpreters of the world around them. If you see something in a rock art panel that looks like something you recognize, who is to say that you are wrong? Remember, however, that there is no way to know, so *do* interpret the rock art from your own personal and cultural background, but know that the interpretation is yours and yours alone, and carries absolutely no meaning for anyone else.

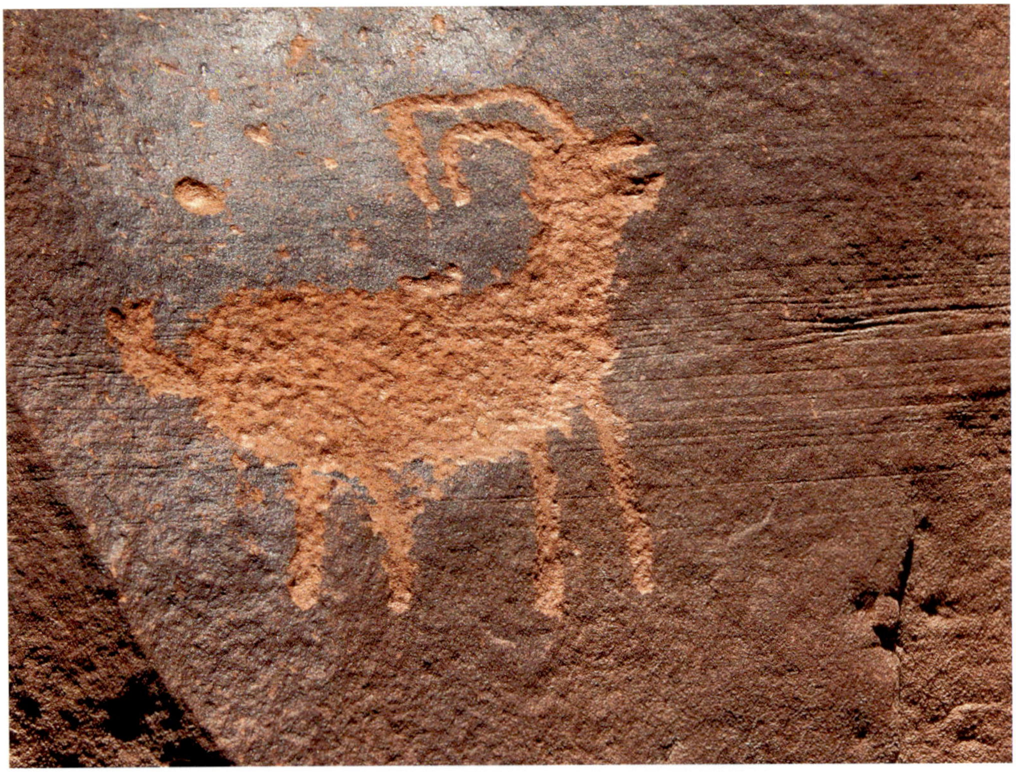

FIGURE 10.4. A Fremont-style bighorn sheep with an open mouth on a wall in Nine Mile Canyon.

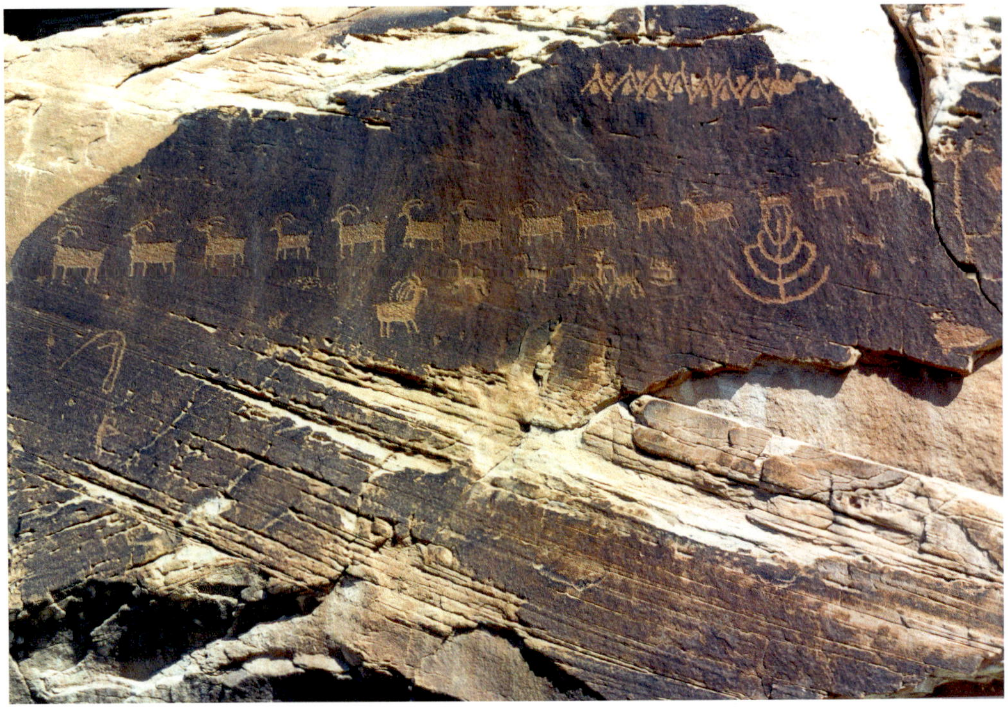

FIGURE 10.5. A row of Fremont-style bighorn sheep making their way along a wall in Nine Mile Canyon.

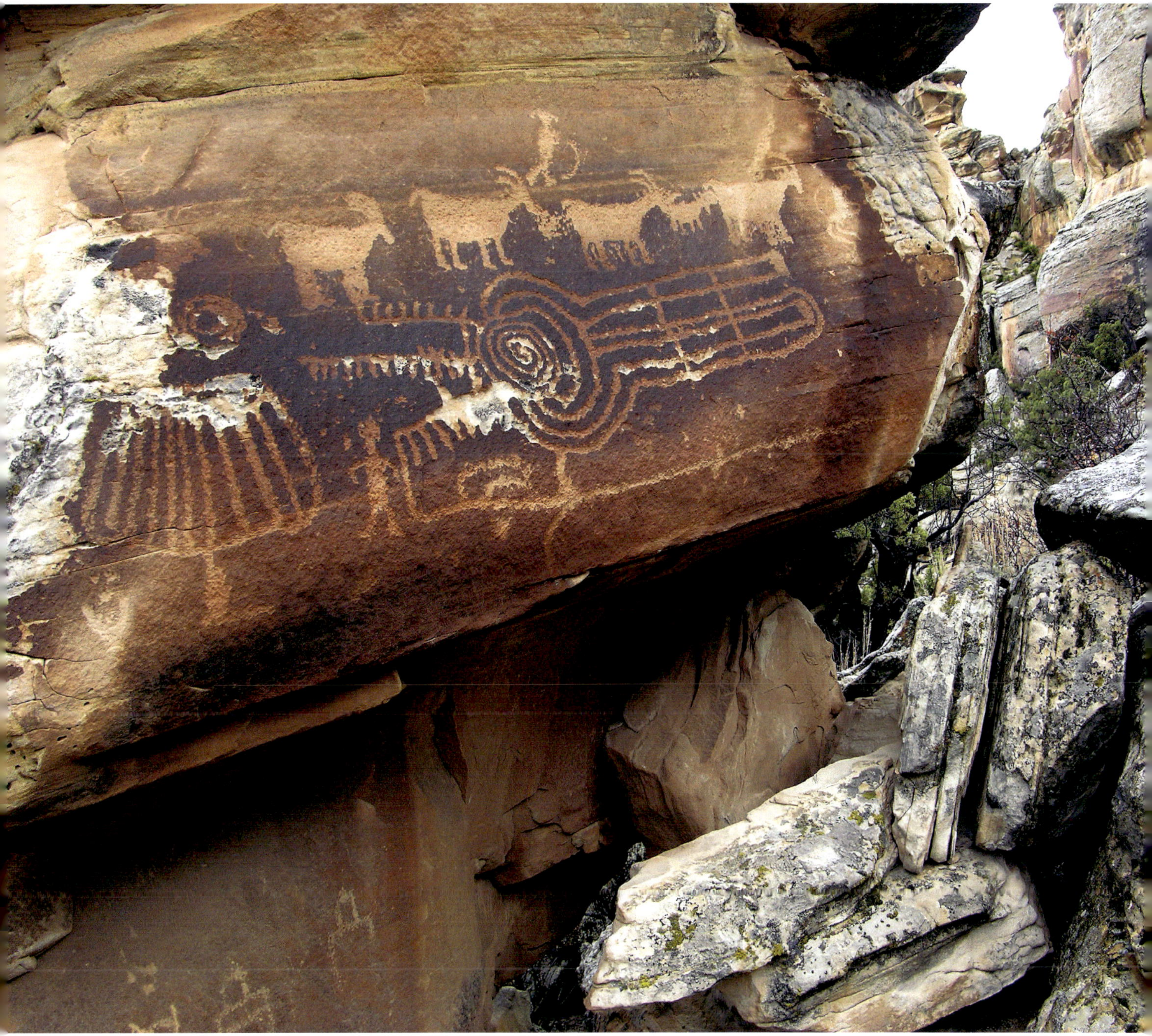

FIGURE 10.6. A multicomponent panel in Ashley Creek Canyon, northeastern Utah, with Fremont-style bighorn sheep and other designs.

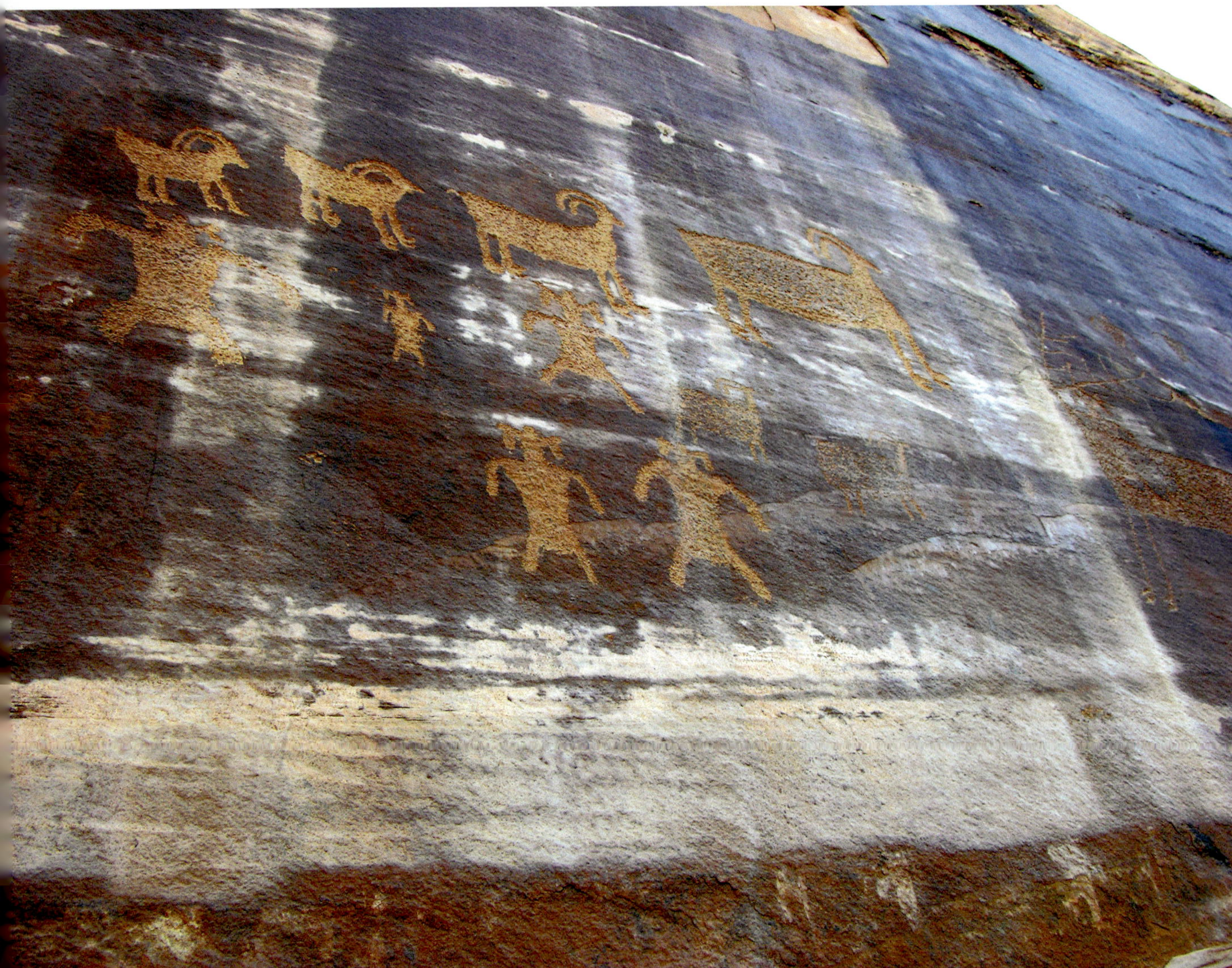

FIGURE 10.7. A Fremont-style petroglyph panel in Ashley Creek Canyon, northeastern Utah. The anthropomorphs have hair whorls similar to those worn by some Pueblo women.

11

THE MAN WITH A HEART OF STONE

I've been floating all week in Desolation
Between the Tavaputs and the reservation.
I talked to the man with a heart of stone
Standing on the wall of time.

I've been hot, I've been cold, I've had every sensation.
To me it's more than recreation.
I've been to a place where time stands still;
It brings me peace of mind.

—*Kevin Jones, "Ancient Places"*[1]

There's a place in Desolation Canyon where a figure stands out, perhaps only to me, on a sandstone monolith covered with petroglyphs: an anthropomorph whose head is haloed by an array of dots, whose torso is pecked solid save for one spot in the center of his chest and two where his testicles would be (figure 11.1). A nearby figure in the same style depicts a female whose breasts are likewise highlighted. Each time I see this couple, my surroundings rush away as though I am hurtling through time, entering hyperspace, and I am immersed in, and part of, this wall of time.

The Man with a Heart of Stone has adorned the canyon for at least 500 years, perhaps much longer. How many others has he beckoned? How many others have relinquished the present to vault lightspeeding through time-space as they stood transfixed in the very spot where so long ago an outstanding artist altered this stone in a way that speaks across centuries? Across cultures, across languages and beliefs, he speaks in a complete and universal way, the language of humanity. And he speaks directly to me, seemingly to me alone.

He shows as much as speaks. He shows me a long view of time. He has stood in that same place since before machines and moon landings and missiles, and will be there when an unimaginably different future flows by—and then some. My conversation with him centers me in time.

Desolation Canyon is a strip of wilderness, some of it even designated as such. We may think of wilderness as untouched by humans, but that is a very ethnocentric view. Over millennia, Native people have been through and over every square inch of this land. They have been intimate with it. The traces the ancient ones left behind may be subtle, but they are there, and they speak to us.

The Man with a Heart of Stone and his companion were incised by a master stone carver of what we call today the Fremont culture, which flourished all across this region for nearly a thousand years. From what is now Cedar City to Vernal, from Green River to Brigham City and beyond, the Fremont people were farmers, builders, dreamers, and thinkers, and they mastered the art of living in this harsh land, occupying and thriving and decorating the canyon walls with their mysterious, evocative images.

Climate change rocked the foundations of the Fremont culture. To the south, the related Anasazi/Ancestral Puebloan culture was torn asunder, as were farming communities and emerging civilizations all across North America. Economies collapsed and social organization fell into chaos. As their farms failed and cultural institutions crumbled, the Fremont people disappeared from the archaeological record in all but the deep clefts in the Colorado Plateau, in the northeastern part of the Fremont world, including Desolation Canyon. The last refuge of the once-vast Fremont empire appears to have been in the vicinity of the Man with a Heart of Stone.

Modern Europeans have spent a mere few hundred years or so in the American West, but they have left their marks nearly everywhere, and the gouges are not subtle. Roads, dams, bridges, wells, mines, trails, and structures mark the so-called progress of the modern world, and they are nearly everywhere. Each time a new something is imposed on the land, it erases the traces of those who came before. It muffles the softly spoken universal tongue that can so powerfully penetrate the ages. It crushes the walls of time and topples them.

Desolation Canyon, a sanctuary for the ancient ones, is under assault. Oil and natural gas, tar sands, oil shale, and who knows what lucre will lure another generation of boom-and-bust profiteers to the shores of the Green River, ready to pierce and tear at the earth, to rip the heart from the man of stone.

Why is the last refuge of the Fremont important? Where else can we learn about how climate change affected a thriving culture? Where else do traces of the past beckon us to investigate, examine, see? Where else can we stand at the wall of time and learn from the Man with a Heart of Stone? Where else does time stand still?

Note

1. From the song "Ancient Places," by Kevin Jones, recorded by The Lab Dogs on the album *Ancient Places* (© 2010, Howlin' Good Records, Salt Lake City).

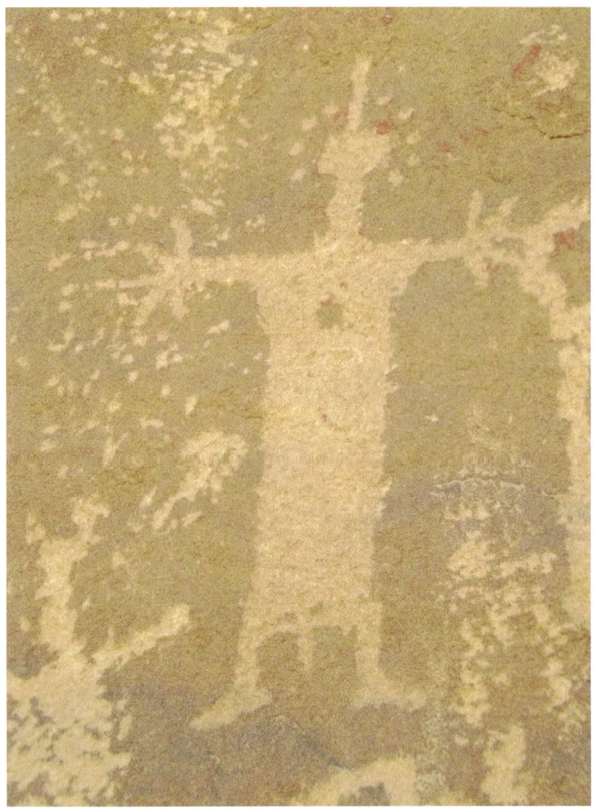

FIGURE 11.1. The Man with a Heart of Stone in Desolation Canyon. Photograph by Kevin Jones.

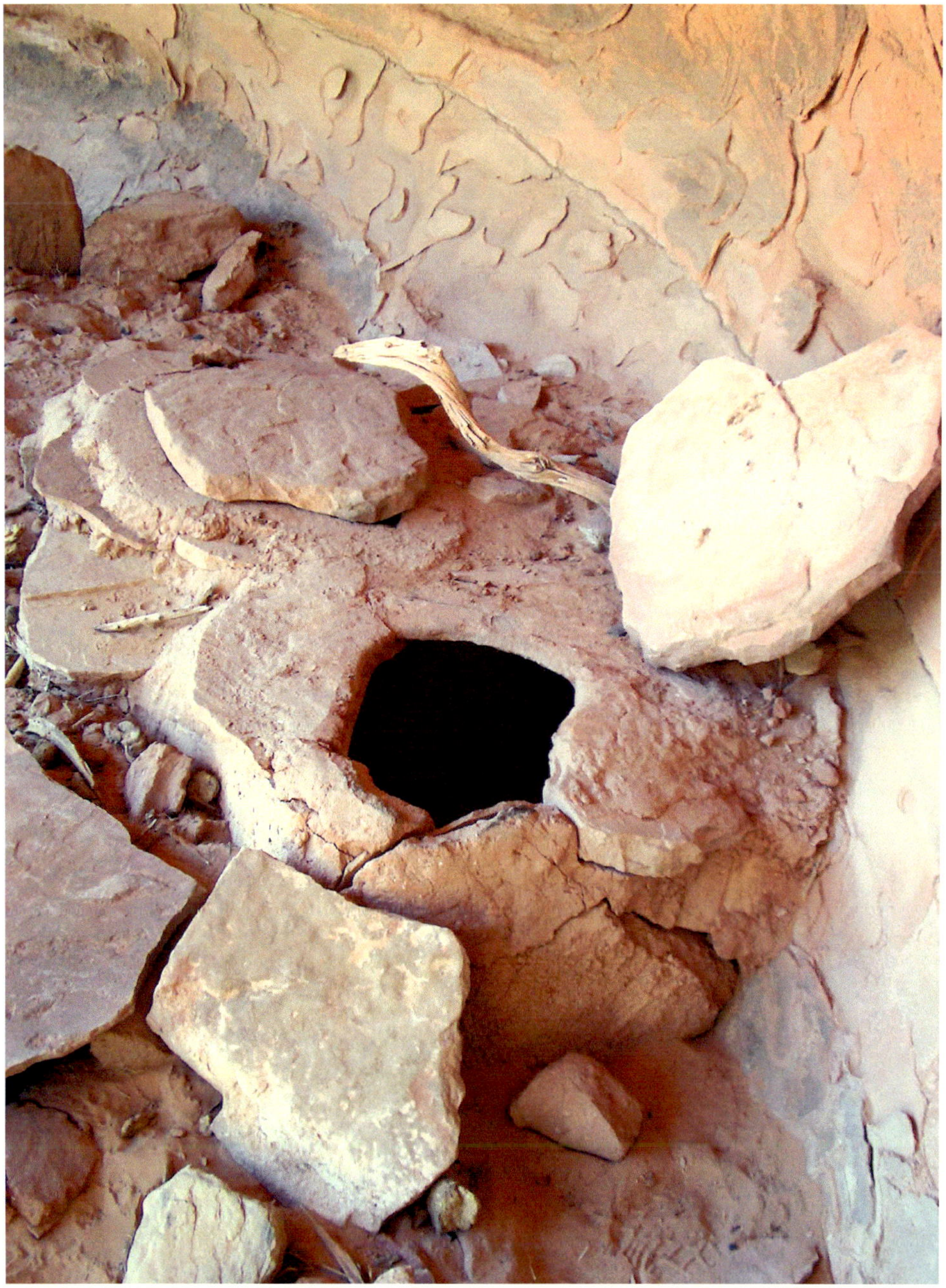

FIGURE 11.2. A storage granary in the Robbers Roost area, which was a popular hideout along the so-called Outlaw Trail.

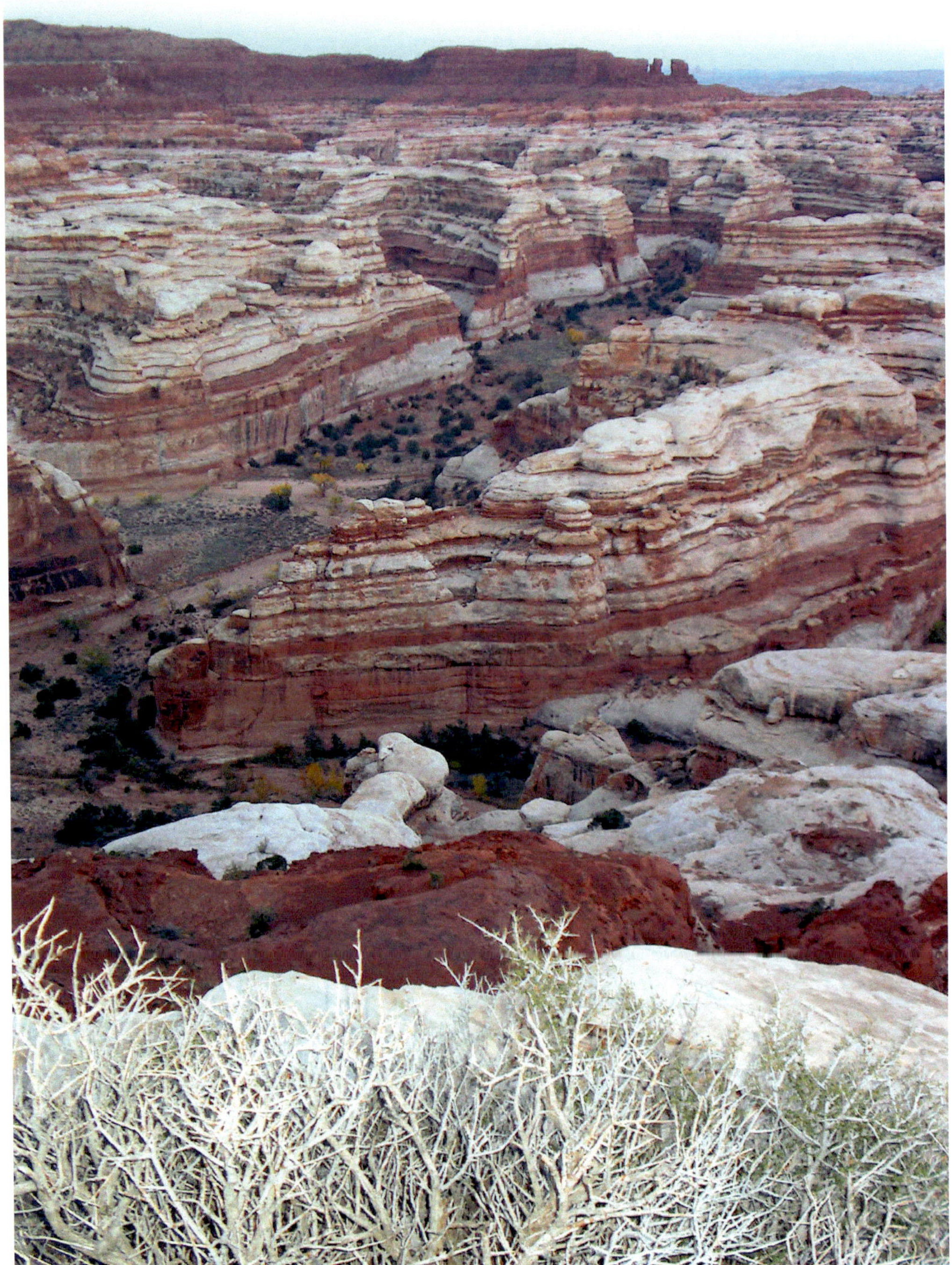

FIGURE 11.3. A view into the Maze District of Canyonlands National Park illustrating the area's apt name.

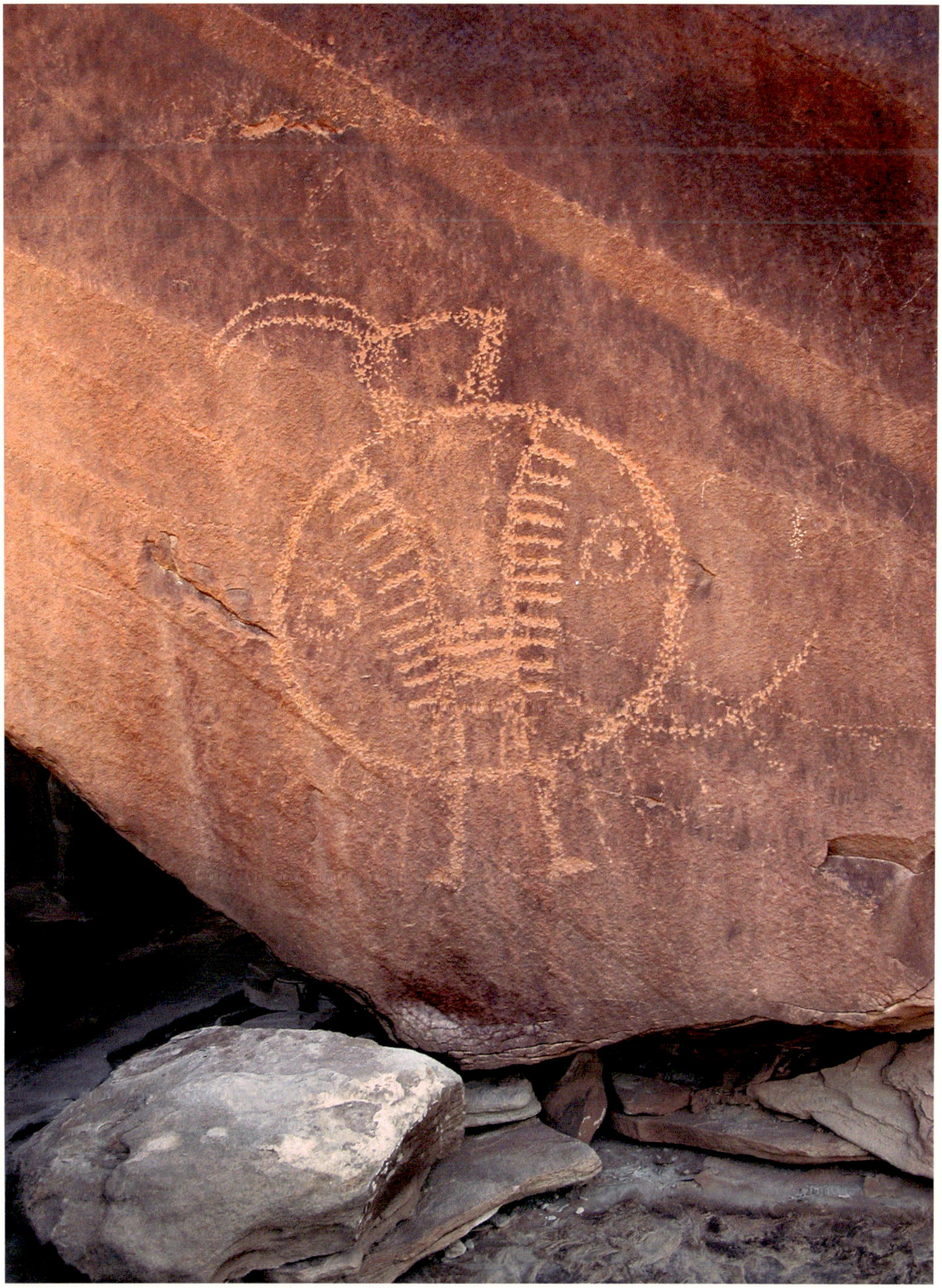

FIGURE 11.4. A large petroglyph panel above Range Creek. It is probably affiliated with the Fremont culture.

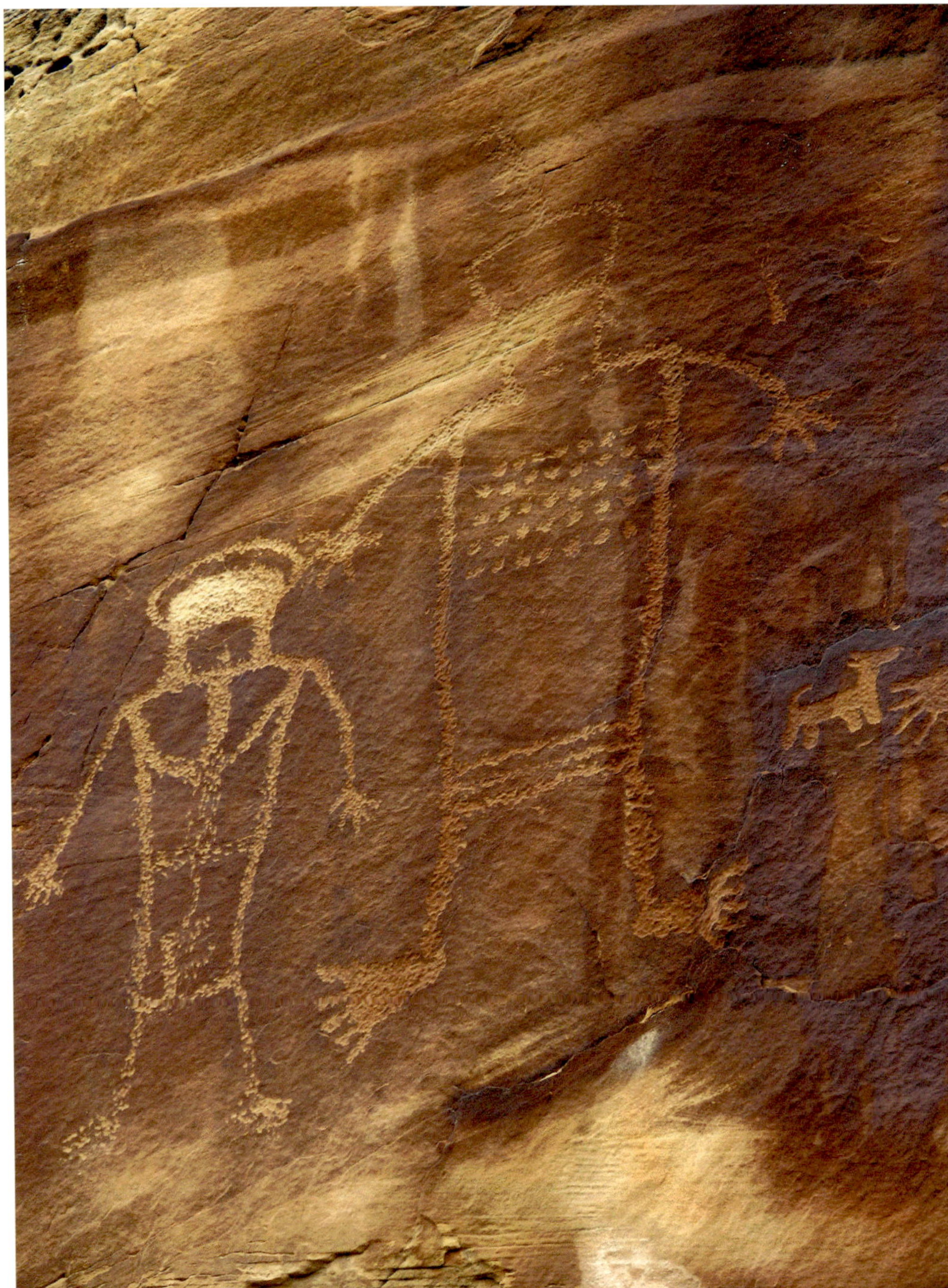

FIGURE 11.5. These Fremont-style figures are found in Ashley Creek Canyon near Vernal, Utah. Note the dog-like figure in the center right of the photograph.

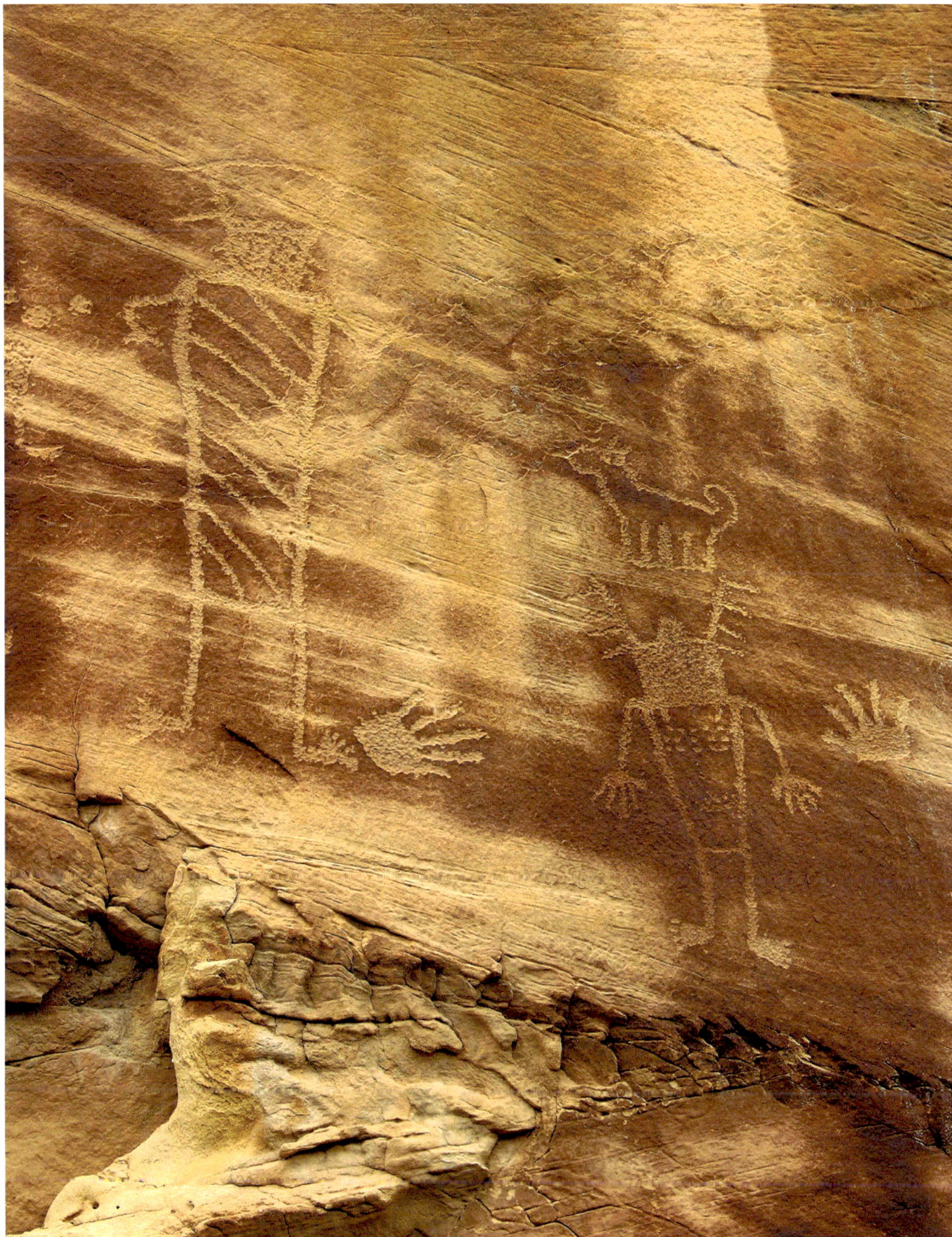

FIGURE 11.6. Fremont-style petroglyphs in Ashley Creek Canyon near Vernal, Utah. Note the dog-like figure on the right.

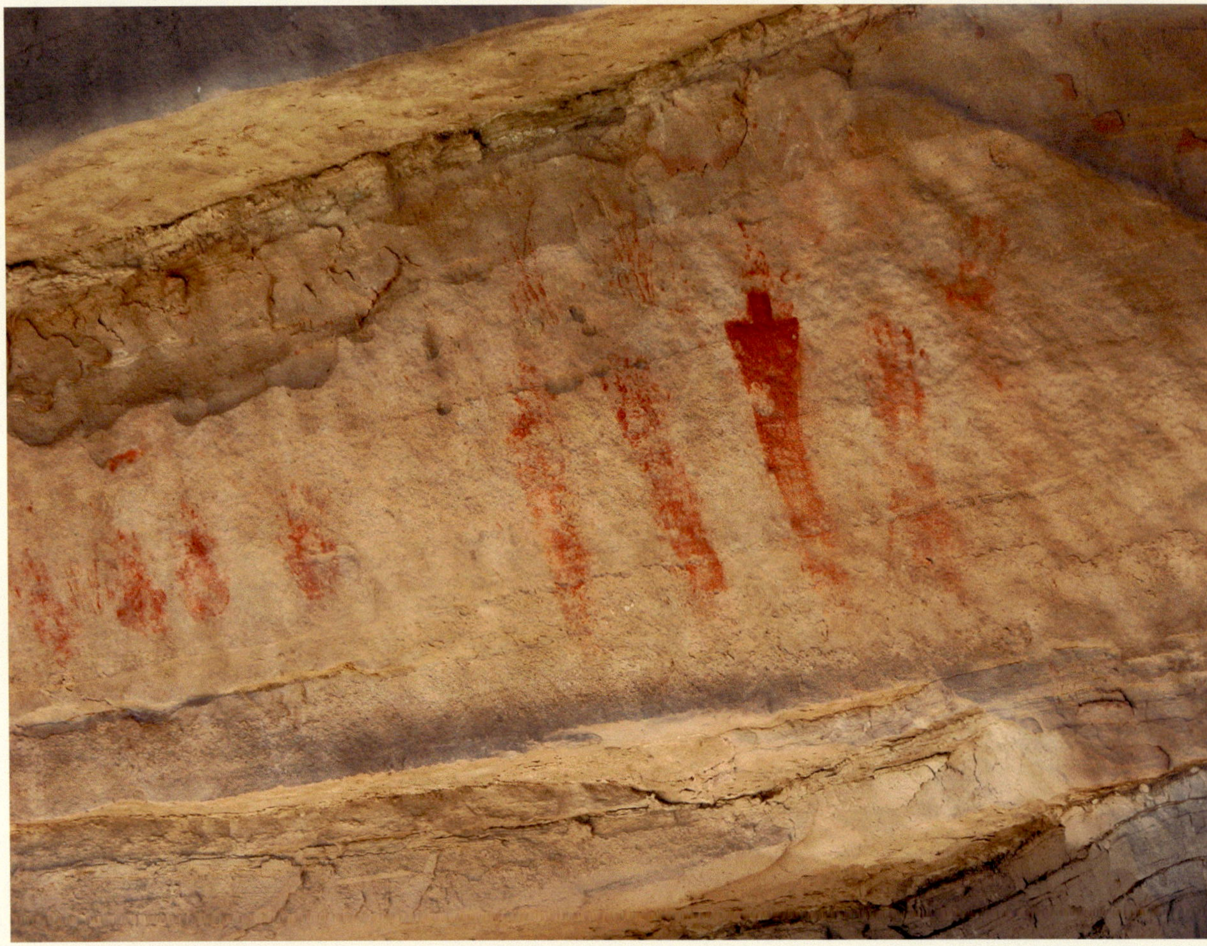

FIGURE 11.7. Fremont-style figures in Ferron Box painted on the canyon wall.

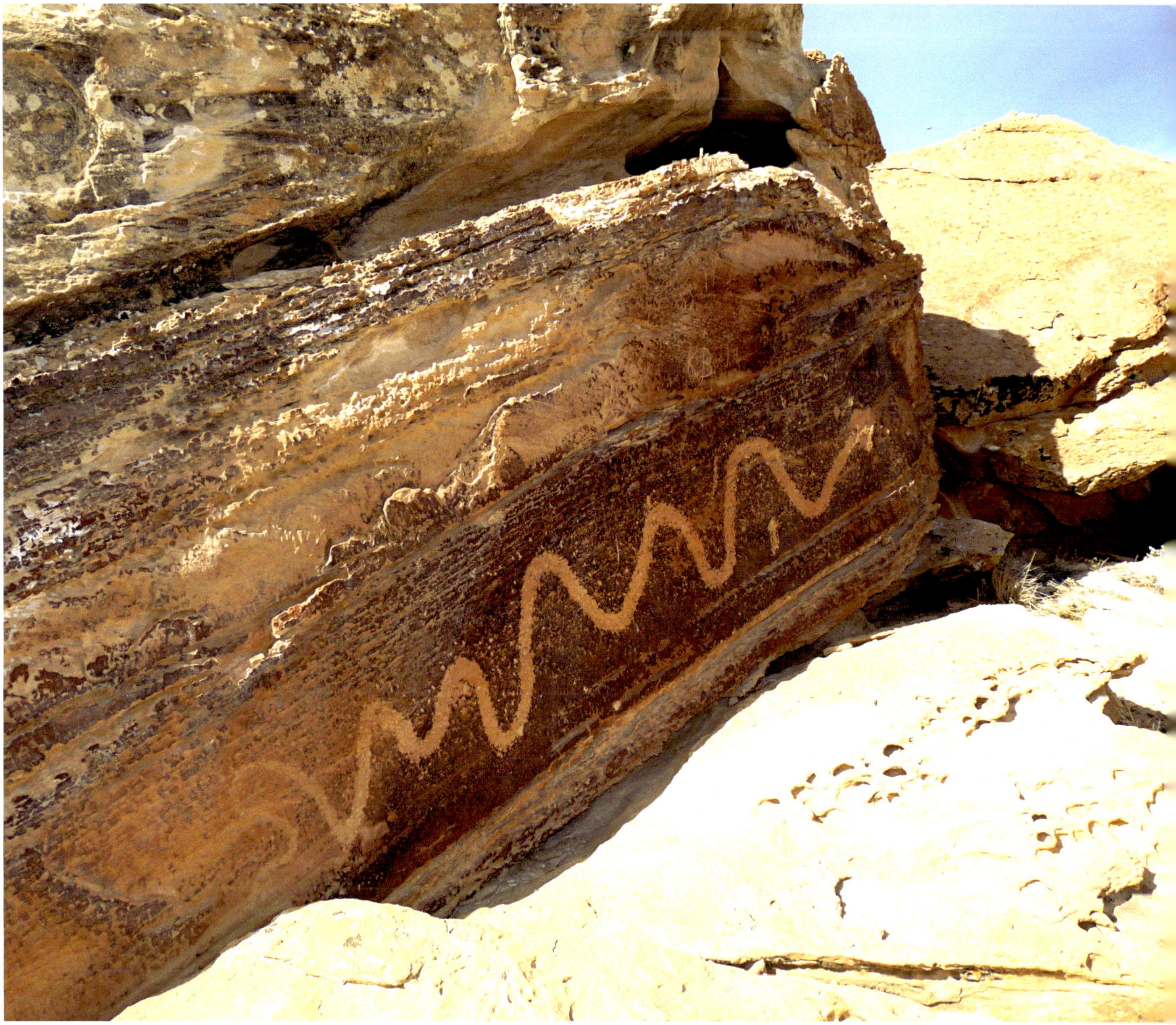

FIGURE 11.8. A large snake-like petroglyph thought to be of Fremont origin in Dry Wash, near the Moore Cutoff Road in the San Rafael Swell.

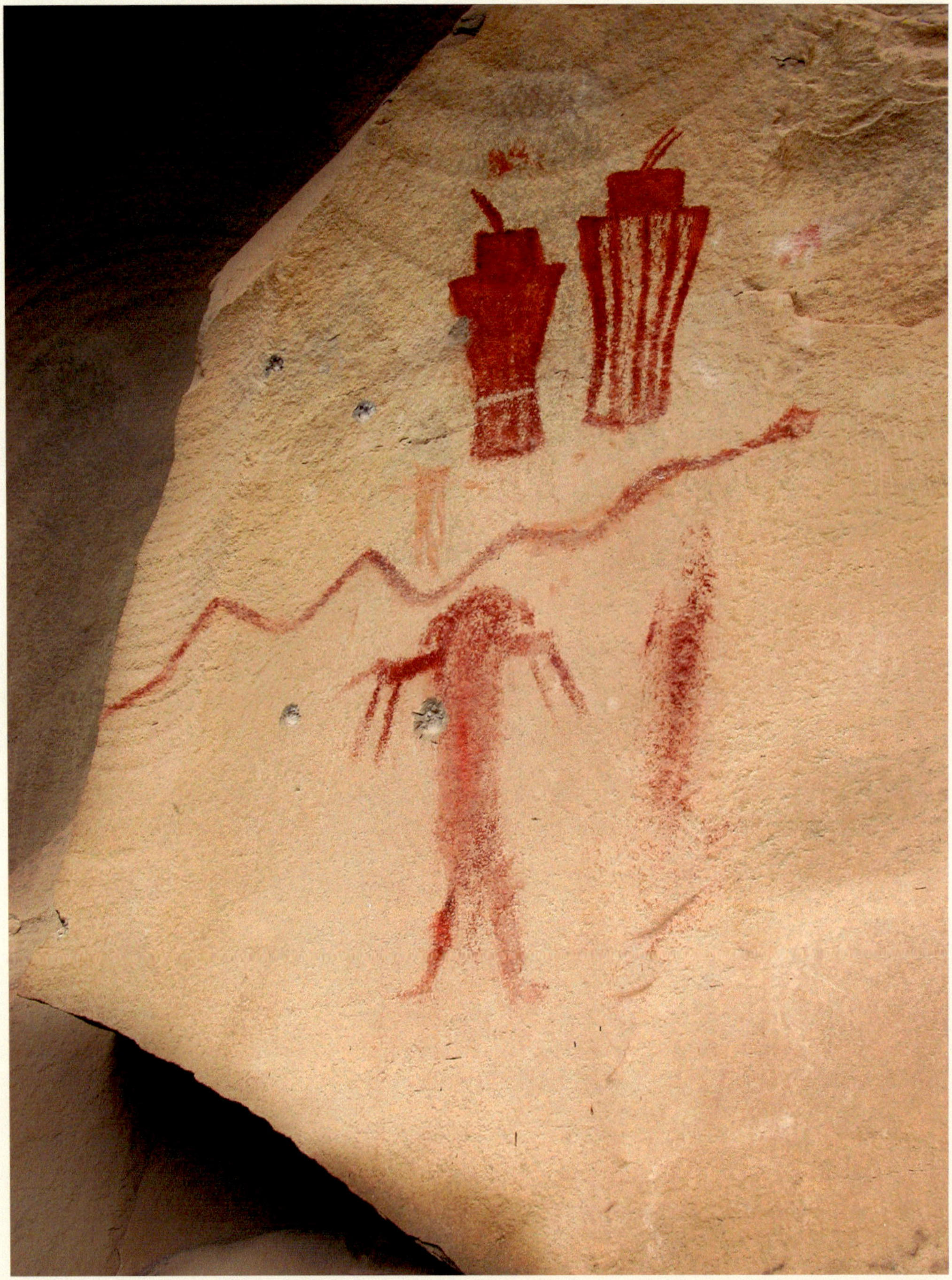

FIGURE 11.9. A Fremont-style panel in Ferron Canyon, eastern Utah, with pictographs of anthropomorphs and a snake.

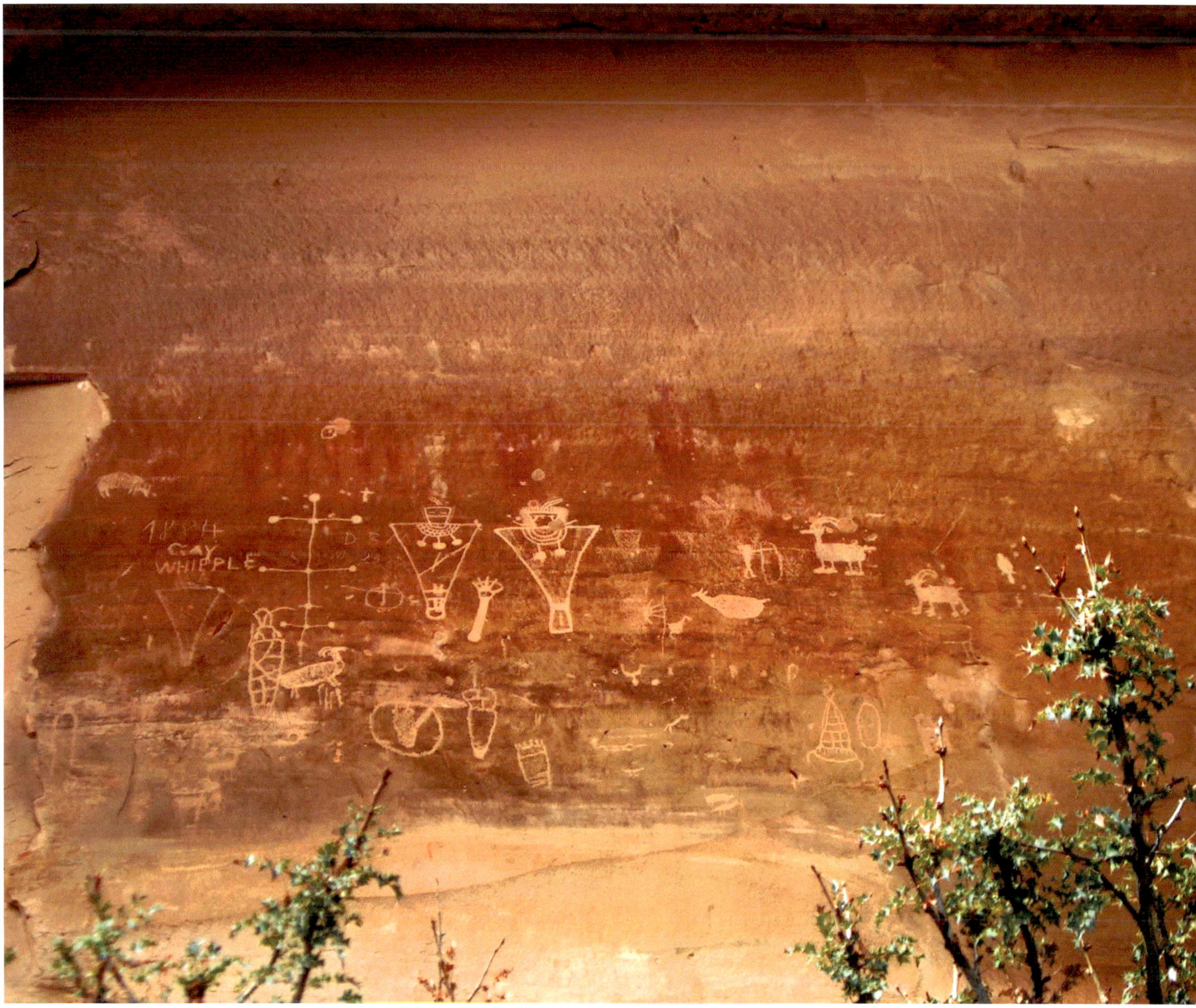

FIGURE 11.10. Fremont-style petroglyphs created on top of older Barrier Canyon–style pictographs in Sego Canyon, eastern Utah.

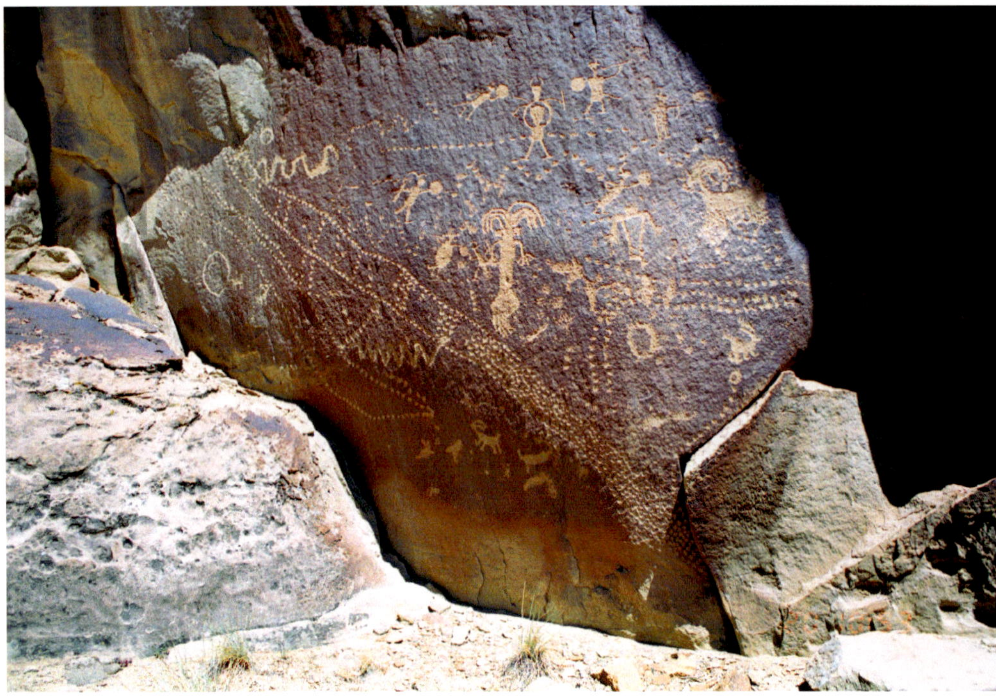

FIGURE 11.11. A complex petroglyph panel on Warrior Ridge in Nine Mile Canyon. It is one of several depicting warfare of some type. Bows and arrows and possibly atlatls are shown.

12

HUNTER-GATHERER ART

People have lived in this area—between the Great Basin and the Front Range of the Rockies—for over 10,000 years, and we know that they were creating incredible works of art the entire time. As humans, we seem compelled to share the stories and visions we have with others, to create something unique, to enhance our world with new human things, and to leave a mark—to indicate to the world and others that we were here.

For most of the time since people first arrived here, we were hunter-gatherers. We sustained ourselves and our families with food and other resources we could glean from the lands and waters around us. For most of human history, since the time our ancestors first become distinct in the fossil record from our now-extinct forebears, we have hunted and gathered. And we were very good at it, eventually occupying a wider array of habitats than any other mammalian species.

Feeding, clothing, sheltering, and protecting yourself and your family is a full-time job, yet hunter-gatherers find time to enhance their lives with stories and art. We add paint or carved lines to tools to enrich and enhance them, perhaps to add identity to them. We make necklaces, earrings, hats, and clothing that go beyond mere utility. Despite living at the edge, we have always enhanced our lives in ways that make us uniquely human, not merely mammalian.

And some of the ways we decorate our lives are truly astonishing. Remember that no hunter-gatherer ever attended art class. No hunter-gatherer ever went to the art supply store for paints and brushes. No hunter-gatherer ever had the luxury to be a full-time artist, which makes the quality and richness of the artwork they created even more incredible.

While we may be tempted to think that modern artists possess some degree of sophistication that foragers lacked, that sophistication is likely limited to having a greater array of tools and media to choose from in expressing ourselves. The creative minds of our forebears were exactly the same as ours today. And artists have always tapped into the same sorts of cerebral inspiration in their work.

Ancient artists, like modern ones, had a fascination with designs: spirals, mazes, complex abstract patterns, repeating elements, combinations of techniques, ab-

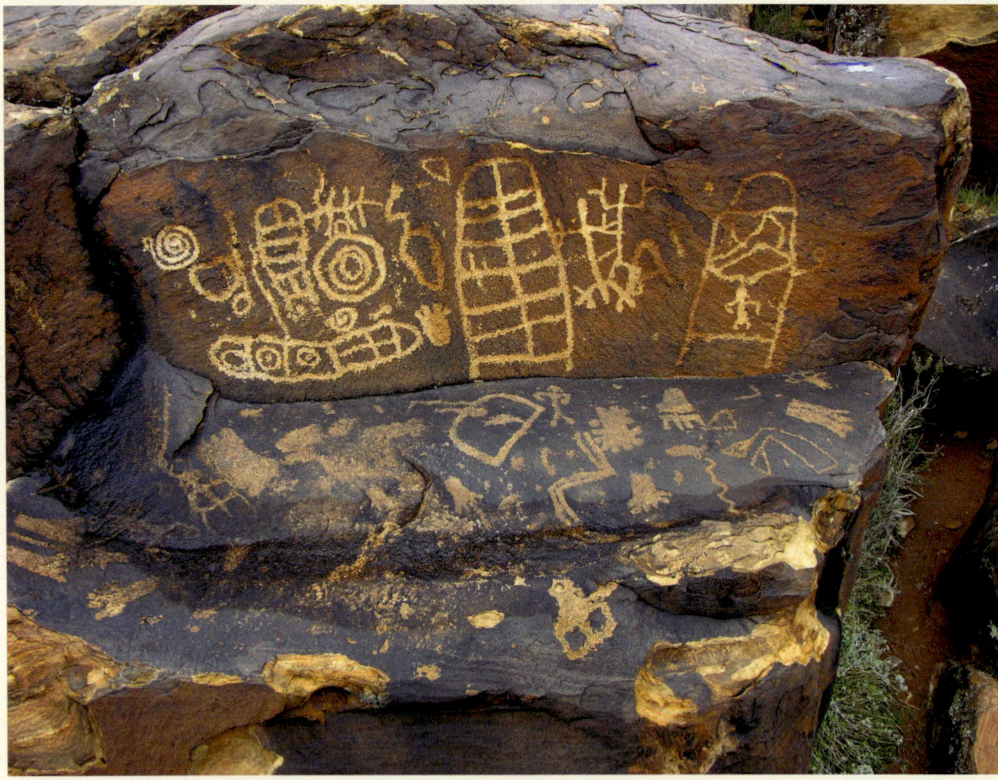

FIGURE 12.1. A petroglyph panel above the Santa Clara River in southeastern Utah, an area used by both Ancestral Puebloans and Southern Paiutes.

stracts mixed with references to the real world. This universality shows that ancient art is not merely a simple depiction of an event or an illustration of a story; it is an exploration of the human mind, its senses, its nervous system. It is art true and pure, and projects the mind of a person, a messenger from antiquity, straight to you. To me. A connection profound and meaningful if we take a moment to let it in.

Some think of the ancient people as being less intelligent and creative than modern ones. They think of our hunting and gathering ancestors as primitive, savage, barbaric. But these people who so quickly dismiss the work of our ancestors are the primitives, the deplorables who will use ancient art for target practice. Those people do exist and—as with any who denigrate those of other cultures, races, and religions—make up the ranks of the sad, angry, and hate-filled segments of society that we must continually work to educate, work around, ignore, and at times, leave behind. The richness of humanity is our vehicle to the future, our salvation, and we are buoyed along by the creative artists of long ago.

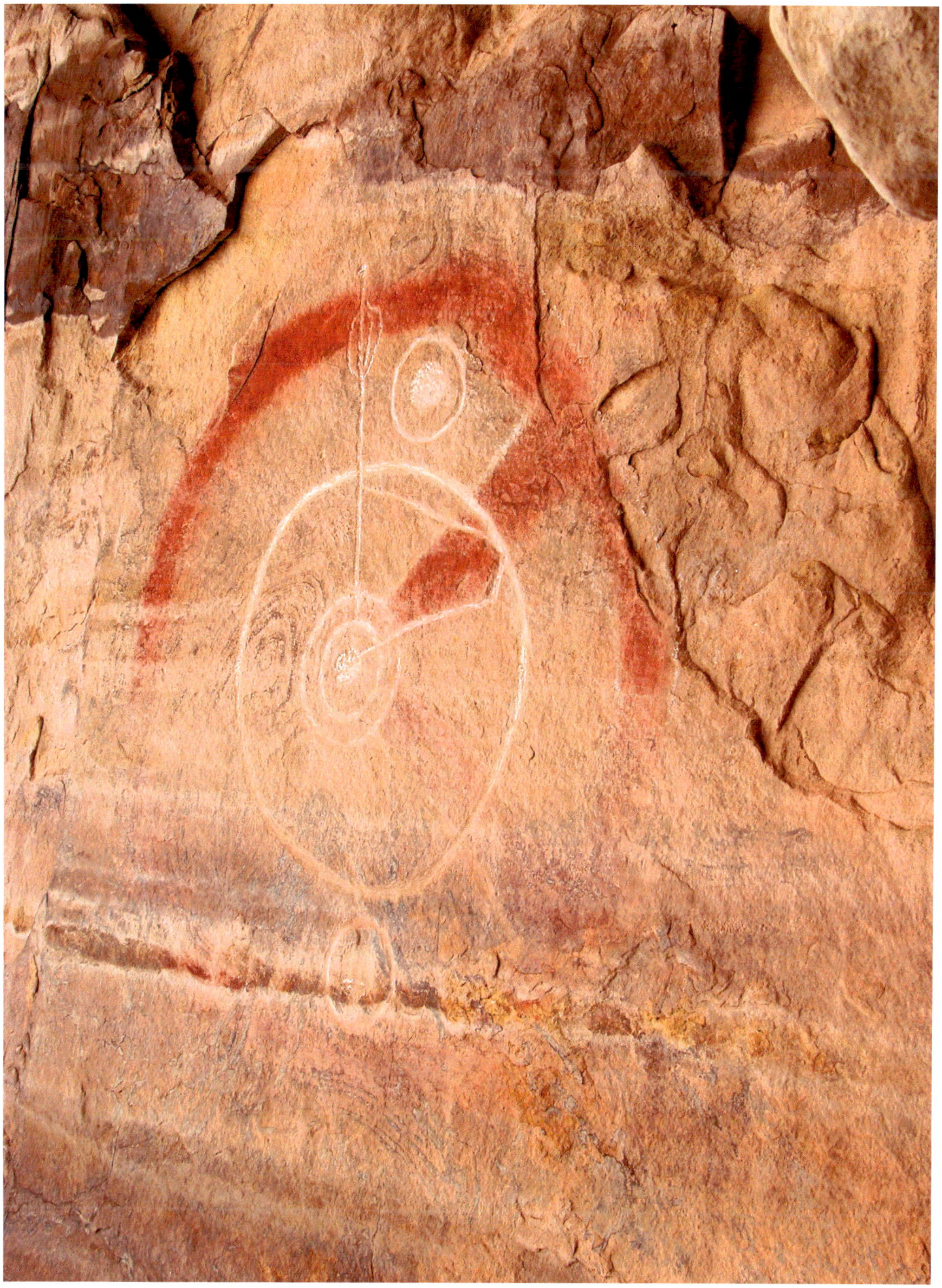

FIGURE 12.2. A Ute-style shield and arrow on a wall in Dry Fork Canyon in the Uinta Basin.

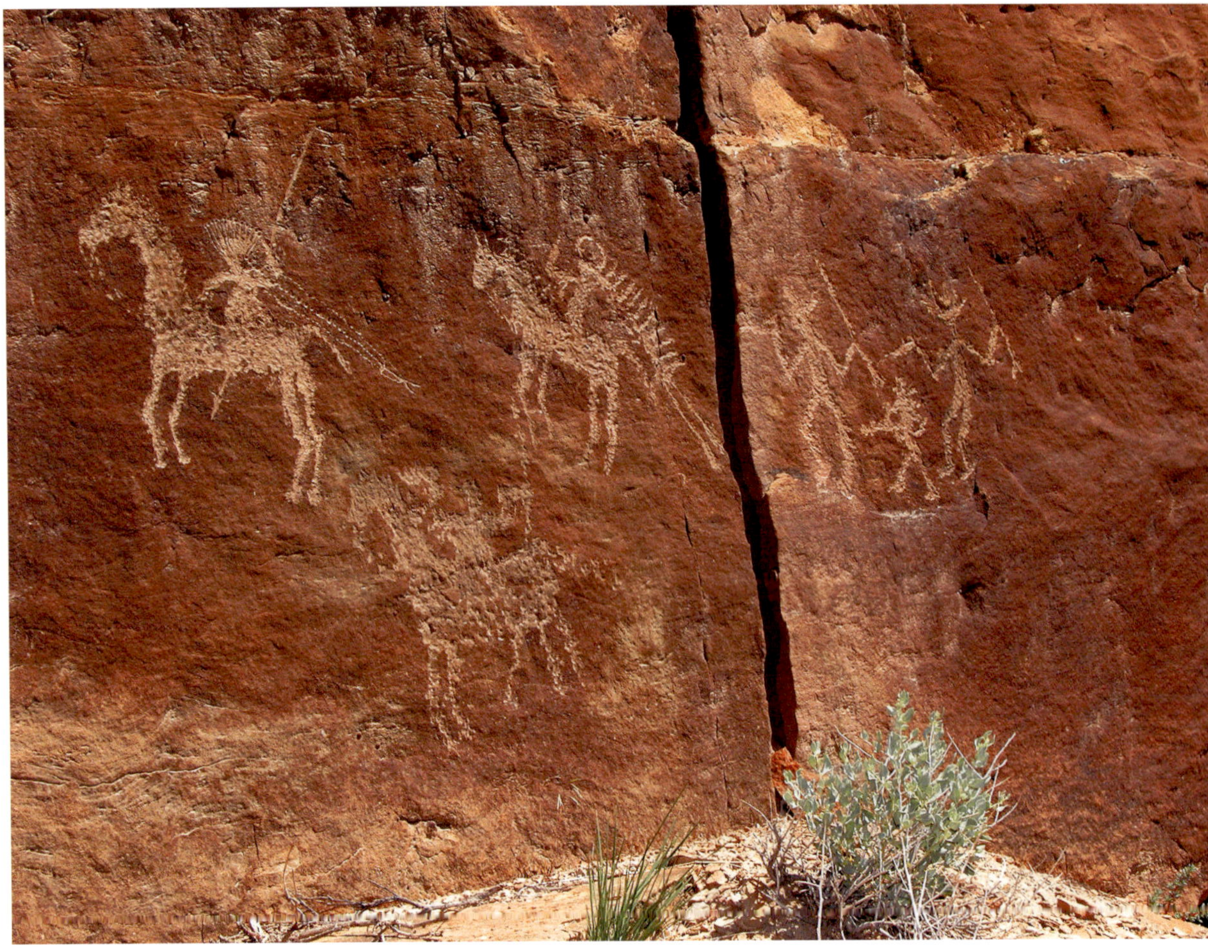

FIGURE 12.3. A panel in Nine Mile Canyon depicting mounted Ute warriors with headdresses and lances on the left, and Anglo cowboys wearing hats and carrying guns on the right.

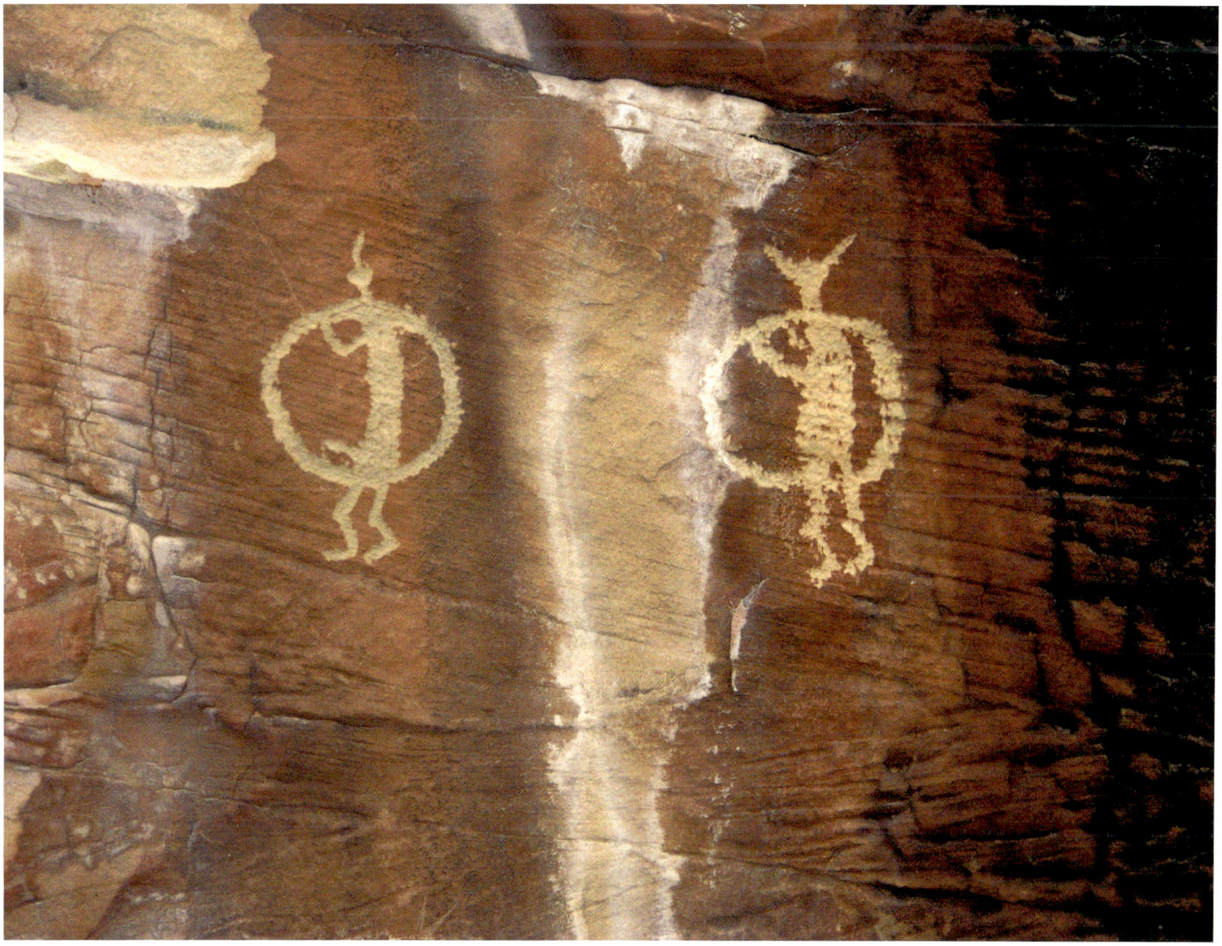

FIGURE 12.4. Hoop or shield figures in the Ashley Creek area. They could be affiliated with the Ute tribe based on their fresh appearance and unusual style.

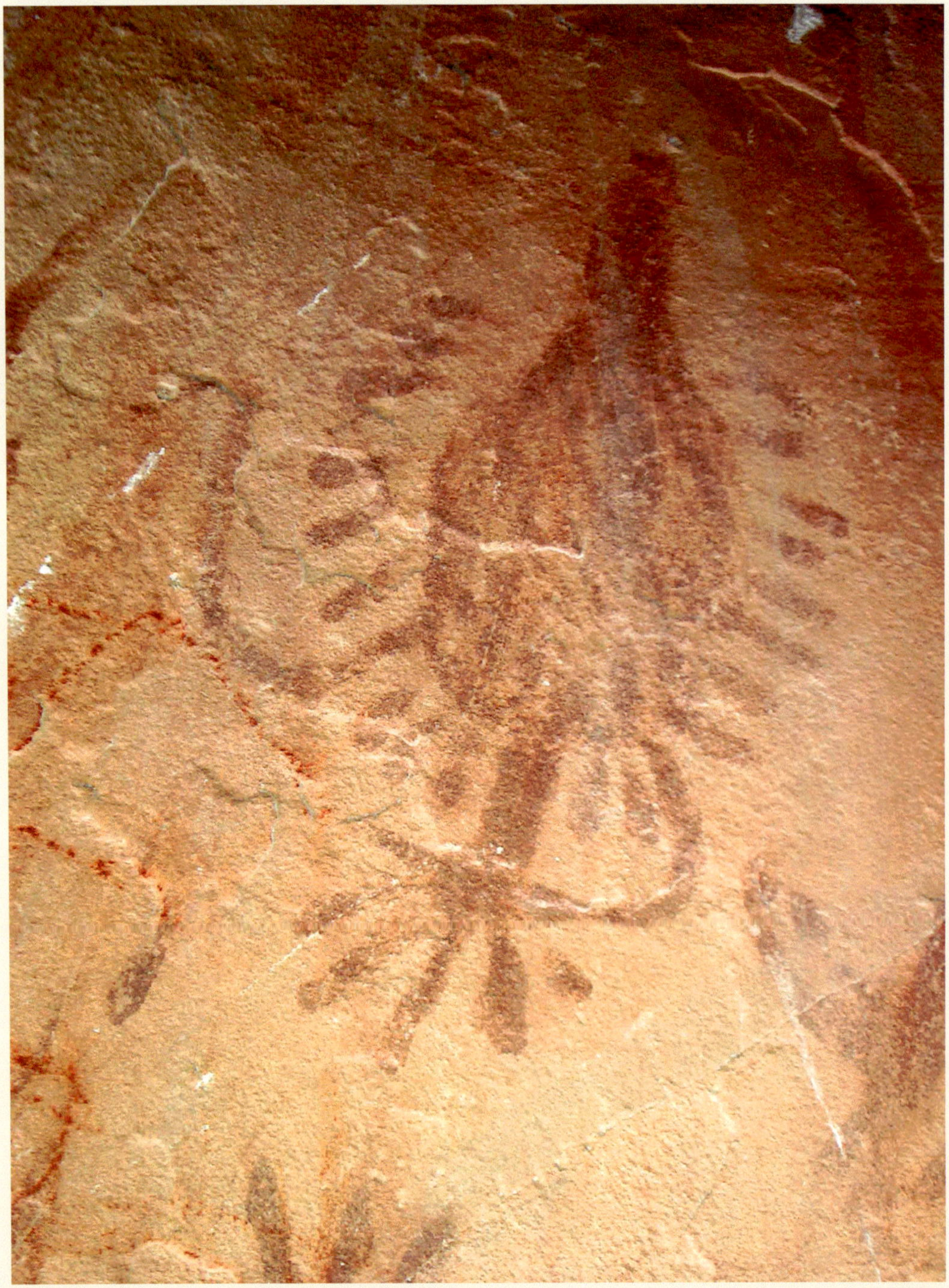

FIGURE 12.5. A rock art panel in a shallow wash near Moab with very unusual pictographs that might be of Ute origin.

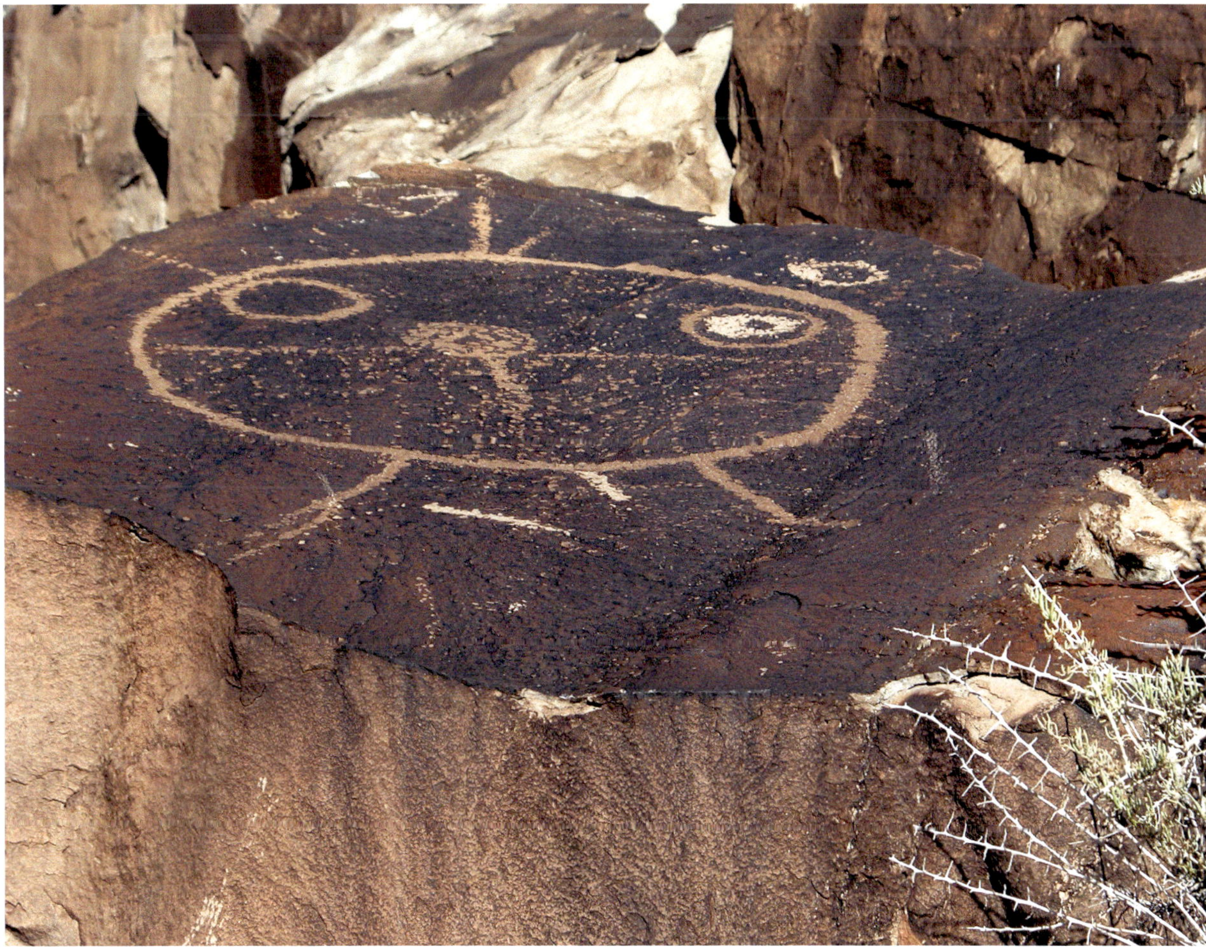

FIGURE 12.6. A large shield figure in the Grassy Trail Creek area in eastern Utah. The cultural affiliation is unknown.

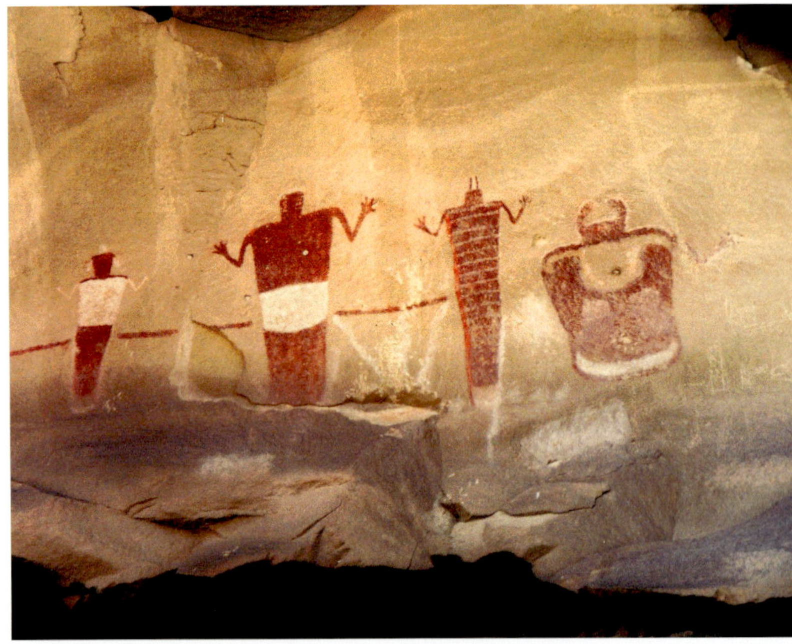

FIGURE 12.7. Pictographs in the Nine Mile Canyon area. This panel is remarkable for its preservation and artistry. It appears to some to be a transitional style between the Barrier Canyon and Fremont-styles.

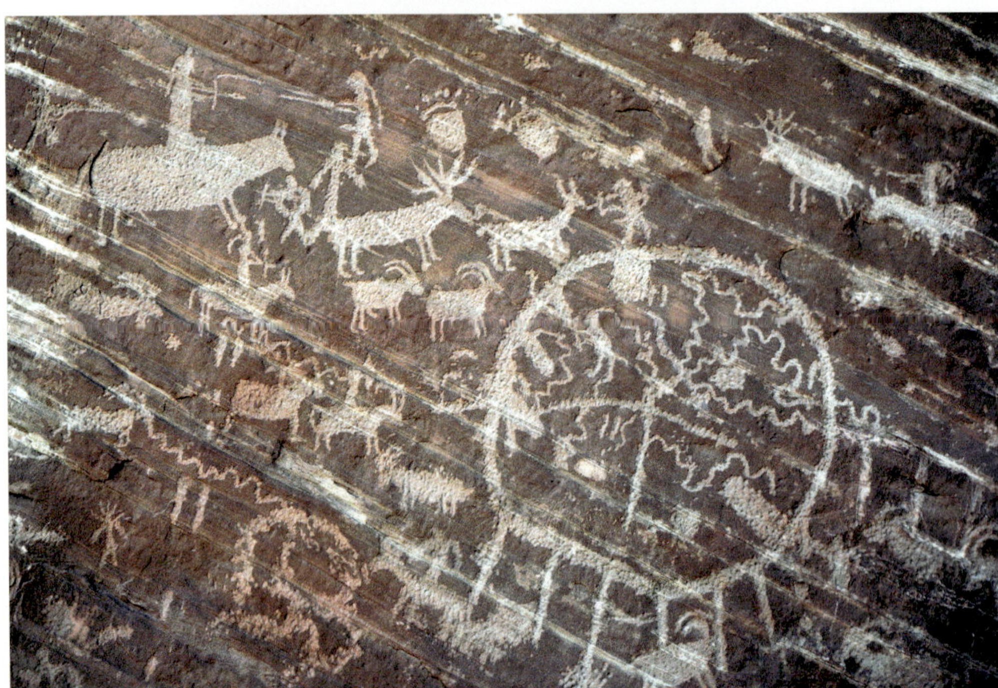

FIGURE 12.8. A complex Ute-style petroglyph panel in Comb Wash, southeastern Utah, with bear tracks and a mounted anthropomorph shooting a bow. It may depict a battle of some sort.

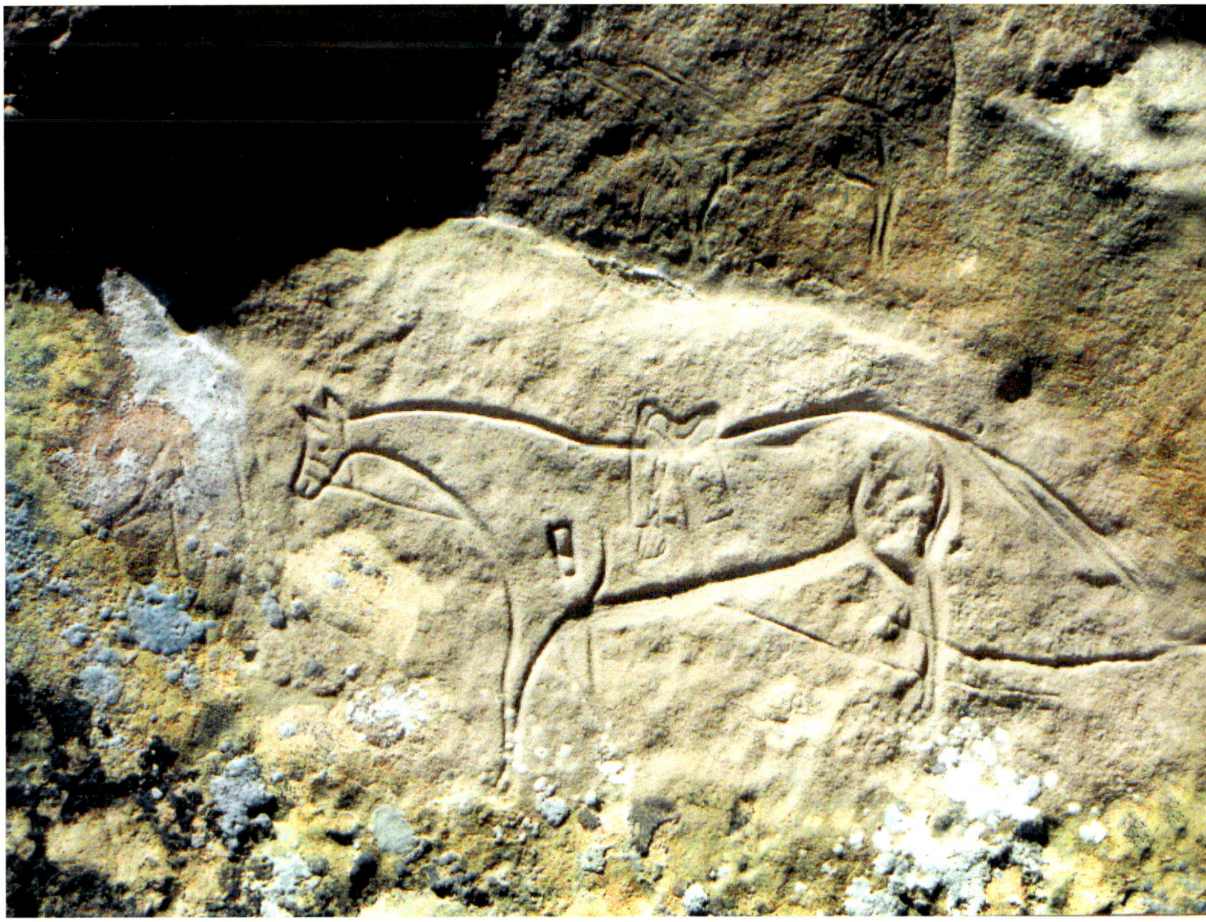

FIGURE 12.9. A large horse chiseled into the rock on the Navajo Reservation near Bluff, Utah.

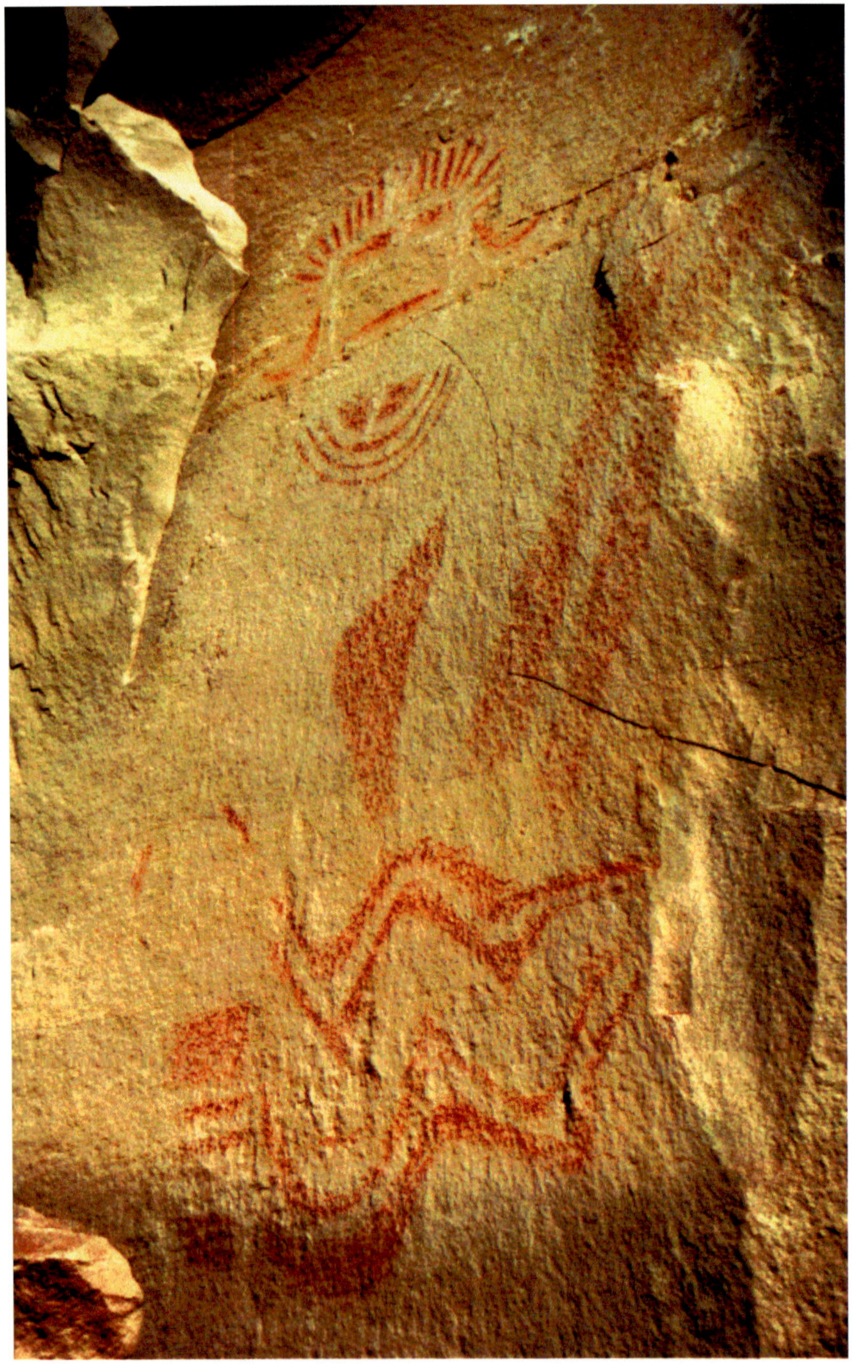

FIGURE 12.10. A large anthropomorph high above the road in the eastern Book Cliffs. It appears to be Fremont-style and may have been created using a stick of pigment, which is sometimes seen in Ute-style pictographs.

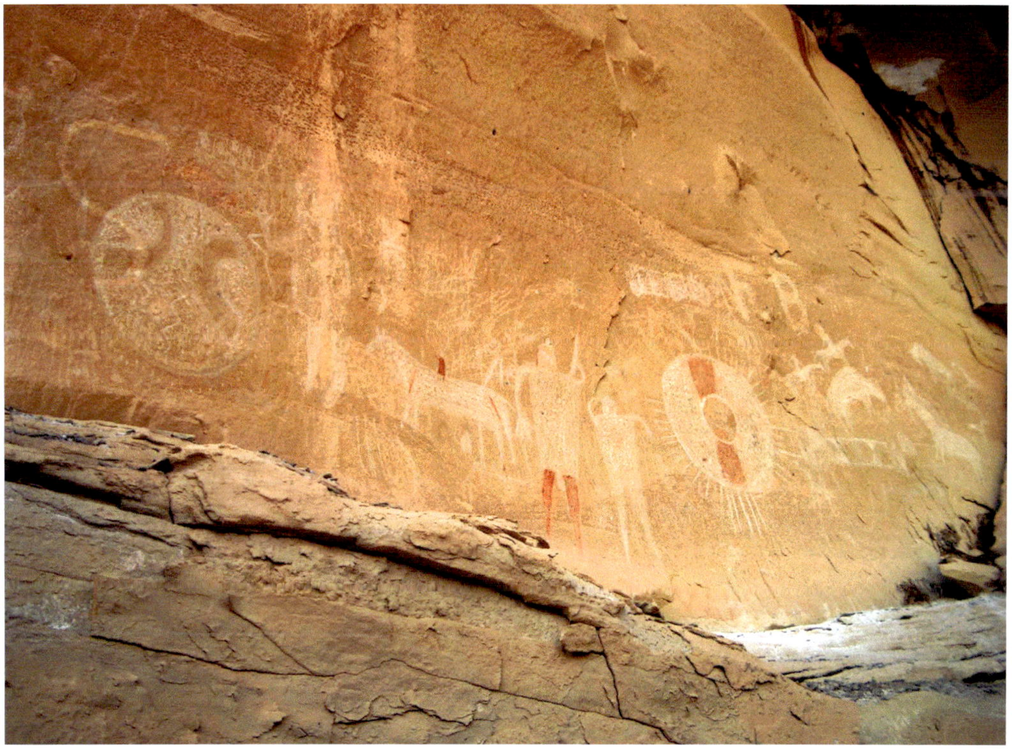

FIGURE 12.11. A Ute-style pictograph panel in Sego Canyon, part of the Book Cliffs of eastern Utah.

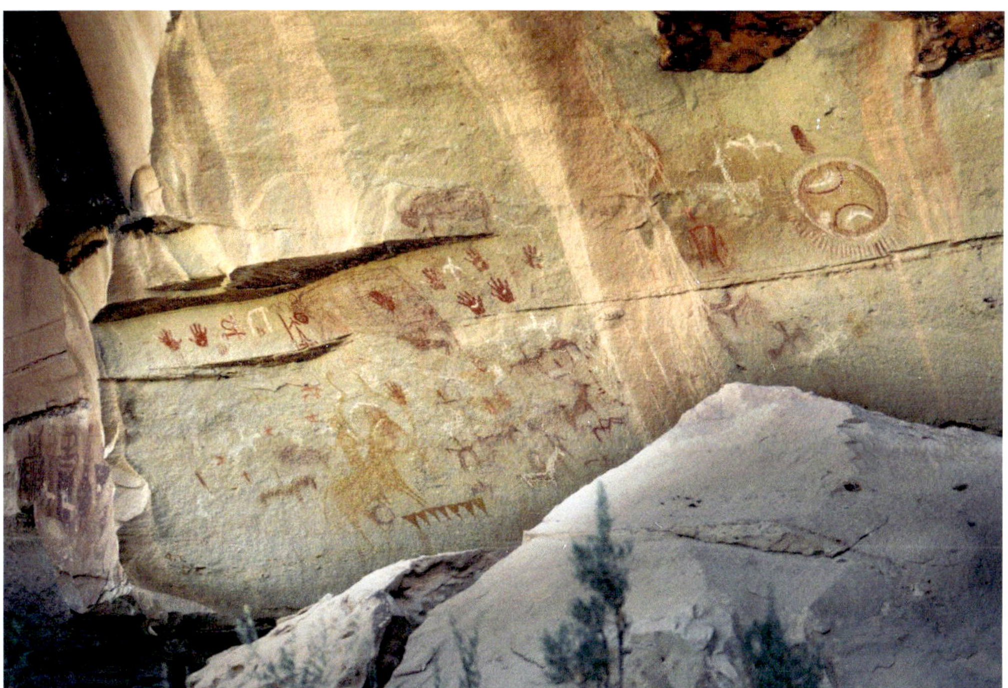

FIGURE 12.12. A Ute-style pictograph panel near a much older Barrier Canyon–style panel in Sego Canyon.

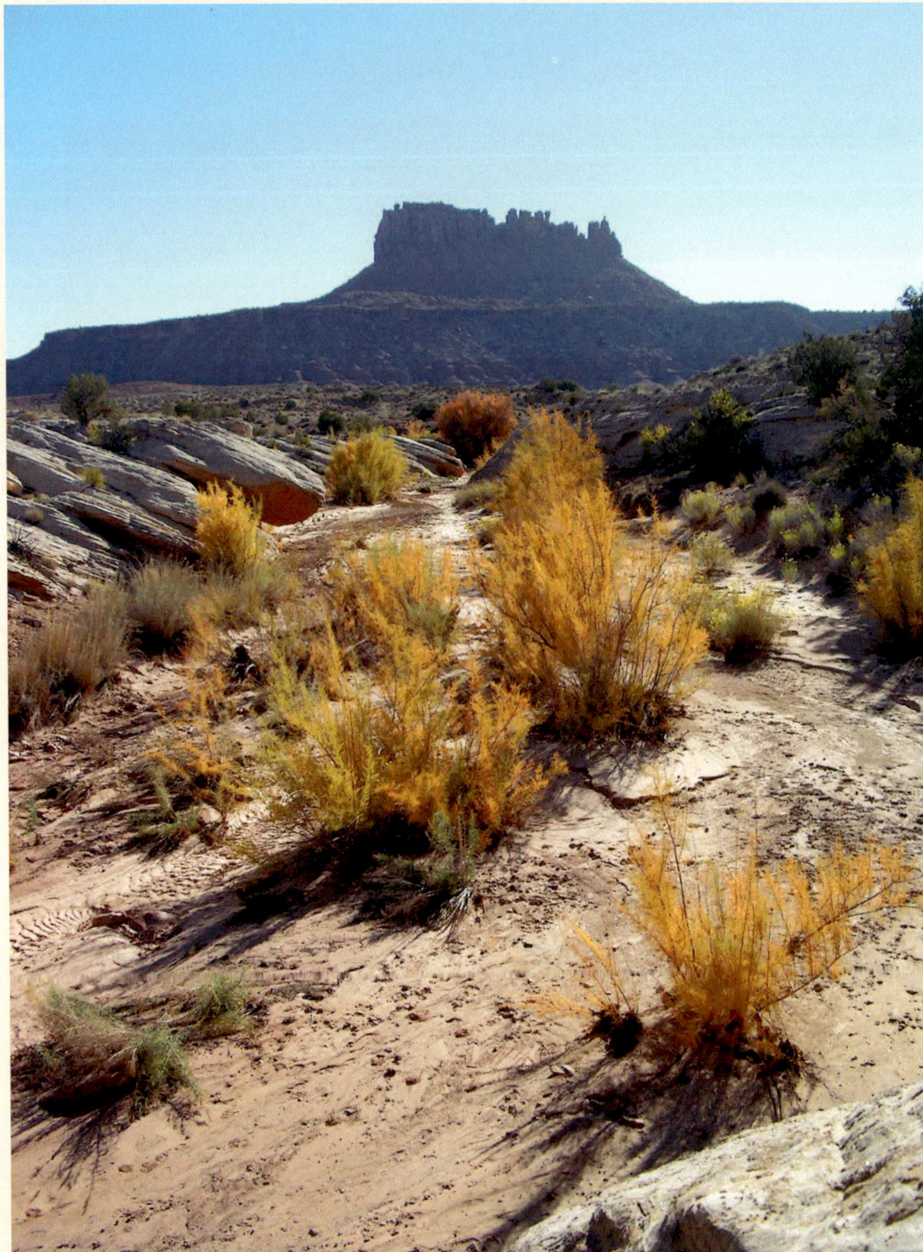

FIGURE 13.1. Elaterite Butte in the Maze District of Canyonlands National Park.

13

ART AND THE MIND OF THE CREATOR

When I look at an artistic creation, I am initially drawn to the art itself—the effect the images have on me, what they look like, what they make me think of, how they affect the way I feel. And rather quickly I begin to think about the creator, the artist. I wonder about her or his intention, about what the circumstances of the creative act might have been. For me, this desire to understand the artist is not unlike my desire to know who is speaking when I hear voices, or to know the identity of the author of a book or poem. I am interested in the human who is creating the work that affects me. And I do think of it as someone creating, not someone who created, even if the work is hundreds or thousands of years old, for the work has not changed. It may have faded or become less distinct. In the case of a written work, changes in language since it was written might make the work seem dated, but the content, the artistic expression, the human outpouring, is no less fresh than the day it was created. I may not see the work through the eyes of the creator, may not understand her or his intent or meaning, but I am being affected, being reached, being spoken to. And I want to be a worthy listener. I want to concentrate, to see, to hear, to pay attention, to give proper audience to the creator, the artist. I would not want to have been merely present when an orator gave a speech—present but thinking about other things, not listening. I want to listen. I want to hear. I want my mind to be receptive to what their mind has created, what their mind has expressed. I want to grow and take in what others have gleaned from their experiences as humans. Some of what I hear and see I will discard and reject, but some I will retain and incorporate into my own mind, my makeup.

We are here only a relatively short time. We will never meet all the people, learn of all the ideas, hear all the music, see all the artistic creations people have made or will make. But we are better for having seen—and listened. When we open our minds to the minds of others, we become greater than we were before. I have been enriched by opening my mind to the expressions others left on the cliff walls and scattered boulders of this desert region many lifetimes ago. And by viewing photographs of those artistic and cultural expressions, those who cannot travel to see them in person can also, almost magically, be touched by the creative mind of someone they will never meet.

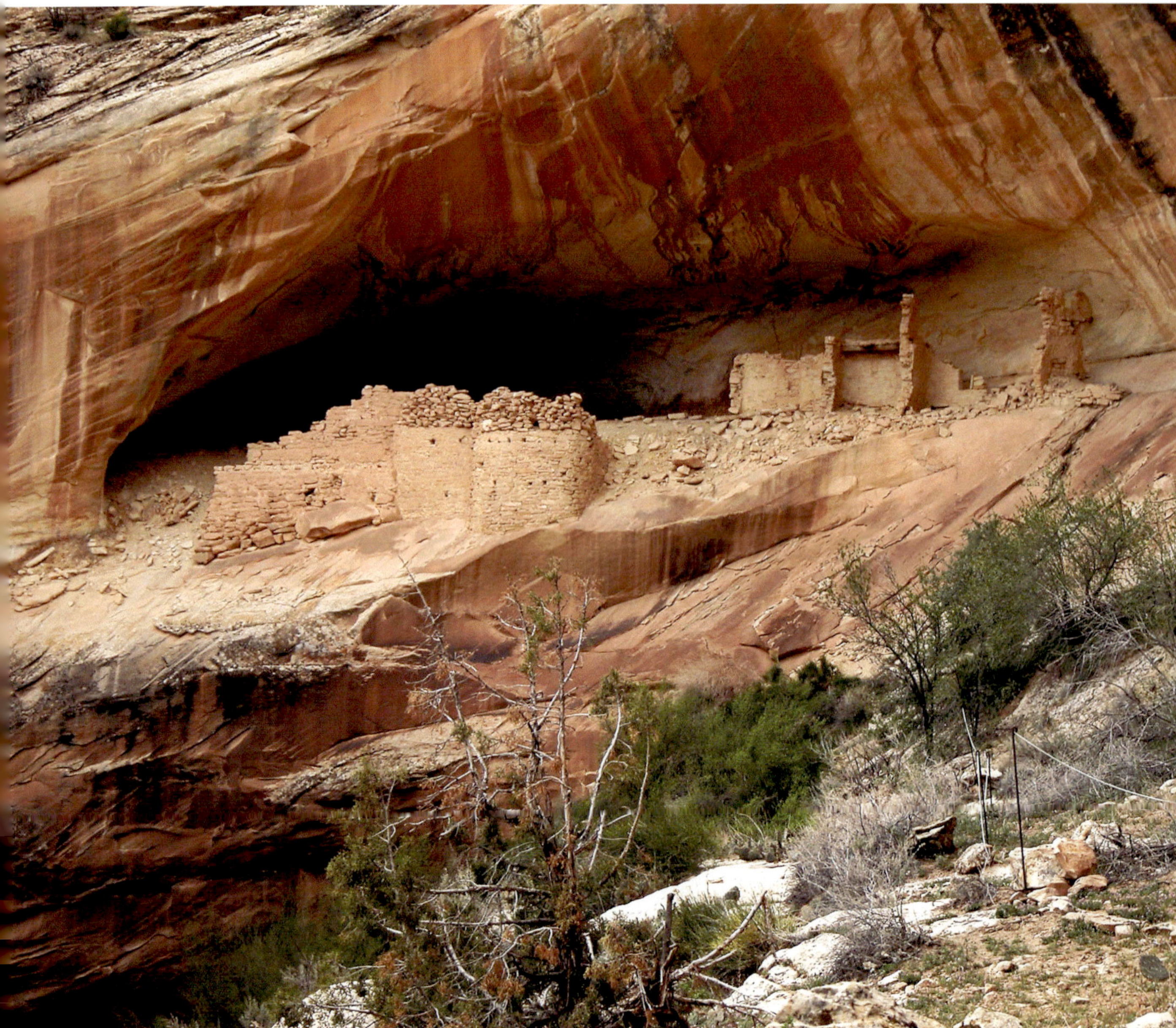

FIGURE 13.2. A large multiroom Ancestral Puebloan habitation known as Monarch Cave near Butler Wash, southern Utah.

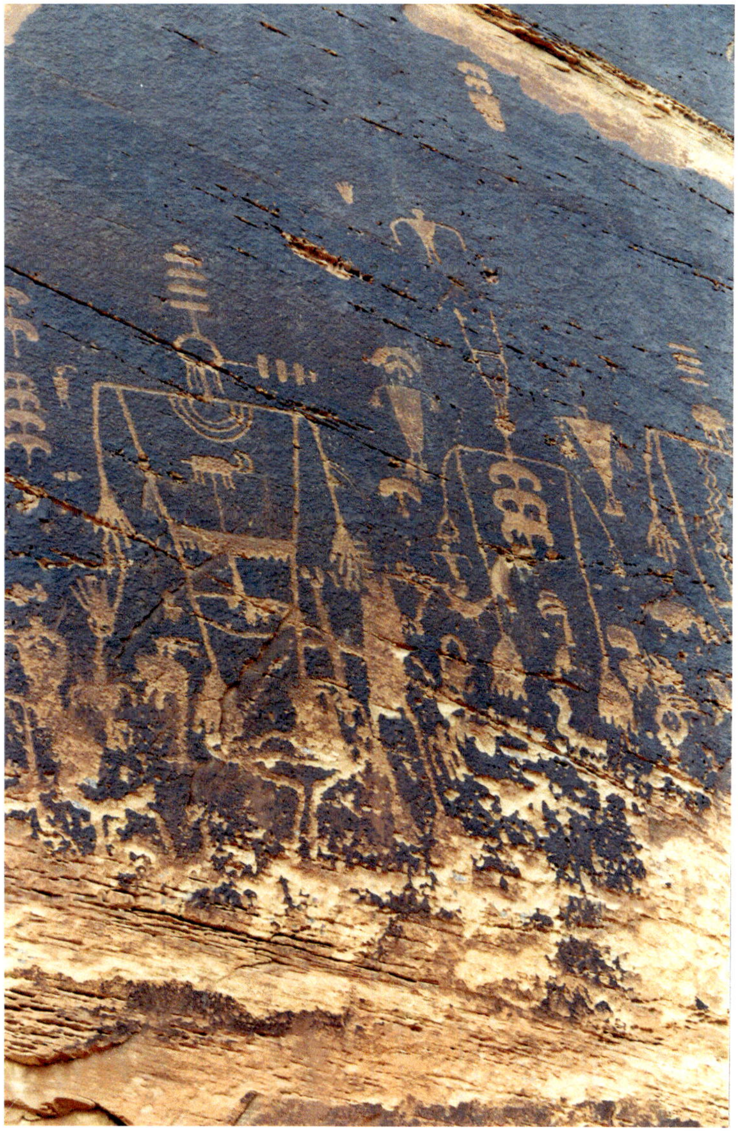

FIGURE 13.3. A spectacular example of the San Juan Basketmaker-style on a panel next to the San Juan River. The large anthropomorphs are nearly life-sized

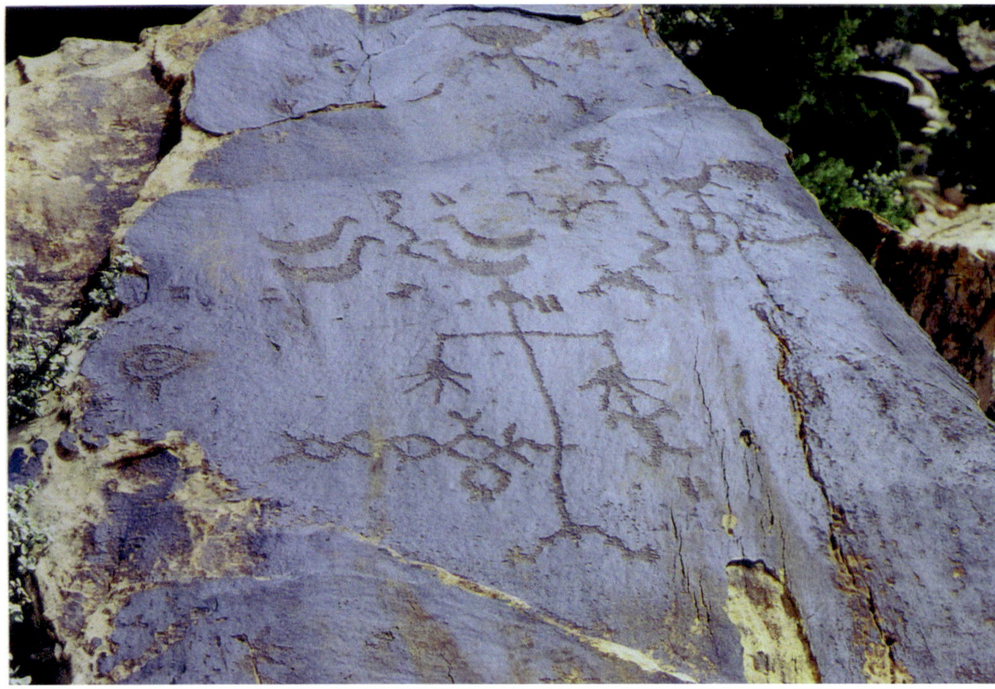

FIGURE 13.4. A San Juan Basketmaker panel near Cedar Mesa. The blue-black patina provides a terrific canvas for rock art.

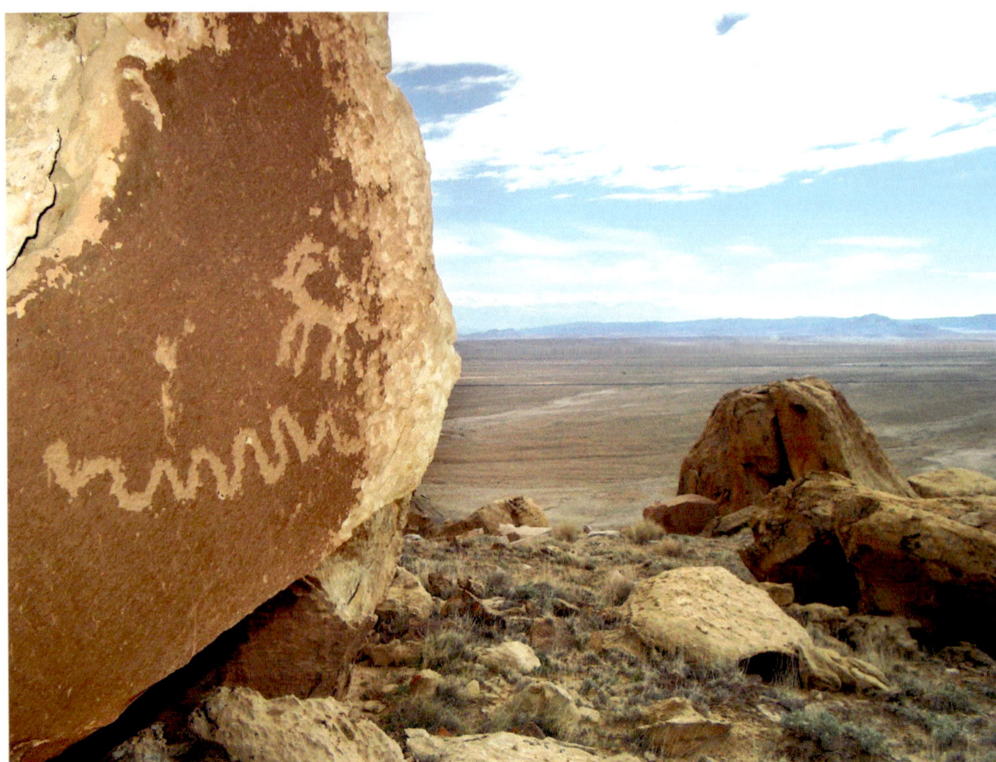

FIGURE 13.5. Fremont-style petroglyphs of a snake and bighorn sheep overlook the landscape.

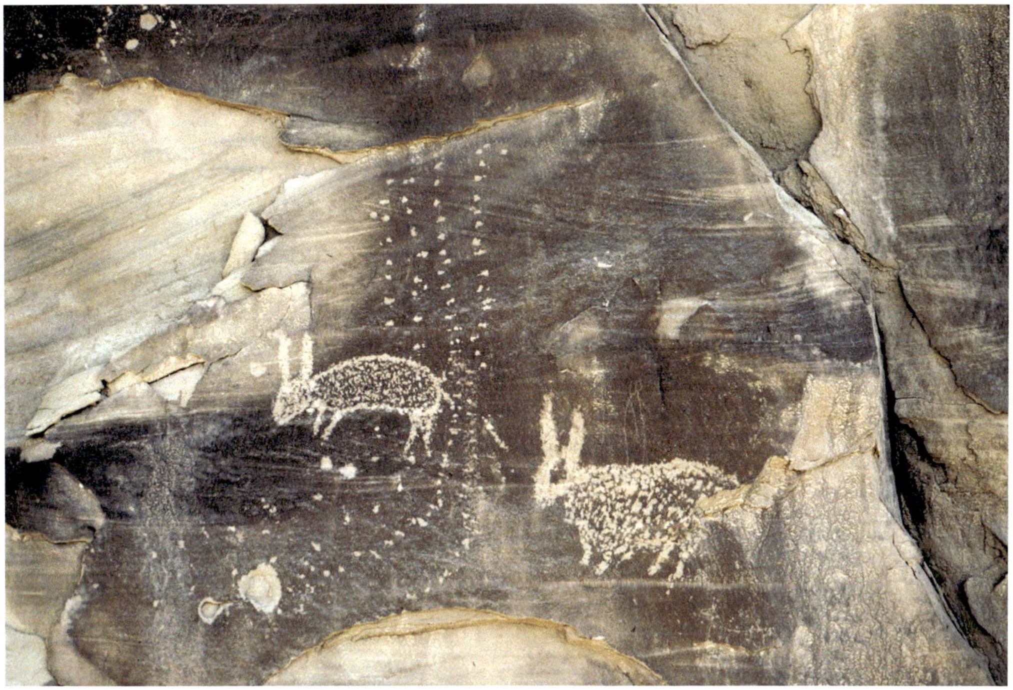

FIGURE 13.6. A Ute-style petroglyph panel alongside Willow Creek, a tributary of the Green River, featuring rabbits and other designs.

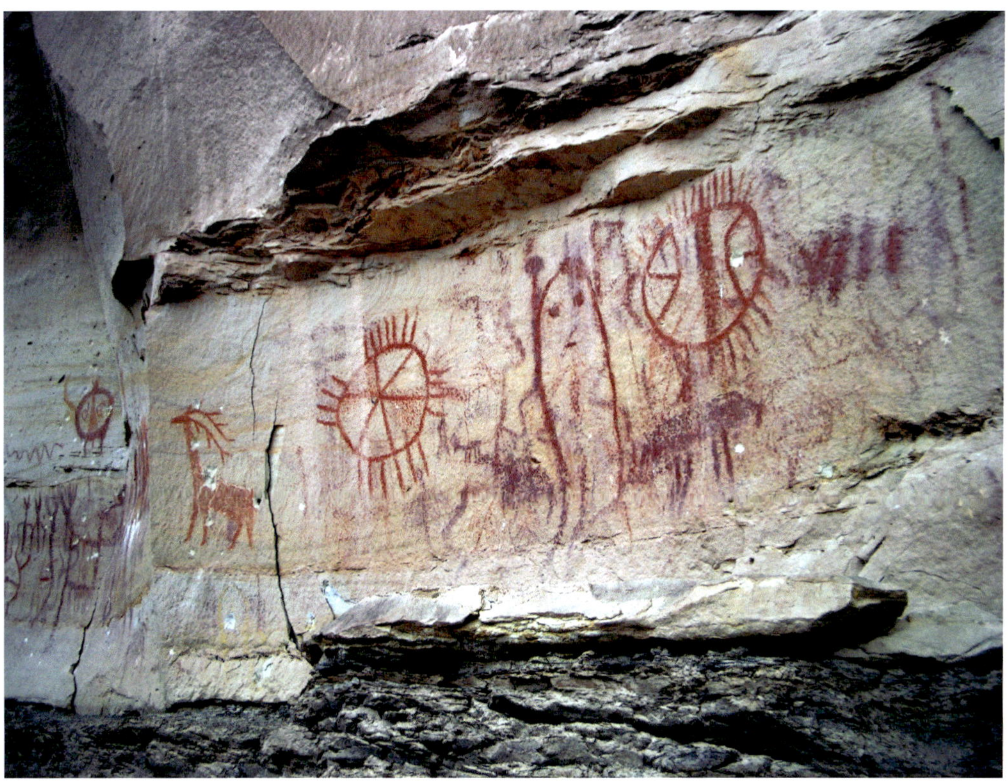

FIGURE 13.7. A painted Ute-style panel in Westwater Canyon of the Colorado River.

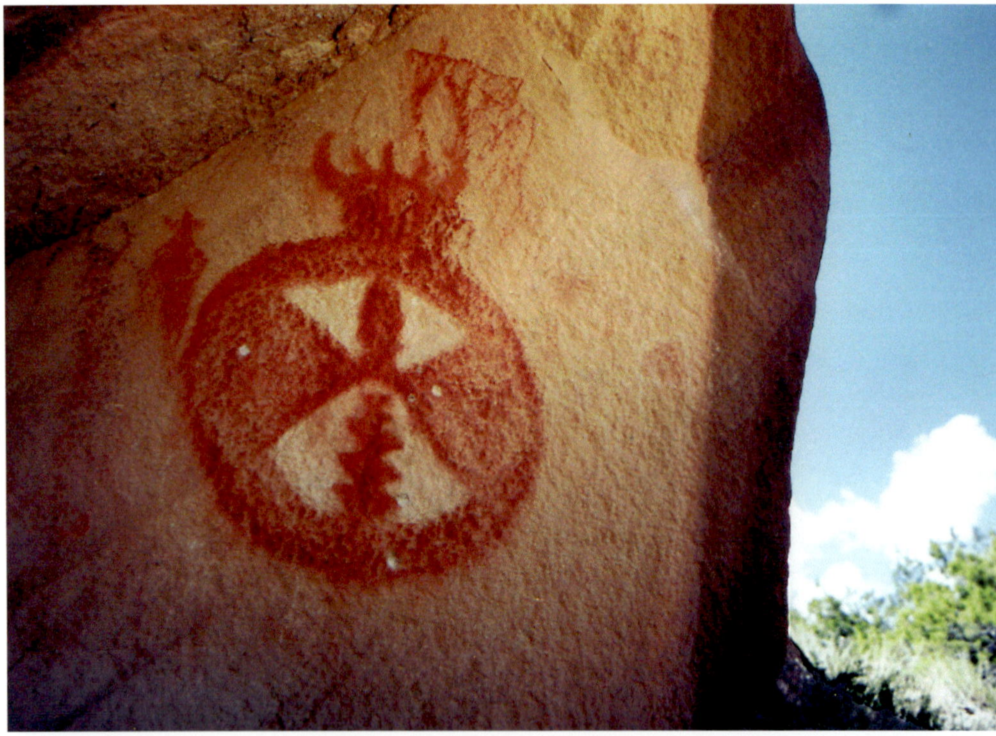

FIGURE 13.8. A painted Ute-style shield figure in Diamond Canyon, in the Book Cliffs of eastern Utah.

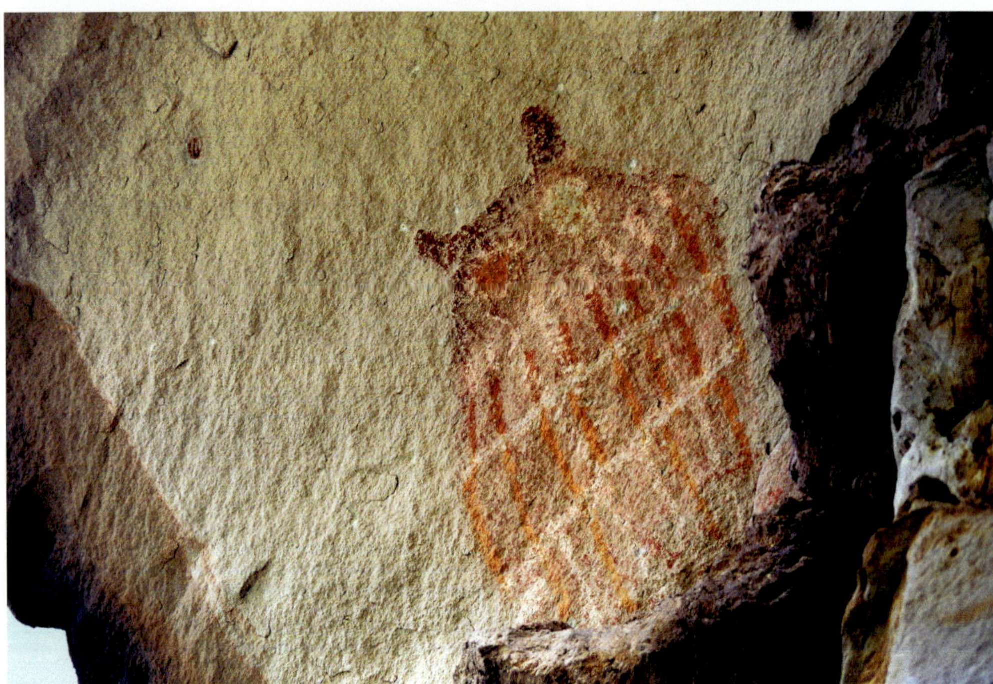

FIGURE 13.9. A painted owl figure thought to be Ute style in Diamond Canyon, in the eastern Book Cliffs.

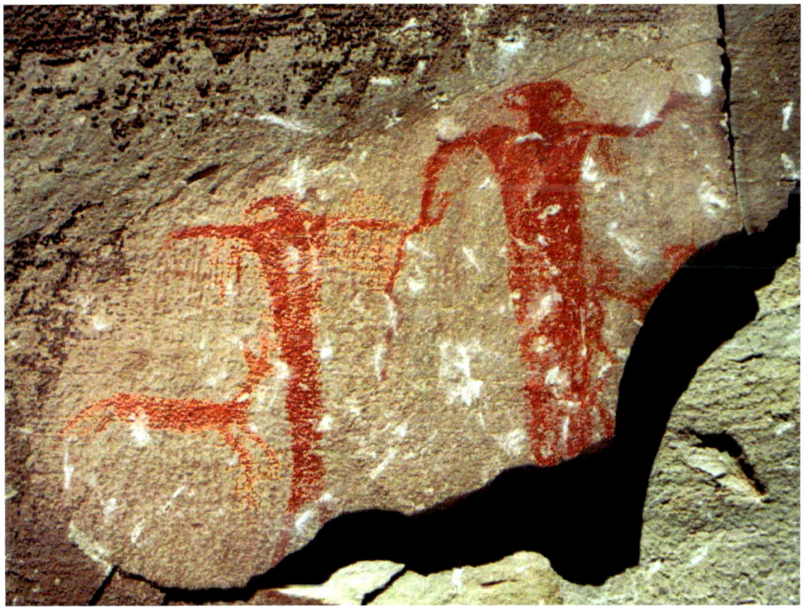

FIGURE 13.10. A Barrier Canyon–style pictograph panel in Cat Canyon near the San Rafael Swell, central Utah.

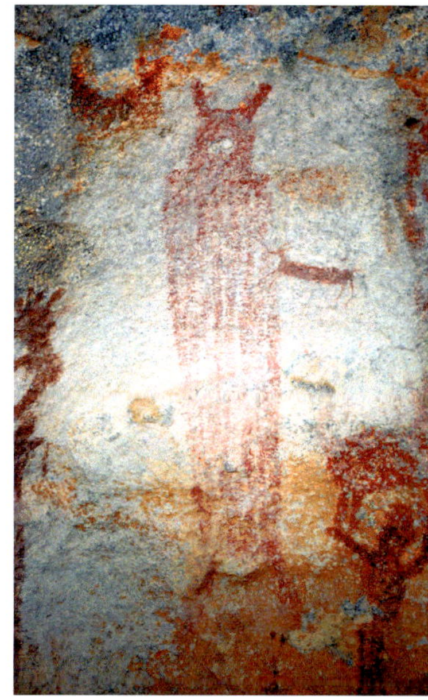

FIGURE 13.11. A Barrier Canyon–style anthropomorph south of Hanksville, Utah.

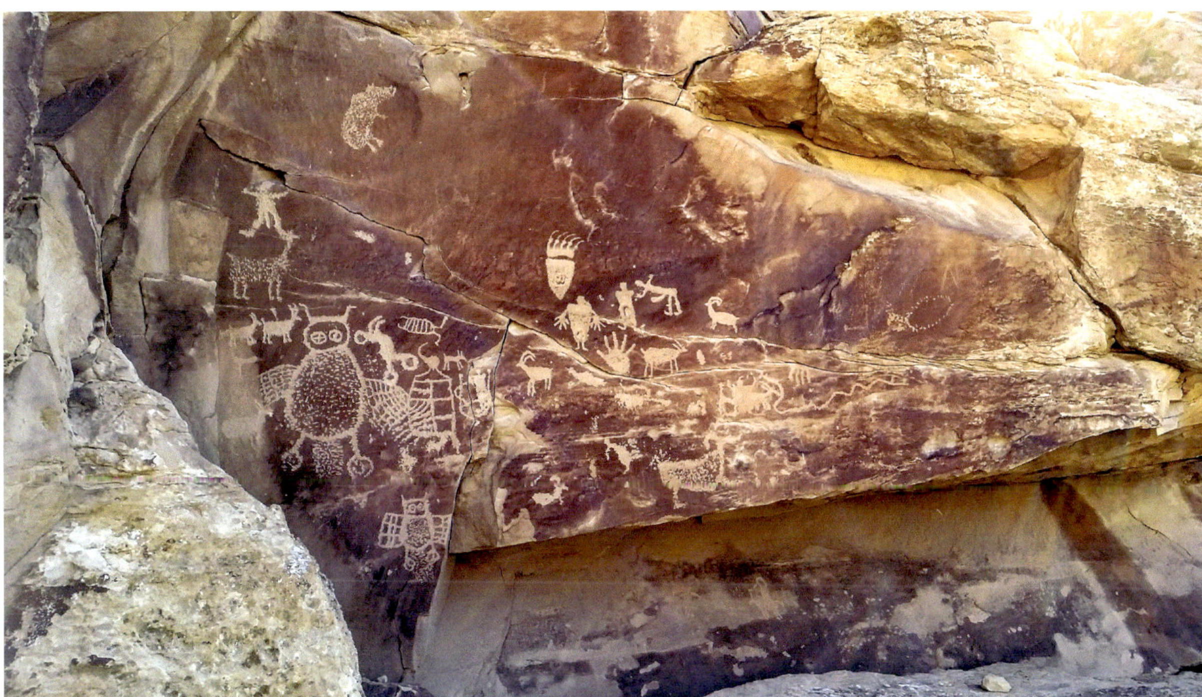

FIGURE 14.1. A beautiful Ute-style petroglyph panel in Nine Mile Canyon. A portion of the panel appears to have been created using a metal tool.

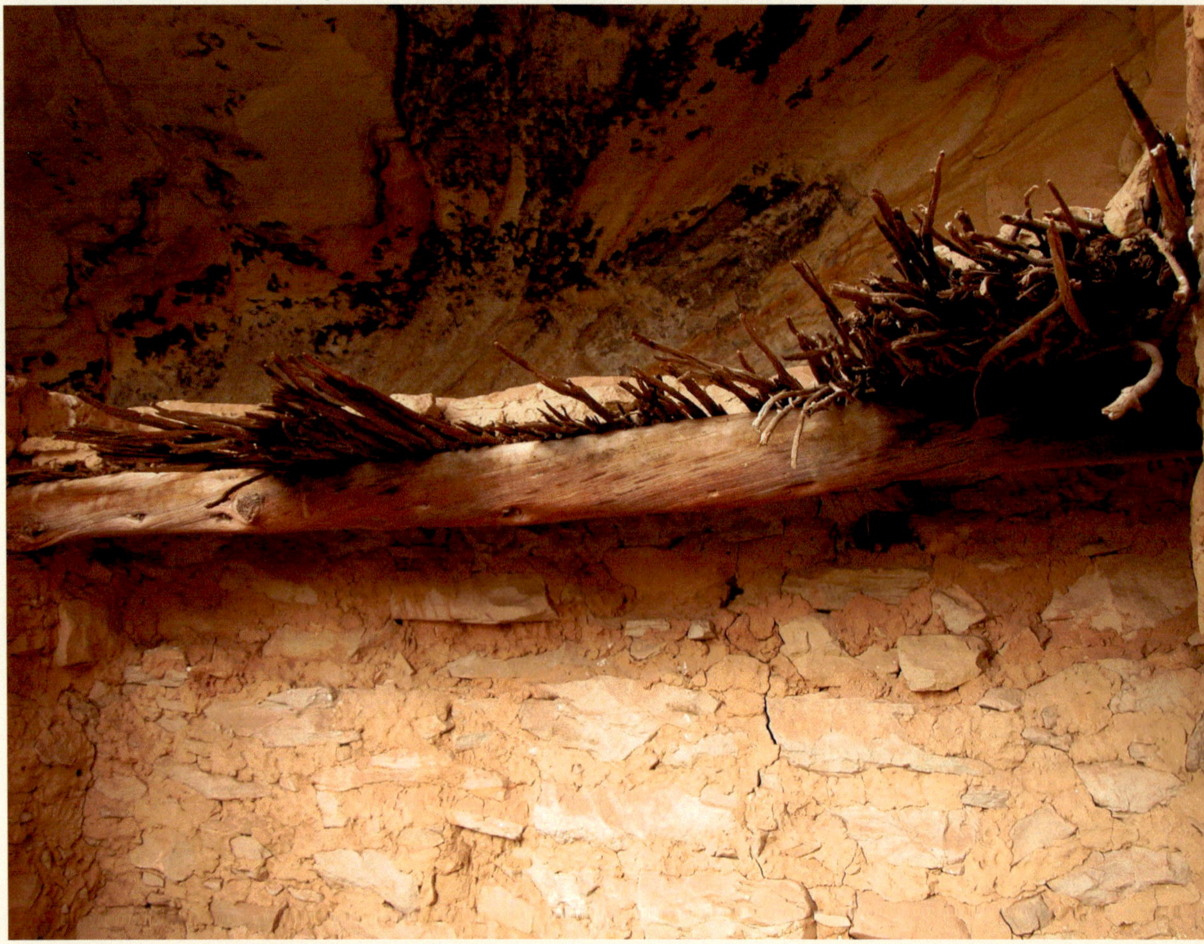

FIGURE 14.2. A wall and part of a roof in an ancient agricultural habitation site in southern Utah.

14

A HUNDRED YEARS FROM NOW

A hundred years from now I won't be crying.
A hundred years from now I won't be blue.
My heart will have forgotten
That you broke every vow.
I won't care a hundred years from now.

—*Traditional song recorded by Lester Flatt and Earl Scruggs*

When Lester Flatt sang this song nearly 50 years ago, he was referring to his heartbreak. It would be gone in a hundred years, as he would be gone, and therefore he would not care any longer about the wrongs he felt had been done to him.

I will not be here in a hundred years, and perhaps then I won't care what happens to the canyon art of the Colorado Plateau, but I am here now, and I do care about a hundred years from now, for if we do not take steps to protect these delicate treasures, despite their having graced the walls of stone for millennia, without care they may not last another hundred years.

A panel of figures pecked or painted on a cliff wall a thousand years ago has usually faced only the benign and indifferent neglect of the natural world. Sunlight, rain, wind, rushing floods, wildfires, lichen, spalling rock, avalanches, and freeze-thaw cycles have affected the works of art—destroying some, diminishing others, leaving some largely intact. Prehistoric people sometimes placed subsequent artworks over older ones, and they might have defaced or destroyed some for reasons all their own. Perhaps we see today only a fraction of the art that was created on these cliff faces by ancient artists, but assuredly, most of the damage and destruction came from undirected natural agents. The modern situation is markedly different.

In recent times, since Spanish explorers, mountain men, and settlers arrived in this country, followed by tourists, partiers, thrill-seekers, free-range cattle, climbers, gun enthusiasts, art thieves, vandals, fools, and well-meaning but uninformed visitors, the rock art of this region has endured an unprecedented onslaught of harm. Bullet holes, gouged names, prurient scratching, saw and chisel cuts, pitons, itchy hide rubbings, spray paint, latex, handprints, reservoir water, industrial chemicals, explosive charges, and more have taken a great toll on once-magnificent artworks (e.g., figures 1.9, 2.8, and 4.5). Without effective advocacy, the cultural stories depicted on the walls of time will be ground to dust. Without effective advocacy, we may have little left in a hundred years but a few pictures and fading memories.

What can we do?

Spread the word. Educate our kids and neighbors. Help them to feel connected to the people who came before, help them feel a sense of ownership and stewardship.

Care for them. Put up interpretive signs. Invite visitors to sites that can be protected and cared for, but do not publicize locations of fragile, endangered panels. Guides can give visitors a rewarding experience while delivering a message of conservation. Create subtle barriers to keep people from touching or getting too close to precious art. Sometimes subtlety is not enough, and real, substantial barriers are warranted. Some people must be fenced out.

Repair the damage. Not that which comes from nature: we do not want reconstructed or repainted rock art. But we should, when possible, without damaging or otherwise affecting the authentic art, try to mask or remove graffiti and malicious damage. This should only be done by professional art conservators with approval of the land manager, and following consultation with all responsible and interested parties. We advocate removing or masking bullet holes and graffiti to reduce the chance of more being added to the same spot. Bad behavior invites more bad behavior.

Document. Document every bit of rock art. As much as can be photographed, drawn, and described should be. For some fantastic rock art, despite our best efforts, only the documentation will exist in a hundred years. And if an undocumented site disappears, it and its significance are forever lost.

Share the documentation. All sites should be recorded according to standards established by state and federal agencies. Each state has guidelines and forms that aid in collecting relevant data. All who are concerned about the future of these precious traces of the past are obligated to record them in the appropriate way, and to make certain that the information gets to the relevant agencies. Without proper data, agencies cannot manage their resources. If they do not know where sites are, they cannot protect them. If they have no record of a site's condition, they cannot determine if it is deteriorating or has suffered recent damage.

While some take pride in keeping site locations secret and only sharing them with "trusted" associates, this does nothing to protect sites. Hoarding special knowledge may be good for your status among friends, but it is self-serving and not beneficial to the resource.

Sharing your love and appreciation of ancient art *is* beneficial, as it enables better management and protection of sites and brings more allies into the ranks of caretakers and stewards. Take photographs. Share them with your friends. Post them on social media without revealing exact locations. Enjoy and love these gifts from those who lived before us, and those who live after us, those who live a hundred years from now, will likewise be able to enjoy and love them.

Be a site steward. Adopt a site. Many agencies have site stewardship programs. Interested citizens visit a particular site or series of sites on a regular basis and check on their condition. This helps agencies better manage sites, and it gets you out to a great place on a regular basis. Look into site stewardship programs in your area. If one is not available, create one!

If we work now to protect these messages from the past, in a way we are helping send messages to future people. Let's make those messages good ones!

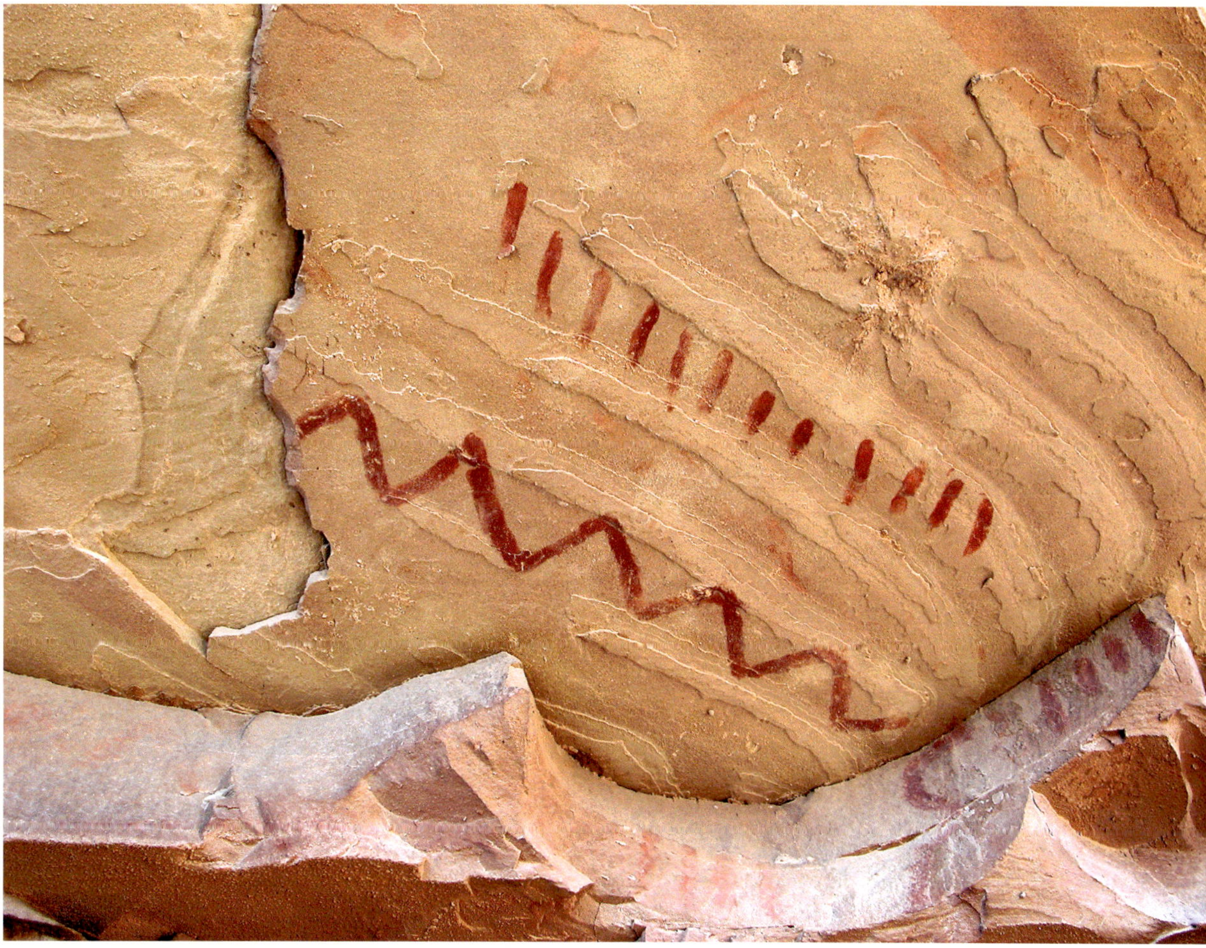

FIGURE 14.3. Pictographs near the Carbon County Golf Course. They seem to have been drawn with the artist's fingertips.

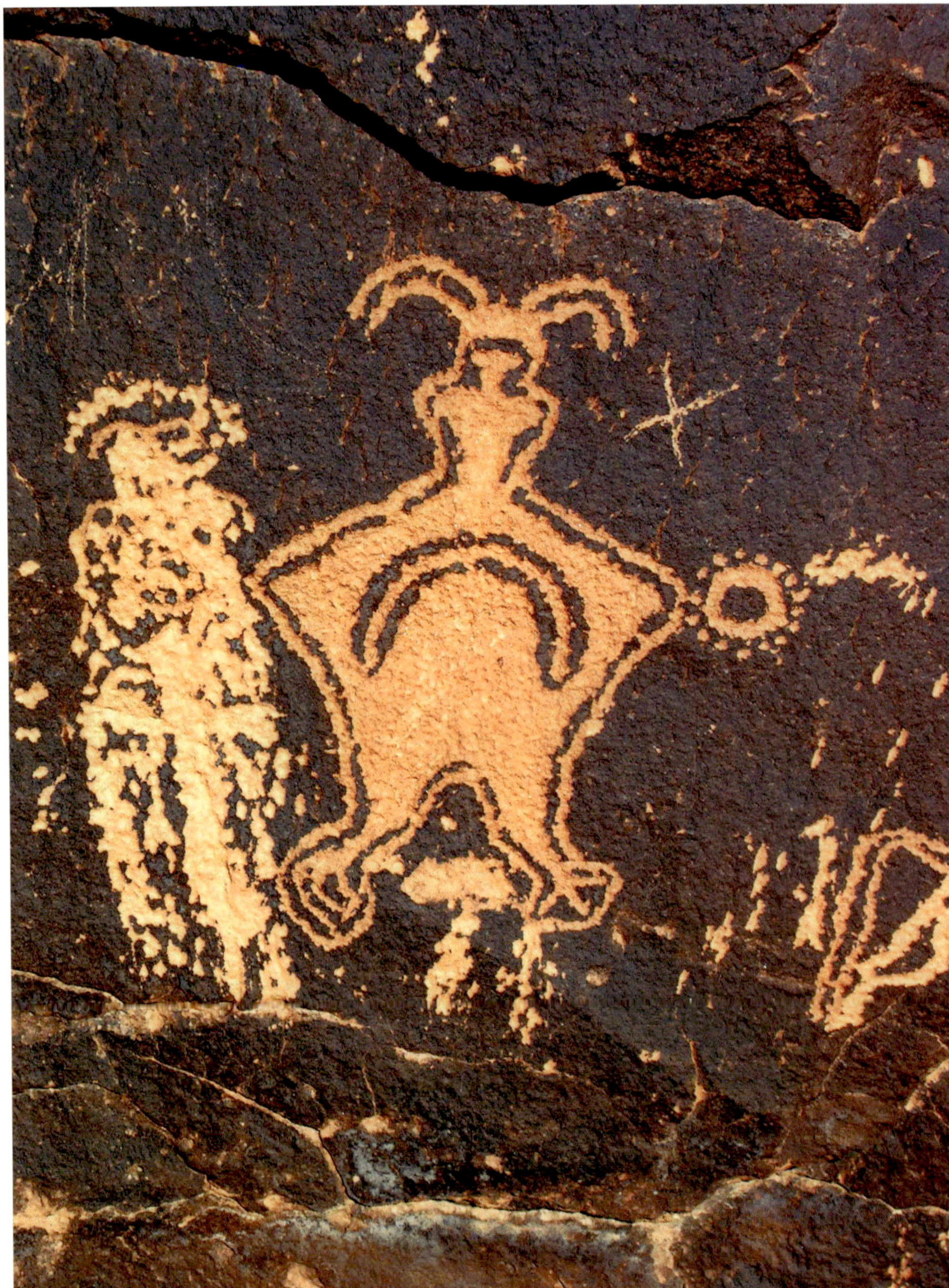

FIGURE 14.4. An unusual petroglyph of unknown cultural affiliation alongside the Green River near Willow Creek.

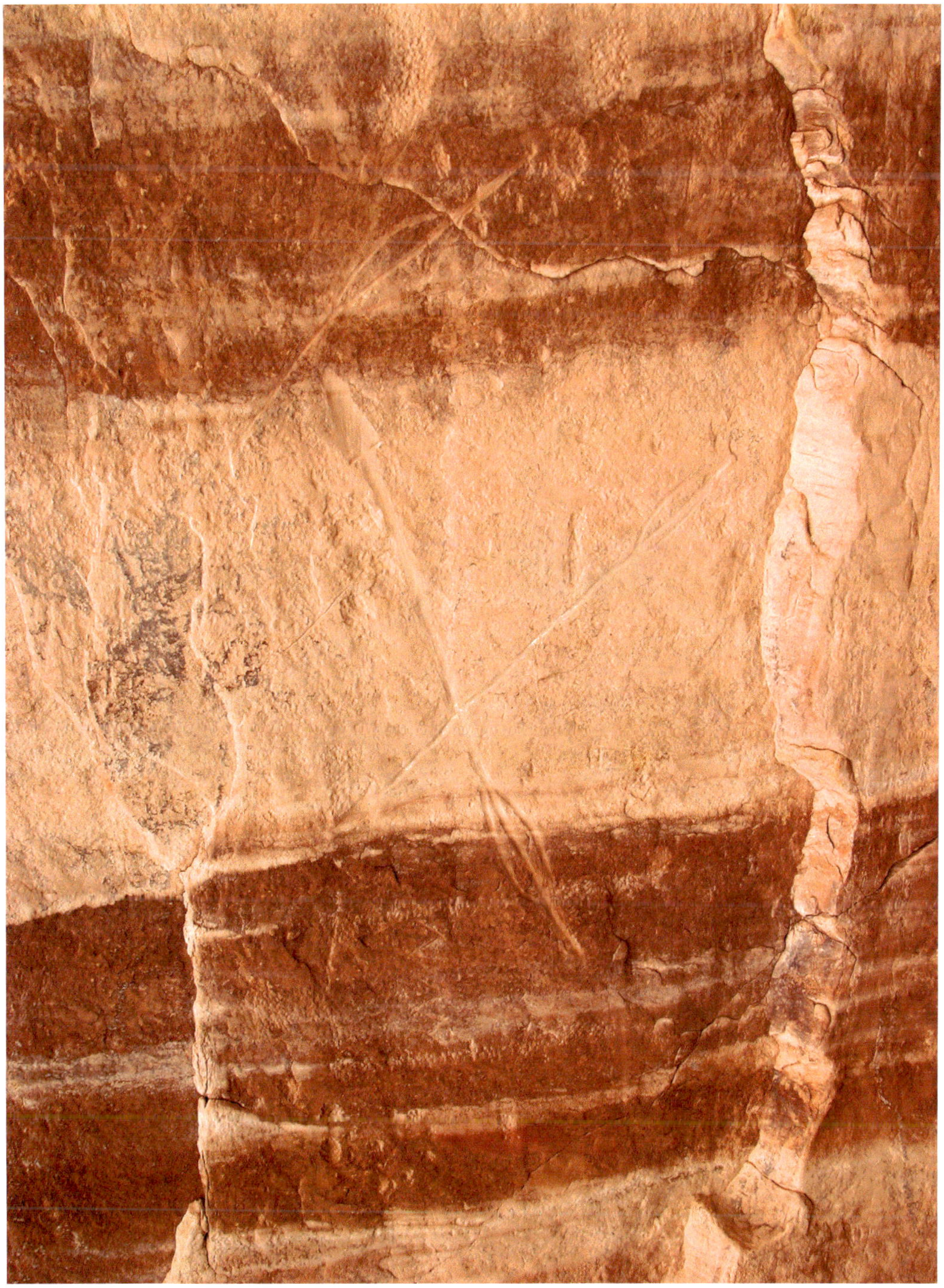

FIGURE 14.5. Arrow petroglyphs near Vernal, Utah, thought to be Ute in origin.

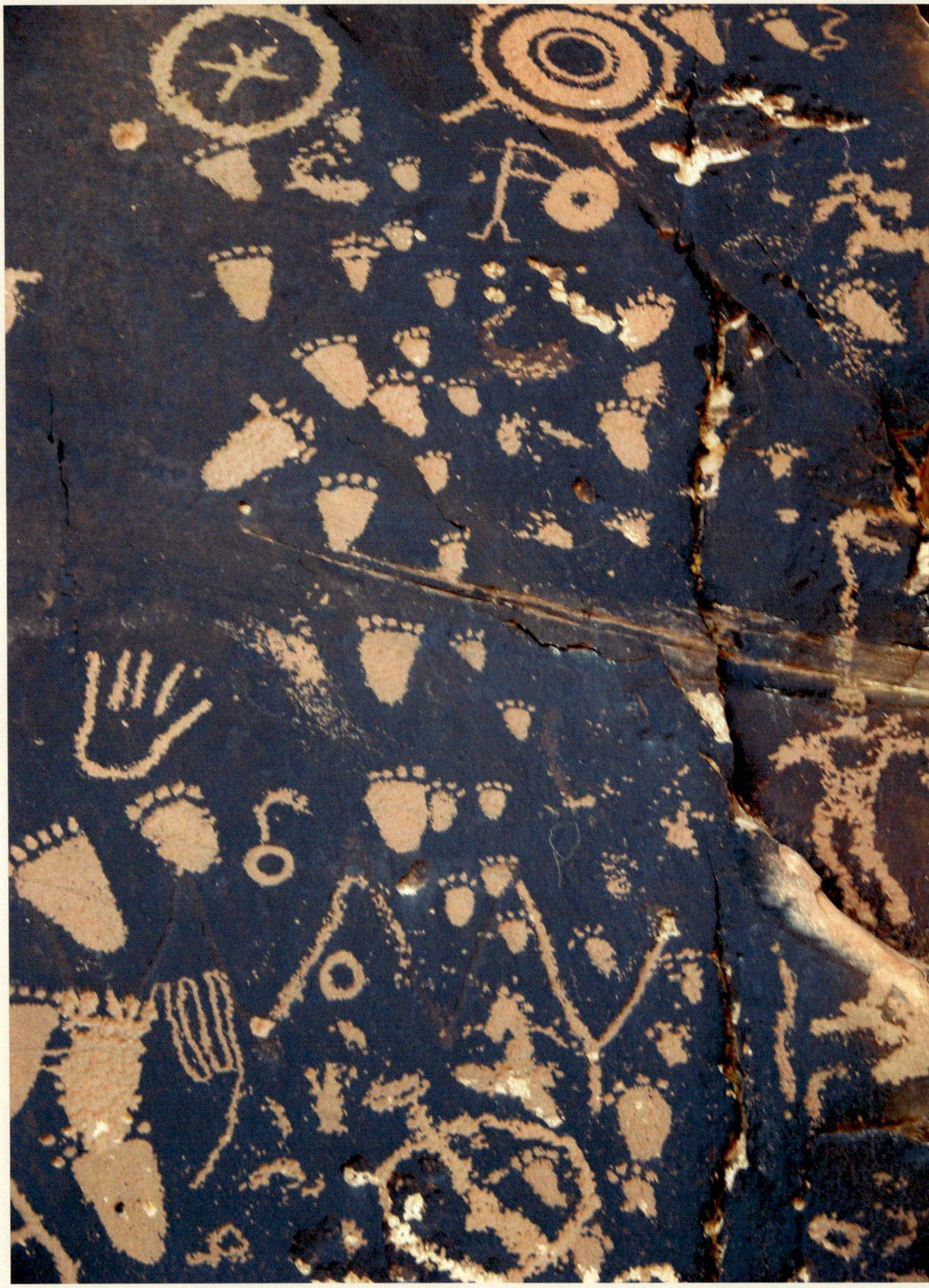

FIGURE 14.6. A close-up view of a section of Newspaper Rock in Indian Creek Canyon, south of Moab, dominated by footprints.

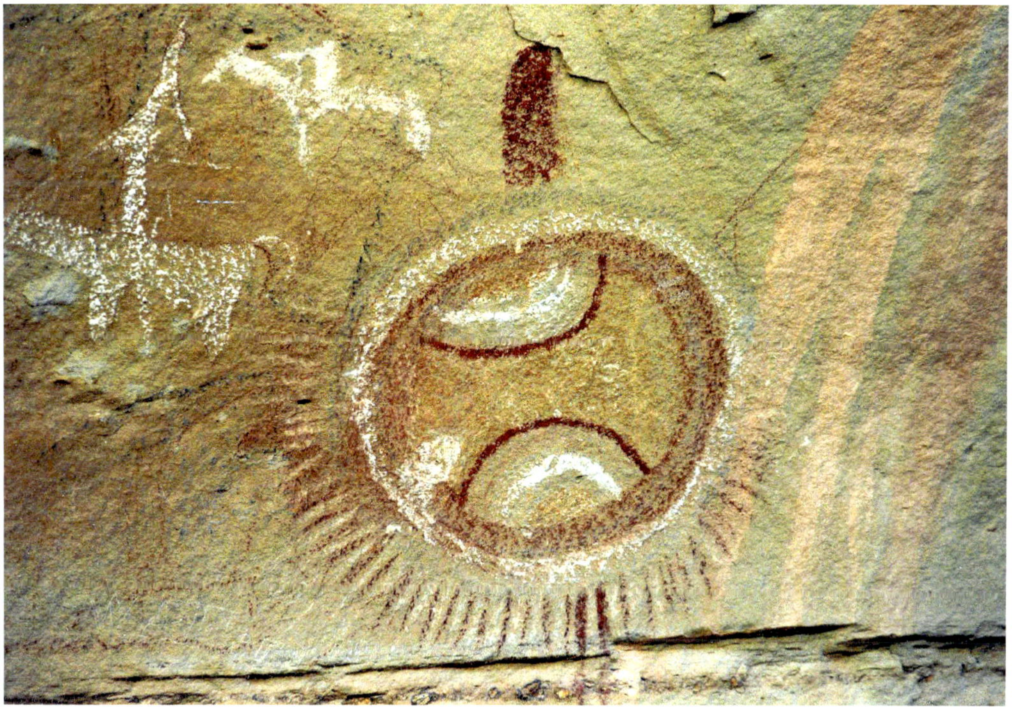

FIGURE 14.7. A Ute-style shield pictograph in Sego Canyon, in the eastern Book Cliffs.

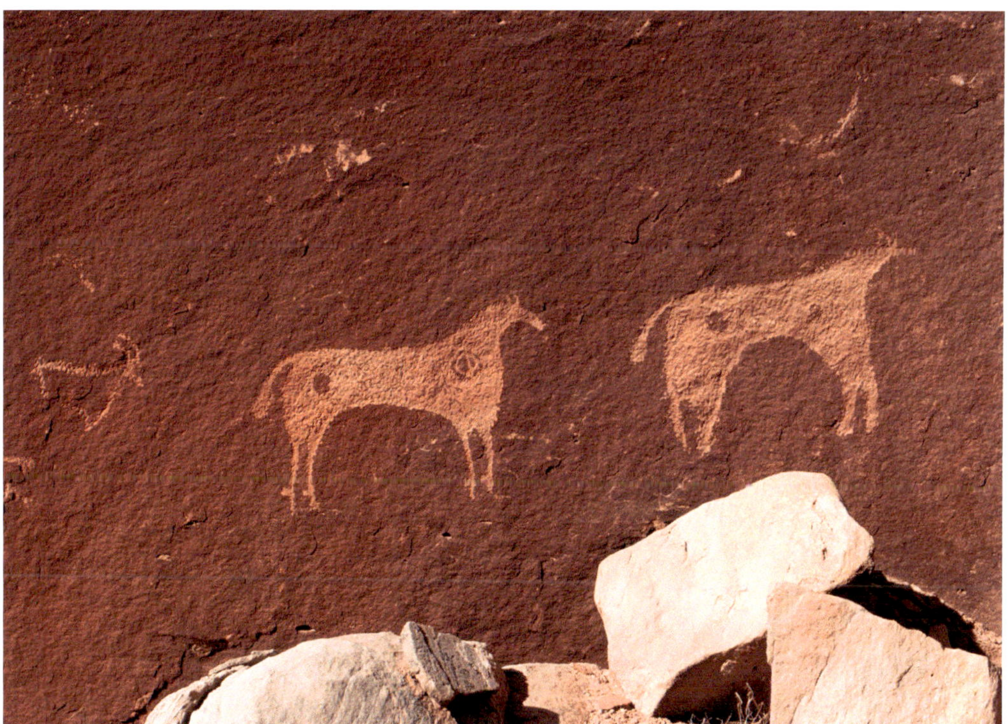

FIGURE 14.8. Two graceful Navajo-style horses on a cliff in Montezuma Creek Canyon. The creek is a tributary of the San Juan River.

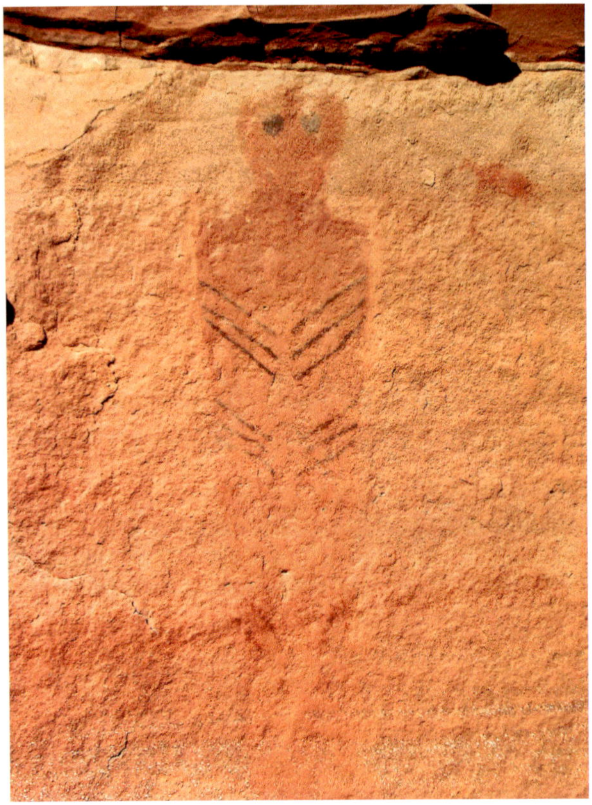

FIGURE 14.9. The Blue-Eyed Princess looking out from a very isolated location in southern Utah. Her eyes are probably not blue, but gray.

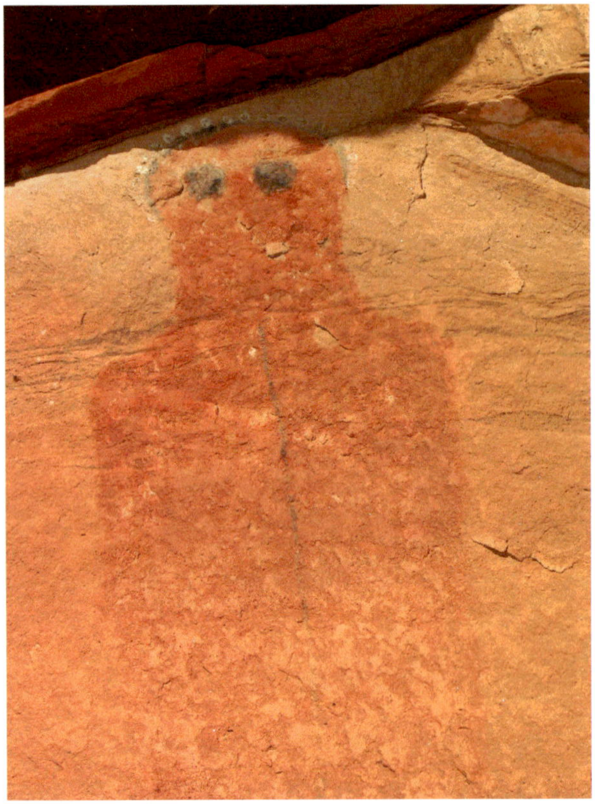

FIGURE 14.10. A close-up of another "blue-eyed" figure (see figure 14.9).

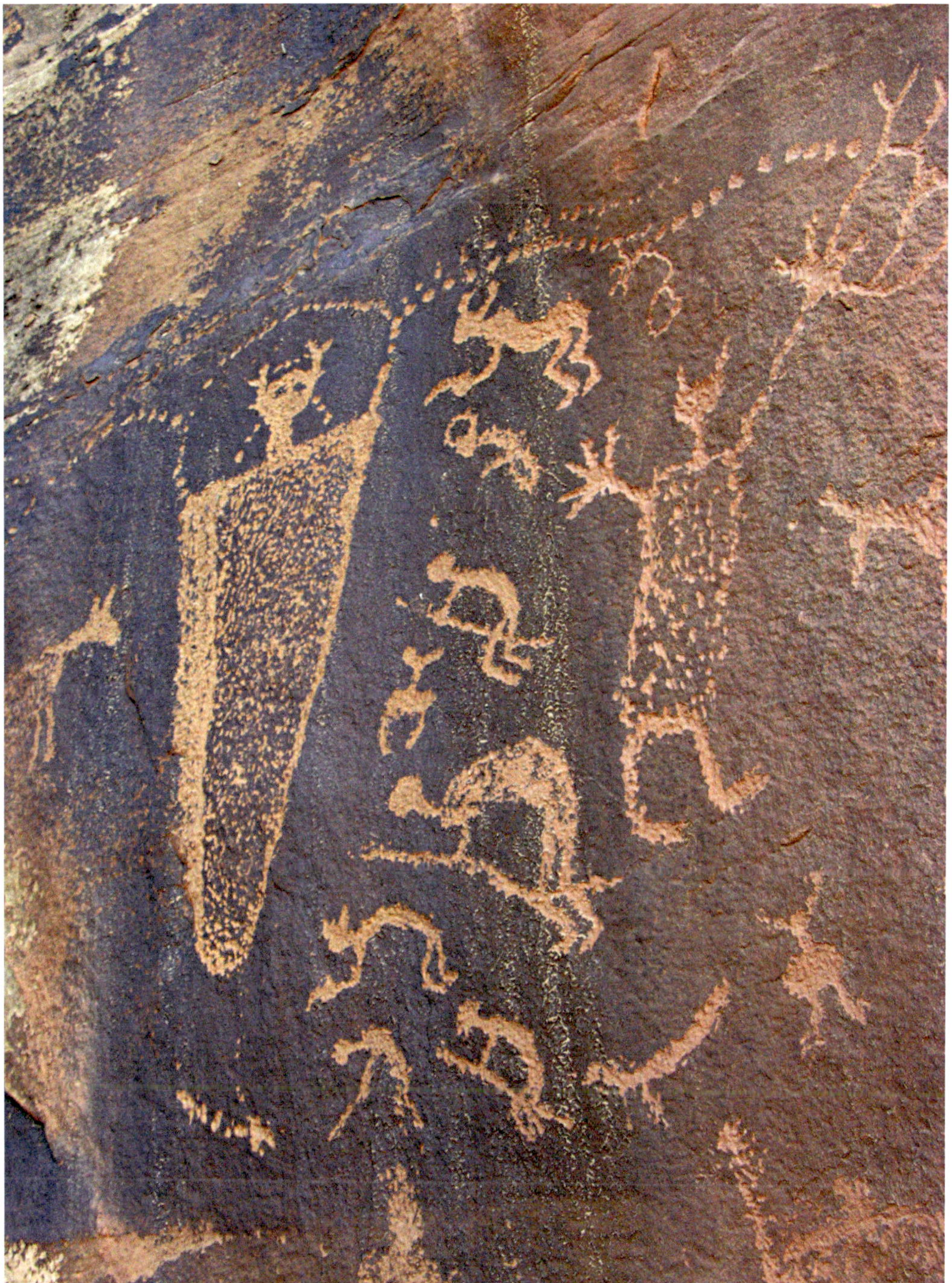

FIGURE 14.11. A petroglyph panel near Moab, Utah, that is unique in its style and individual elements.

GLOSSARY

Anasazi: A term for an archaeological culture of the Four Corners region of North America characterized by stone and adobe architecture, sophisticated agriculture, decorated ceramics, elaborate rock art, and significant variation through time and space. May also be referred to as Ancestral Puebloan or Hisatsinom.

Ancestral Puebloan: The term preferred by some for the archaeological culture commonly known as Anasazi.

Archaic: A general term used to classify the hunting and gathering cultures that occupied the American Southwest from approximately 8,000 to 2,000 years ago.

Barrier Canyon style: A style of rock art generally characterized by mostly painted figures, including large anthropomorphs and fantastic designs. Thought to date to the Archaic period.

Basketmaker: A term for the earlier Anasazi/Ancestral Puebloan archaeological cultures of the American Southwest, characterized by horticulture, pithouse dwellings, and the development of pottery-making technology. Generally thought to date from approximately 3,000 to 1,200 years ago.

Fremont: A name given to an archaeological culture characterized by horticulture, ceramics, pithouse construction, aboveground adobe structures, stone and adobe granaries built in overhangs and on cliff walls, and exquisite rock art. Sites associated with the Fremont culture are primarily found in Utah and northwestern Colorado.

Grinding slick: A place on stone worn smooth by abrasion from people grinding or sharpening another stone on that spot (see figure 4.1).

Handprint Positive: A representation of a human hand made by pressing a painted hand against the stone or by pecking such an image (see figures 1.5, 2.12, 3.8).

Handprint Negative: A representation of a human hand made by spraying or blowing paint over a hand pressed against the stone to create an outline or by pecking such an image (see figure 8.6).

Horticultural: People who gain some of their sustenance through agriculture, but with substantial contributions to the diet coming from hunting and gathering.

Hunter-gatherers: People who gain all or nearly all of their sustenance from gathered or hunted wild foods.

Paleo-Indian: A term that refers to the early inhabitants of the New World who hunted and gathered from the end of the Pleistocene (the last Ice Age) to about 8,000 years ago. Paleo-Indian people lived during a time when mammoths, giant ground sloths, short-faced bears, and other now-extinct megafauna were present across North America.

Petroglyphs: Inscriptions on stone made by pecking, abrading, incising, or otherwise physically altering the rock surface.

Pictographs: Inscriptions on stone made by applying paint or other pigments.

Shield figures: Images having a generally round shape and often appearing in front of an anthropomorphic figure, like a shield held for protection. These figures can appear as round-bodied anthropomorphs and also stand-alone round figures. Shield figures may bear decoration ranging from simple to very complex.

REFERENCES AND FURTHER READING

Bailey, Jonathan

2016 *Rock Art: A Vision of a Vanishing Cultural Landscape.* Photographs by Jonathan Bailey. Johnson Books, Boulder, CO.

Castleton, Kenneth B.

1978 *Petroglyphs and Pictographs of Utah,* vol. 1: *The East and Northeast.* Utah Museum of Natural History, Salt Lake City.

1979 *Petroglyphs and Pictographs of Utah,* vol. 2: *The South, Central, West, and Northwest.* Utah Museum of Natural History, Salt Lake City.

Castleton, Kenneth B., and David B. Madsen

1979 The distribution of rock art elements and styles in Utah. *Journal of California and Great Basin Anthropology* 3(2): 163–175. Banning, CA.

Chaffee, Scott D., Marian Hyman, and Marvin W. Rowe

1994 Radiocarbon dating of rock paintings. In *New Light on Old Art: Recent Advances in Hunter-Gatherer Rock Art Research,* edited by David S. Whitley and Lawrence L. Loendorf, pp. 9–12. Monograph 36. Institute of Archaeology, University of California, Los Angeles.

Cole, Sally

2004 Origins, continuities, and meaning of Barrier Canyon style rock art. In *New Dimensions in Rock Art Studies,* edited by Ray T. Matheny, pp. 7–78. Occasional Papers 9. Museum of Peoples and Cultures, Brigham Young University, Provo, UT, and the University of Utah Press, Salt Lake City.

2009 *Legacy on Stone: Rock Art of the Colorado Plateau and Four Corners Region.* Updated. Johnson Books, Boulder, CO.

Francis, Julie E., and Lawrence L. Loendorf

2002 *Ancient Visions.* University of Utah Press, Salt Lake City.

Grant, Campbell

1967 *Rock Art of the American Indian.* Thomas and Crowell, New York.

Heizer, Robert F., and C. W. Clewlow, Jr.

1973 *Prehistoric Rock Art of California.* 2 vols. Ballena Press, Ramona, CA.

Hurst, Winston, and Bruce D. Louthan

1979 *Survey of Rock Art in the Central Portion of Nine Mile Canyon, Eastern Utah.* Publications in Archaeology, n.s., 4. Brigham Young University, Provo, UT.

Hurst, Winston B., and Joe Pachak

1989 *Spirit Windows: Native American Rock Art of Southeastern Utah.* Spirit Window Project, Blanding, UT.

Jones, Kevin T.

2017 Ancient rock art is indeed worthy of Utah's recognition. Op-ed, *Salt Lake Tribune,* March 6. http://www.sltrib.com/csp/mediapool/sites/sltrib/pages/printfriendly.csp?id=4996092

2017 The man with a heart of stone. In *Red Rock Stories: Three Generations of Writers Speak on Behalf of Utah's Public Lands,* edited by Stephen Trimble, pp. 31–33. Torrey House, Salt Lake City.

Kelen, Leslie, David Sucec, N. Scott Momaday, Craig Law, John Telford, and Philip Hyde

1996 *Sacred Images: A Vision of Native American Rock Art.* Canyonlands Natural History Association, Moab, UT.

Keyser, James D., and Michael A. Klassen

2001 *Plains Indian Rock Art.* University of Washington Press, Seattle.

Madsen, David B.

1989 *Exploring the Fremont.* Utah Museum of Natural History and the University of Utah Press, Salt Lake City.

Manning, Stephen

1990 Barrier Canyon style pictographs of the Colorado Plateau, Part 1: Hypothesis and evidence of post circa A.D. 1300 panels. *Utah Archaeology* 3(1): 43–81.

Matheny, Ray T., ed.

2004 *New Dimensions in Rock Art Studies.* Occasional Paper 9. Museum of Peoples and Cultures, Brigham Young University, Provo, UT, and the University of Utah Press, Salt Lake City.

McKern, W. C.

1978 *Western Colorado Petroglyphs.* Edited by Douglas D. Scott. Cultural Resources Series 8. Colorado Bureau of Land Management, Denver.

Morss, Noel

1931 *Ancient Culture of the Fremont River in Utah: Report on the Explorations Under the Claflin-Emerson Fund, 1928–29*. Papers of the Peabody Museum of American Archaeology and Ethnology 12(3). Cambridge, MA.

Olsen, Nancy

1985 *Hovenweep Rock Art: An Anasazi Visual Communication System*. Occasional Paper 14. Institute of Archaeology, University of California, Los Angeles.

Pederson, Joel L., Melissa S. Chapot, Steven R. Simms, Reza Sohbati, Tammy M. Rittenour, Andrew S. Murray, and Gary Cox

2014 Age of Barrier Canyon–style rock art constrained by cross-cutting relations and luminesence dating techniques. In *Proceedings of the National Academy of Sciences Early Edition*, pp. 1–6.

Russ, J. M., Marian Hyman, Harry J. Shafer, and Marvin W. Rowe

1990 Direct radiocarbon dating of rock art. *Nature* 348: 710–711.

Schaafsma, Polly

1971 *The Rock Art of Utah*. Papers of the Peabody Museum of American Archaeology and Ethnology 65. Cambridge, MA.

1980 *Indian Rock Art of the Southwest*. University of New Mexico Press, Albuquerque.

1992 *Rock Art in New Mexico*. Museum of New Mexico Press, Albuquerque.

Schaafsma, Polly, and M. Jane Young

1983 Early masks and faces in Southwest rock art. In *Collected Papers in Honor of Charlie Steen*, edited by Nancy Fox. Papers of the New Mexico Archaeological Society, Albuquerque.

Simms, Steven R.

2008 *Ancient Peoples of the Great Basin and Colorado Plateau.* Left Coast Press, Walnut Creek, CA.

Simms, Steven R., and Francois Gohier

2010 *Traces of Fremont: Society and Rock Art in Ancient Utah.* University of Utah Press, Salt Lake City.

Spangler, Jerry D.

2004 Categories and conundrums: The rock art of lower Nine Mile Canyon. In *New Dimensions in Rock Art Studies*, edited by Ray T. Matheny, pp. 119–143. Occasional Papers 9. Museum of Peoples and Cultures, Brigham Young University, Provo, UT.

2013 *Nine Mile Canyon: The Archaeological History of an American Treasure.* University of Utah Press, Salt Lake City.

Spangler, Jerry D., and Donna Kemp Spangler

2003 *Horned Snakes and Axle Grease: A Roadside Guide to the Archaeology, History, and Rock Art of Nine Mile Canyon.* Uinta, Salt Lake City.

2016 *Last Chance Byway: The History of Nine Mile Canyon.* University of Utah Press, Salt Lake City.

Steward, Julian

1941 Archaeological reconnaissance of southern Utah. In *Bureau of American Ethnology Bulletin* 128: 277–356. U.S. Government Printing Office, Washington, DC

Warner, Jesse

1984 An analysis of head form and head gear of the inverted bucket head hunter. In *Utah Rock Art*, vol. 3, edited by Cindy Everitt, Rex Madsen, and Phil Garn, pp. 70–82. Utah Rock Art Research Association, Salt Lake City.

Wenger, Gilbert R.

1956 An archaeological survey of southern Blue Mountain and Douglas Creek in northwestern Colorado. Master's thesis, Department of Anthropology, University of Denver.

Whitley, David S., and Lawrence L, Loendorf, editors

1991 *New Light on Old Art: Recent Advances in Hunter-Gatherer Rock Art Research*. Monograph 36. Institute of Archaeology, University of California, Los Angeles.

Wormington, H. M.

1955 *A Reappraisal of the Fremont Culture.* Proceedings no. 1. Denver Museum of Natural History.

Young, M. Jane

1985 Images of power and the power of images: The significance of rock art for contemporary Zunis. *Journal of American Folklore* 98(387): 2–48.

ABOUT THE AUTHOR

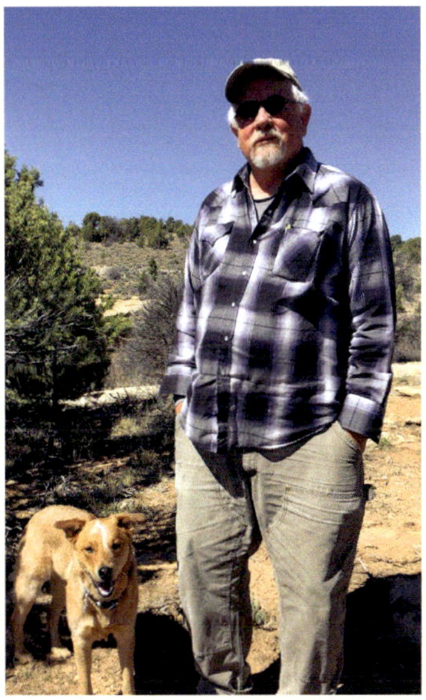

Kevin Jones is an archaeologist and writer. He was State Archaeologist of Utah for seventeen years. He and his wife, Barbara Evert, live off the grid on forty-two acres in Pleasant View, Colorado. Kevin is the author of the anthropological novel *The Shrinking Jungle* (University of Utah Press, 2012), set among the Aché, hunter-gatherers of Paraguay among whom Kevin lived while conducting his dissertation work in the early 1980s. Kevin plays mandolin and loves bluegrass music.

ABOUT THE PHOTOGRAPHER

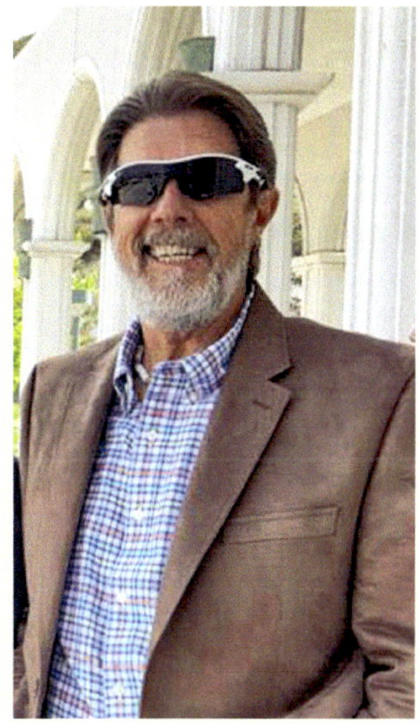

Layne Miller has been involved with rock art for nearly forty years. He is a founding member of the Utah Rock Art Research Association and the Nine Mile Canyon Coalition. He guides public tours to Nine Mile Canyon, the San Rafael Swell, and Range Creek, helping visitors enjoy and learn about rock art while practicing respectful site etiquette. He has taught classes on rock art at Utah State University Eastern and spends much of his time documenting and visiting sites while he enjoys life retired from full-time work.